D0280722

MATTHEW SMALL

DOWN AND OUT TODAY

NOTES FROM THE GUTTER

Paperbooks Ltd,
175-185 Gray's Inn Road, London, WC1X 8UE
info@legend-paperbooks.co.uk
www.legendtimesgroup.co.uk / @legend_press

Contents © Matthew Small 2015
The right of the above author to be identified as the author of this
work has been asserted in accordance with the Copyright, Designs
and Patents Act 1988. British Library Cataloguing in Publication Data
available.

Print ISBN 978-1-7850799-6-2
Ebook ISBN 978-1-7850799-7-9
Set in Times. Printed in the United Kingdom by Clays Ltd.
Cover design by Simon Levy www.simonlevyassociates.co.uk

All rights reserved. No part of this publication may be reproduced,
stored in or introduced into a retrieval system, or transmitted, in
any form, or by any means electronic, mechanical, photocopying,
recording or otherwise, without the prior permission of the publisher.
Any person who commits any unauthorised act in relation to this
publication may be liable to criminal prosecution and civil claims for
damages.

Matthew Small is a fiction writer and freelance journalist, currently living and writing in the limestone city of Bath in south west England.

Matthew has travelled through many parts of the world exploring different cultures and societies across five continents. His debut novel, *The Wall Between Us - Notes from the Holy Land* explores humanity behind the Israel Palestine conflict.

Visit Matthew at
thewordsisaw.co.uk
Follow him
@TheWordsISaw

Just because people are poor or have little, doesn't mean that their dreams aren't big and their soul isn't rich.
Eva Rodriguez – *Searching for Sugar Man*

Preface

What does poverty mean today? What does it look like? How does it feel to those living in the midst of it? Why, and despite humanity's incredible capacity for innovation, does poverty persist?

This book will be an exploration into some of the ways poverty can be defined at the beginning of the 21st century. It will be a narrative following my journey into bearing witness to some of the different and distinct guises of poverty today. I will seek to engage with it, to see the symptoms of poverty in my attempt to better understand the causes. It's a book that has been taking seed inside me for some time.

In early August 2014 I was walking across a bridge in Paris which spanned the railway tracks just north of Gare du Nord. The central divide that ran between the two roads was wide, but still, the sight of fifty or more souls inhabiting it was nevertheless shocking. They were sat on bare mattresses with their clothes draped over the surrounding wire fence. I stood still and stared at all the waiting faces as they watched the cars driving quickly by them, while others moved further beneath the overhead metro line in order to escape the sun's hot glare. Children lay beside mothers and men sat in circles talking, the air around them troubled by car fumes and the clatter of trains on the tracks below. I was struck by many questions: where had they come from? What had led them to Paris and, from where I was standing, to certain poverty? If they were immigrants, what poverty had they left behind to instead seek shelter in an unforgiving city in Europe?

This community of down and outs is just a snippet of the poverty and hardship displayed on Parisian streets. But Paris is not exceptional in its high rate of rough sleepers or people struggling to meet their daily needs. Poverty is a global condition and an ill that humanity has failed to cure.

I do not claim that this book will provide an answer. It will be pursued on the basis that to address something we first have to be willing to touch it, to not look away because poverty is an ugly thing and it taints the otherwise beautiful world we try to paint around ourselves. This isn't to say that we shouldn't paint and admire.

I write this in an environment of natural beauty and relative comfort; it is mid-September in south west France and I am beside the river which is flowing slowly through the grounds of the meditation centre where I have just volunteered for the summer. The late afternoon sunshine is shimmering through the oak trees and bamboos while birds are happily singing at their tops. Despite finding an inner richness throughout my time here, a question or two has been awoken in me about poverty. This largely comes when reflecting that I do not earn money while I'm here. I don't, for that matter, necessarily need to spend money either, except for the odd razor blade and tube of toothpaste, or *un petit café* on a rare trip to Périgueux, the old cathedral city 20 kilometres away. My daily needs are met; I have enough food to eat and, once my chores are done, time to write, to meditate, and to give to creative engagement or long discussions with others after supper.

I want to make note of my present setting and situation as next week things will be very different. I'll be heading home to the city of Bath in south west England, where I presently don't have anywhere to live and where my daily needs, primarily food, drink and shelter, will need to be paid for.

I have a rough idea where this book will take me; firstly, I will walk the streets in the city I've come to call home, seeking to know what poverty means to different members of society in an English heritage city; then I'll travel to India, to see what similarities and differences exist in a country that has been accelerating up the global financial charts, but nevertheless is still home to a population of over 100 million human beings deemed to be poor. This book, for the most part, will be written as it is lived.

Brown crinkled leaves are falling from the big linden tree behind me, scattering over the pebbles before the main house. I imagine the end of summer arrives with some foreboding for those who sleep on the bridge just north of Gare du Nord – the chill of autumn and winter is coming. I invite you to journey with me as I begin to search out my notes from the gutter.

Matthew Small
17th September 2014

BATH, ENGLAND
Late September to November, 2014

I

As the train's steel wheels screamed to a stop in the limestone city I was met with a view to material wealth. Opposite Bath Spa station is the Southgate shopping centre, built on the site of a previously demolished complex with the buildings constructed with a Bath stone façade, in keeping, if not meticulously so, with the honey-coloured dress of the city. There are restaurants with menus perhaps out of a poor person's sights (I have to look away from most) as well as the familiar golden arches whose marketing won't let us forget that *We're loving it!*, along with an array of other fast food outlets. There are clothes shops, phone shops, department stores, a market stall selling relatively cheap fruit and veg – call by at the end of the day and they're practically giving broccoli heads away – there's a flower stand and the street performers who are usually found strumming their guitars and beating their drums at the end of Stall Street, playing to the consumers as they march on by to spend, spend, spend.

Running along the eastern edge of Southgate and away from the train station is Manvers Street; home to a few shops, cafés, nightclubs, and a wonderful old second-hand bookshop, George Gregory. There's also the council building and city police station with Manvers Street Baptist Church next door. The Julian House night shelter and Bath Foodbank operate from the basements of the building and it is not uncommon to find a group of the charities' 'clients' sitting on the steps outside the church's café, or leaning against the stone wall around the police station car park. They're a diverse bunch; a thirty-something man with the top buttons of his shirt undone to display the outstretched wings of the tattoo across his chest; an elderly woman with her tired face often covered by the dreadlocks that fall out from beneath the woollen hood she has pulled up over her head, despite the warm September sun, along with others whose clothes are frayed and cheeks somewhat pale.

I observed this group as I walked along the pavement and a voice inside my head said, *Poor*. But do they see themselves in this way? Julian House uses the phrase 'socially excluded' to identify the people it comes into contact with. I looked back over my shoulder, questioning. Most were holding bottles in their hands, sipping at whatever was inside as they talked (the bottles were not labelled so I cannot say if they contained alcohol). Most would be deemed as scruffy in comparison to the tourists, commuters, consumers and students walking past them on the pavement and, standing huddled in a group with the rest of the city swirling by, they would likely be identified as being in poverty. But what does that mean?

I arrived in the city two days ago and, financially speaking, I guess I could also be placed on some statistical chart as being poor, although this I do not feel or identify with. I can, for the time being, buy enough food to meet my needs and even go to my friends' coffee shop and sit checking emails with a cappuccino beside me. This is where a part of the complexity of understanding poverty begins; it is primarily recognised aesthetically. Sitting at the brew bar at Colonna & Small's, tapping at my laptop and enjoying my drink made from beans grown on a remote farm in Ethiopia, I, in most people's eyes, would not look to be poor. But in truth I have around £140 in my bank account and £350 cash on my being. Before arriving in the city, a quick search online told me that the average starting price to rent a room in Bath is around £300 to £350 per month, normally requiring a deposit of £200. I do have a part-time job in a local inn but my first wage slip won't come until the end of October, one month away, and the only other immediate income I can expect is the advance I'm due for my previous book, *The Wall Between Us*, which would also not be enough to cover a room.

If I was forced to rent somewhere, with unforeseen bills and council tax to pay, then I would quickly find myself in a situation faced by many millions across the world: struggling to exist. That's why I'm writing this from a small, slightly mouldy and altogether little bit poorly caravan, situated at the bottom of a sweet lady's garden on one of the hilltops surrounding Bath. I've promised to give it a lick of paint and Clare, my landlady, has let me stay rent-free. I don't have electricity, running water or even a toilet (although Clare is happy for me to come into the house if nature calls). I am incredibly fortunate, even if I don't presently have a desk where I can write. I think most writers go through the same thought process when they move into somewhere new; the owner might be pointing out the light coming through the window but we're only interested in where we're going to be able to sit down and write.

After finishing work last night and locking up the inn around midnight, I walked through the drunken city which is now inebriated most days of the week, with students falling over each other after having knocked back trays of cheap shots, and hindered further by the school ties knotted together around their legs as they take a pub crawl to mean just that: crawling. I carried my sleeping bag under my arm, crossed a footbridge over the River Avon and began my walk up the long hill to where the caravan and my new home awaited. My first night was spent using John Steinbeck's *The Grapes of Wrath* as a pillow. It's not a thick book, more's the pity. What this has shown me is that without the graciousness of another, I would have had to stay in a hostel until my money ran out, or on the street with only my sleeping bag and Steinbeck to fend off the chill and my vulnerability. It showed me how close we can come.

II

My work at The Griffin Inn mostly entails pulling pints, cleaning glasses and engaging with whoever decides to drink at the bar. In days gone by, the inn was the drinking den for locals, pub brawls, dominoes and singing songs. Occasionally an old timer will call in and tell me a story or two about 'the old days' when there was an Alsatian sat at the door, eyeing up limbs of the punters on entry, and a pool table which was where most of the brawls broke out. It was the type of establishment where you'd be hard pushed to pick out the landlady and landlord from the punters, stood smoking at the end of the bar and as drunk and merry as the rest of the inn.

"It was a little bit like EastEnders, that sort of thing," a man at the bar told me one autumnal night, his fingers tobacco-stained and his skin weathered. He and his wife had called in to see what The Griffin had become after holding onto many memories from two decades prior. He sipped at his pint of Griffin Gold and his wife a Bacardi and Coke. "It's the first time me and the missus have come back into town, like. If the landlord and lady ever went on holiday then we'd run the place for them while they were away."

"Was it very different back then?"

"I'd say so," he replied, now leaning on the bar.

His wife smiled as she looked towards the window which dislodged a view to yesterday. She turned to her husband.

"Remember that Bath Rugby lot, doing their dares

when they'd get here?"

"Course I do."

"Dares?"

"They'd do silly things," she continued. "There used to be an aquarium in the window, just over there. They dared one of them to eat a fish. He walked straight over and stuck his hand into the water and pulled out a little one, before putting it in his mouth. He swallowed it straight down."

"No!"

"He did," confirmed the husband.

I looked towards the window, imagining the fish tank with glass stained by green algae on the inside and spilt beer on the outside. The husband and wife drank their drinks and continued surveying the inn. I watched nostalgia shape their expressions; it wasn't the same inn for them anymore, so many lives and stories had been scratched into the heavily worn wooden floors – all that remained of a place where they had passed days and nights, shared embraces and good times. I pulled them more drinks and they brought some of those stories back to life for me.

But The Griffin has moved on from those days when beer was cheap and smashed glasses were as common as fresh lime in slimline tonics. It's had a couple of coats of paint; the eight rooms upstairs are listed as 'Four Star' and, due to being five minutes from the Roman Baths are, generally full most days of the week. The tourist season has no end in a city famed for its *Englishness*.

After living in Japan for two months, I came to understand the draw of this small heritage city nestled in the Somerset valleys, it's in Bath's stoned conformity. The city has been constructed, for the most part, out of the stone of one man, Ralph Allen. Prior Park House, Allen's 17th century home and built in Palladian grandeur on a hill overlooking Bath, was commissioned in celebration (and promotion) of the stone. It certainly had an effect.

His stone is the city and the city has become his stone. Of course the tourists also flock here because Jane Austen lived and wrote in the city, capturing the pomp of the bath houses so astutely in *Northanger Abbey*; they also come to see the Roman edifices and it's only a short coach trip to Stonehenge. However, I still believe the main reason for their visit is to admire the sunlight sinking into the limestone walls, to watch the River Avon being split into three channels as it flows beneath the iconic arches of Pulteney Bridge, with Bath stone buildings speckling the tops of the distant hills like gold dust. The real reason the tourists arrive in coachload after coachload, with a recorded five million visitors in 2012, is to simply amble around the beautiful Georgian city of Bath.

A few nights back I was pulling a pint for a guest at the inn. His job was to drive tourists, mostly Australian and American, on coach trips around the UK. He was one of those guests who would sit at the bar for a couple of hours or more, leaving only to pick up some dinner in a nearby fast food outlet. His days were spent on motorways or sat in laybys and coach parks waiting for his group to return. So with a pint and me before him, he inevitably wanted to talk.

"She's from the Mediterranean, so everything's got to be a bloody drama." He was talking about his co-driver who had just called him to report another coach having hit her wing mirror, pushing it inwards. "I told her, 'Don't worry, push the thing back and it will be fine,' but she's from the Mediterranean, so she's all stressed and getting me stressed. But I don't get stressed."

He sipped at his drink and rested it back down on the bar. It would not be unreasonable to say that he had a beer belly; his hair was cut short and his eyes were watchful. He wore jeans and a long-sleeved top that was one big Union Jack. The red, blue and white were perhaps the boldest colours to be found within the dimly lit room. I stood on the other side of the bar, polishing glasses and, as the place was empty except for the coach driver, offered him my full attention.

"So you've written a book about Israel and Palestine?" He was referring to *The Wall Between Us* that was being released the following week. "That's a complicated subject."

"It's been made complicated," I said.

"And you're going to write another book?"

"I'm just starting."

"About what?"

"Poverty."

"Where do you begin with that?"

"I think that's what the book's going to be about."

He drank and I placed a clean glass back on a shelf with many others beneath the ale pumps. The coach driver leaned forward on his stool as he spoke.

"Poverty isn't just on the streets. Poverty isn't just in the council houses. It's also in the houses you see as affluent."

"You're right," I said. "But this poverty isn't easy to engage with, it's hidden. I'm still not sure how to find a way to capture it."

This was something that had been niggling at me. How do you speak to people who do not want to be defined by their poverty, living day to day on the breadline, stuck in an unending cycle of bills and not knowing where the money would come from to cover them? Or people who had fallen into poverty for the very reason that they did not want to appear poor, living and purchasing on credit which had led to debts that felt like a heavy slab of concrete resting on your chest, pushing out the remaining pockets of air from your lungs? The bar was so quiet it was fit for tumbleweeds and this meant the coach driver's voice commanded the empty tables, and easily lifted over the music playing out of the two small speakers on the paint-chipped walls.

"You got to think outside of yourself," he continued.

"Take this for an example, you're a woman who is homeless on the streets, you've no money or possessions and then that time of the month arrives. How do you deal with it?"

"God, I've no idea."

"Poverty isn't just about not having enough food or water, it's also about not being able to maintain personal hygiene."

I was starting to wonder what coach drivers got to be thinking about during those long hours behind the wheel.

"How do you come to be contemplating such things?"

"I used to be a probation officer, before driving coaches. Used to come into contact with lots of people, some were struggling, some were on the streets."

"It's their voices I'd like to include in this book," I said.

"So you'd best get out on the streets then."

"I intend to."

He finished the last of his drink and slid the glass across the bar towards me. I retrieved it and moved to the larger taps, pulling him a fresh one. He watched me on his stool with his back straight and his Buddha belly pregnant with two pints of larger and his evening kebab.

"You want to find that person who chooses to be on the streets," he added. "That person who's happy to be on the streets. They're not looking for a home. They're not looking for work. They're on the street by choice and they're happy to be there by choice."

I placed the full pint glass down before him, the door opened and two guests returned from their evening spent at the Theatre Royal, having enjoyed *The Importance of Being Earnest*. They smiled at me as they passed the bar before climbing the stairs to the rooms. I turned back to the coach driver.

"But why would someone choose to be on the streets?"

"All I'm saying is that you find that person who is quite happy to be on the streets and there you'll have your story."

The door opened again and this time some punters entered, I left the coach driver on his stool at the end of the bar to welcome the arrivals. I pulled pints of ale, measured out a glass of wine and mixed a gin and tonic with fresh lime and ice. I worked. My thoughts, however, lingered over what the coach driver had said. This book is meant to be about the hardship of poverty, not the freedom, and I didn't like the idea of him flipping it upside down; it was a difficult subject as it was. As I tallied up the drinks on the till, the coach driver's phone rang; he lifted from the stool and walked to the door, answering it.

"It's alright, just calm down will you," he said before the door closed behind his words.

It must be the Mediterranean, I thought. I pressed cash on the till and the money drawer rattled open.

III

It was a cold but fine October day, the sun occasionally being concealed by harmless sheep-white clouds, the type of sheep whose wool is pure white like clumps of fresh fallen snow. I'd just come from sitting in the café in Manvers Street Baptist Church, speaking to the coordinator of the Bath Foodbank. I wish to include our conversation in this book but first I want to write about two other encounters I made after finishing the meeting, while walking back through the city en route to the coffee shop to write up my notes.

The first took place on Milsom Street, a main shopping road running through the centre of Bath, and one I often see as the spine of the city, busy with cars and people going about their every day. I was waiting for a break in the traffic when I heard guitar music nearby. Looking along the pavement, beyond a group of youngsters employed by Coca-Cola to give out little cans of the stuff to passers-by, their smiles wide as they handed over the free samples, I could see a guy sat on the stone strumming a guitar. I walked towards him, politely refusing the cans of Coke being offered to me from all directions. I stopped and listened to him play for a while. Placed on the pavement was a bag with some coins in it, a piece of cardboard rested over the bag with words scribbled onto it with marker pen: *Homeless: Busking to get a train ticket to Portsmouth where I can be housed. Thank you + God Bless. Please Help.* He finished playing and I took a pound coin from my pocket, crouching down and placing it into the bag.

"Thanks."

"No problem," I said, my mind secretly racing to find the next right words to say. "I'm... I'm writing a book and it's about people struggling and stuff, and I wonder if you'd mind telling me why you can get housed in Portsmouth and not here?"

He rested his arms on top of the guitar and looked up at me, squinting against the sunlight that reflected off the light limestone all around. His hair was black with a quiff not unlike that of Elvis. I placed him to be late thirties or early forties; he had a prominent nose and ears. His voice was soft:

"I was in Southampton as a witness in a criminal investigation. They then moved me to Bath for my safety. They wanted to put me in a hostel for people who had been in prison. I refused to stay in this hostel so they refused to help me, and because I had refused they refused me help from any other services. I've got nothing here. I don't know anyone. I've an ex-girlfriend living in Portsmouth who might be able to put me up for a bit. I don't know what else to do."

I told him the book I'm writing would seek to give a voice to stories like his, because I don't think they're being heard or listened to.

"No, they're not," he said before resettling his fingers over the strings.

I turned and walked away, running across the road between slow moving cars and passing the building society on the corner of Quiet Street. This street, as it happens, is seldom quiet; instead noisy with traffic, unloading vans and human voices. I was looking straight ahead, beyond Queen Square to my day's first coffee and space where I could write, now wanting to also detail my encounter with the Elvis of Milsom Street (I passed this chap again a few weeks later, he was playing in the same spot only this time his sign had changed, *Looking for work*. I wondered if this meant that his story and history had also changed). Thinking ahead meant I didn't quite capture the voice that came from below. It came again.

"Excuse me, couldn't spare a little change?"

I stopped and turned towards him; a man, mid-fifties with heavy stubble and humble shoulders, looking up at me with his whole being nothing but uncomfortable.

"Sorry to ask," he added.

"No, don't be," I said, suddenly aware that on two adjoining streets there was someone to be found asking for money.

I rummaged for my wallet but in the meantime the writer inside me sat my body down on the step beside him.

"Look," I said, "I'm writing a book about people who are struggling. I've just spoken to another chap about why he was on the street, would you mind telling me why you're here asking for money too?"

"Yeah, I'll tell you, but you ain't going to use my name or nothing?"

He looked at me when he spoke and quickly looked away again when he had finished.

"I don't need to know your name."

He turned to me again and his words erupted out of him, tainted by anger.

"They just suspended my job seekers. I been to that office three times this week and still they told me I've not done enough. Now they suspended my payments and what do I do? I got nothing to get food with. It's disgusting. Now I'm getting all worked up just thinking about what they do to people. It takes a long time to get the money but they stop it in an instant. I'll tell you, this government's got to go."

"Do you have a home?"

"Yeah, I've got a home but I haven't got a job and now they stopped my job seekers."

"I'm going to be in London in a couple of weeks," I said, wanting to offer him some kind of condolence, "there's going to be a protest taking place in Parliament Square about the failings of our democracy and government, including their treatment of the poor."

"Good," he replied. "You tell them a thing or two for me, this government's got to go."

"And what about this campaign recently launched in Bath to encourage people not to give money to people such as you, begging on the street? It's called Your Kindness Can Kill."

It was something I had read about in *The Bath Chronicle*, piloted in 2014 and having received support from the main charities in the city who work with the poor, claiming it stopped funding addiction and dependence and instead forced the vulnerable into channels of support. I had mixed feelings about it; appreciating that it could be easy for some to abuse the kindness of others, but I didn't like the branding and the way it came across, feeling it would only distance people from those on the street for fear of getting into trouble. I also wasn't keen on the stereotyping it evoked that all those on the streets were addicts and if you gave them money it wouldn't help their situation. It might not, but maybe it will buy them a Snickers bar, a cigarette, or a magazine and a little light relief from being poor – after all, not all poor people are drug addicts, just like not all celebrities are propped up by cocaine.

"What do you think about it?" I asked the man sat beside me, his cheeks having become red during the course of our conversation.

"Well they're bloody evil! Trying to stop people from helping people, I mean that's what we're meant to be about, helping those that are in difficulty. It's evil. This is how they want you to feel. I feel like a piece of dirt on the street sometimes. I don't want to be sat here asking for money, but I got nothing to buy food. They just suspended my job seekers in an instant, I got nothing to fall back on. What am I supposed to do?"

He looked away again. I'd just come from the foodbank and knew that he'd need to get a stamp for food assistance from one of the many agencies in the city who were authorised to distribute them, but it was Friday afternoon and the foodbank wasn't open over the weekend. So I thanked him for talking to me and gave him some money, and decided to rely on my own ethics as to whether I truly believed that my kindness could ever kill him.

"Are you sure?" he said, stowing the money into his inner coat pocket as I stood and walked away.

I turned and waved before quickly walking to the coffee shop to write. Two city centre streets had brought two tales of poverty, tinged by injustice. It's an intimidating thought when you begin to question how many streets there might be in the world, with all those tales to go with them.

IV

"We're at the tail end of the process, really… "

I was in the basement of Manvers Street Baptist Church, speaking to Bob and Sally, two volunteers at the Bath Foodbank.

"… although we're also on the frontline in a way," added Bob.

I'd say Bob was mid-sixties and Sally younger – they were sat on plastic chairs, awaiting the next order to be brought down by the *greeter*, the name I shall give to the volunteer who was waiting to meet those in need upstairs in the church's café. The basement was a little like being in a windowless sports hall, with a part of the far wall taken up by lockers containing shelves of food, all neatly stacked and separated. There were small towers of baked bean cans, bags of sugar, packs of pasta, cartons of long-life milk, cereal boxes, jars of instant coffee, and more – all food which had been donated to the foodbank.

Bob and Sally were asking me questions about my want to write about poverty when the greeter walked across the hall towards us, holding two pieces of paper in her hand, one red and the other yellow. The greeter was a middle-aged woman with curly hair and hurried speech.

"Sally," she said, "I've just had two arrive and they're very hungry. One has a slip but his friend hasn't. Can I order him some beans on toast?"

"Of course," said Sally. "I'll come up with you."

The greeter gave the pieces of paper to Bob and left with Sally, their footsteps pattering and then echoing around the hall. Bob saw my eyes settle on the papers in his hand.

"The yellow one's confidential," he said. "Has clients' personal information on, but I can show you what I do with the red one. It tells me what food to give them. You can watch me make up the order if you like."

"I'd like that, thanks."

Bob moved to the lockers of food and I followed. He placed the red piece of paper down on a table and began to trace his finger down the list.

"Five hundred grams of pasta," he said, turning to the food and picking out a pack of spaghetti before returning to the table and placing it into a plastic bag. He returned to the list again, a modern day ration card.

"This is for one person," he said. "If it had been for a family then we'd obviously give out more."

The plastic bag quickly became two after Bob searched out a pack of biscuits, coffee, sugar, a box of cereal, two cans of soup and baked beans.

"We don't accept perishable food, see," he continued, bringing the red piece of paper to his nose to make sure he'd not missed anything. "Come on, we'll take the food up."

I walked with Bob across the hall, holding the doors open for him with the bulging plastic bags held at his side. We climbed the stairs and made our way to the café. Sally and the greeter were sat with the two men, one had a messy beard and was a picture of hunger; he had visible cheek bones despite the hair on his face and was slow in his movements and speech. The other, his friend, a younger man with a shaven head, stood as Bob placed down the bags at his feet.

"Thank you," said the shaven headed man who had arrived with the food stamp, lifting the bags and walking away with his donated provisions.

His friend stayed sitting silently at the table, waiting for his beans on toast. I thanked Bob and Sally for speaking with me and also left, but I wanted to know more about this organisation and the people it assisted. One week later I returned; this time to meet with Grainne, the foodbank's coordinator and also as chirpy as a songbird in spring.

The café in Manvers Street Baptist Church is a popular place for pots of tea and simple cuisine. It's a dying breed on the high street where the majority of cafés now serve up freshly ground 'Arabica' coffee and overpriced paninis. I walked over to the table used by the foodbank, where they meet the people who have been provided with a food stamp, identified as being in need of food assistance by one of the many agencies in the city who come into contact with people in either financial or circumstantial difficulties. There are no banners on the table to say Bath Foodbank, or anything in the way that indicates charity. There is a measure of discretion to the work the foodbank does. Sat at the table was the greeter; she watched me approach and looked to my hands, instantly picking up that I wasn't holding anything.

"Do you have your slips?"

"I'm actually here to meet with Grainne," I replied. "She's going to talk to me about the work you do."

"Oh, I see."

She stood and waved at a woman who was talking to an aging couple on a nearby table. Grainne excused herself and came over.

"Grainne," said the greeter, "this young man is here to talk to you."

"Matthew?" Grainne offered me her hand.

"Thank you for taking the time to meet with me."

"It's a pleasure," she said. "Let's find a table to sit at."

Grainne is the coordinator of the Bath Foodbank, a service that has 'fed more than 6,500 people since its launch in 2011, including 2,000 children'. She spoke with passion and energy and the hum of the café faded into the background as I explained to her that I hoped meeting with charities such as the foodbank would provide me with an insight into the hidden poverty in the UK, people who have incomes and homes but can't afford to put food on the table.

"Of course we see people in that exact situation but we maintain a high level of confidentiality. This is why we don't wear name badges to say who we are while operating in the café. We're discreet so as not to make those who come here feel uncomfortable or exposed. We welcome them, offer them a cup of tea, a chat if they would like it, and provide them with enough food to see them through three days."

The foodbank is, in a way, an emergency response service to assist those in food crises, a stop gap or buffer zone. It does not provide a long-term solution, but instead a lifeline when times are unmanageable. If an unforeseen bill means someone has found themselves in a position where they can't put food on the table, then the foodbank is there to help see them through it. It also helps those in abject poverty, without income or homes, but will always seek to direct them to other services in the city, which will work with them to explore pathways out of poverty. In order to reduce reliance on the foodbank, a guideline has been set that means only three stamps can be issued to one person per month.

"Although this is just a guideline," said Grainne. "We work closely with the local agencies, social services, churches and the council, and will cater for people on an individual basis. For instance if someone is in a period where they are financially unable to buy food, and need to be helped for a time that exceeds three stamps, then the agency will contact us and we can help to see them through."

The foodbank is not unique to Bath, being found

in increasingly more towns and cities nationwide. The growing need for foodbanks in a Western economy has been seen by many as a 'national scandal'. More than 20 million meals were served in the UK in 2013, a rise of 54 per cent on the previous year.[1]

"And how is the food donated to you?"

"Different ways really," said Grainne. "Churches and schools do a lot of collections for us. This time of year is particularly good. We fit in well with Harvest; it's about collecting food for your community. The supermarket collections are where most of our food comes from. All the supermarkets in the city have been very supportive. They let us set up a stand outside with a team of volunteers who hand out a shopping list to customers. We ask if they could just pick up one item on the list for the charity while they do their own shopping. It's incredible how supportive most people are. It's a simple way to help. One day a woman in Sainsbury's came back to us with a full trolley."

I was making notes as Grainne spoke, thinking there was a short story to be found in the woman who donated a trolley's worth of food.

"I can take you downstairs to see where we keep the food if you like?" said Grainne.

"Bob was kind enough to let me watch him make up an order last week," I replied, looking up from my notes. "How do people respond to you in Bath?"

"Now people are used to seeing our collection points, but I still remember when we first set up a stand outside one of the supermarkets, handing out leaflets about the charity and seeking donations. People kept coming up to us and asking why we needed a foodbank in Bath. They were really surprised."

Plates clattered together in the kitchen behind us and spoons chimed against china with the café now busy in service.

"It's not just about food," continued Grainne. "People

leave here with a bag or two of food but it's more than that. They can also sit and have a chat if they want to. We don't tell them what they should do. We don't judge them. We can offer advice about different services that they can contact, but more importantly we are here to share a pot of tea with them and listen."

I explained to Grainne that I was coming to realise the scale of the subject I had set out to write about, and how I felt unable to do it justice. Poverty was so circumstantial that it almost felt silly to search out trends, but Grainne suggested I look at the Trussell Trust website, one of the largest providers of foodbanks in the UK, which compiled statistics about the people it came into contact with. I was still certain however that I wanted to pursue the personal stories that the statistics don't reveal.

"I do remember one woman," said Grainne. "She was a single mum and struggling dreadfully. She would eat less, often miss meals so her son was well nourished. We provided her with some assistance. Poverty isn't simply about not having enough to eat, it's so much more. At night, with her son in bed, this woman would sit alone in her house. She hadn't the money to afford a babysitter, or even the money to go out if she could find someone to look after her son. This meant her chance to form relationships was extremely limited. It costs money to do anything in a city like Bath. So she would stay at home. It can be a very lonely existence for people." Grainne looked over to the table where the greeter was sat waiting next to an empty chair, ready to welcome the next person in need. She turned to face me. "It's about the other things that your life loses out on."

V

At 7pm, each and every night of the year, a huddle of people begin to form in a dark car park at the back of the Hilton Hotel, perhaps a leading contender for the ugliest building to be found amongst Bath's otherwise flattering architecture. The hotel looks like one giant breeze block; fronted by many rectangular windows and drooping Hilton flags.

The car park, poorly lit by street lamps and framed by graffiti painted walls, is the location of the Bath soup run; a service set up and maintained by different churches in the city. I first stopped by on a Saturday evening; a small camp table had already been erected with two men stood behind it, one serving soup and the other cups of coffee. Around twenty to twenty-five down and outs were gathered around, sipping their cups of warm liquid and chatting amongst themselves; the ones that were really hungry focused only on the warm soup in their hands.

I merely observed, thanking the volunteers for allowing me to join them. The old boy beside me, in charge of pouring coffee, fiddled with his hearing aid as I spoke. They were from a church in Widcombe; a small village-like enclave of Bath, across the river from the main city station. I walked through Widcombe high street on my way to and from the caravan.

"And you're here every night?" I asked the gentleman serving the chunky vegetable soup.

"We take it in turns," he replied. "We're here every Saturday; tomorrow will be a different church."

"How are you funded?"

"Our congregation, mostly, we have collections."

I was beginning to realise how many of the services assisting the poor in the city were Christian based, and so far I hadn't sensed anything in the way of being motivated in the name of missionary aims and conversion – they were motivated by their faith in helping those in need. It was refreshing, and unlocked little moments of guilt in me about my previous tendencies to tense up around institutionalised religion, particularly Christianity, seeing it as a distasteful joke in light of the life of Jesus. Jesus taught about maintaining a deep compassion for life and those among us who are vulnerable, and the charities I had met so far, rooted in Christianity, certainly acted out of this same compulsion. Standing on the edge of this giving, it was much like being at an unglamorous feast.

A woman was walking among the crowd, carrying a plastic bag.

"Would you like some biscuits?" she asked a soup sipper who had faded tattoos across his knuckles and a once hard face, now softened by age and poverty which will disarm even the toughest of characters.

"Have you got Hobnobs?" he asked.

She peered into the bag.

"Just Custard Creams, I think."

"Alright then," he replied, accepting a pack and stuffing it in his coat pocket.

"Sandwiches? Anyone not had a sandwich?" Another man walked past, handing out sandwiches wrapped in cling film.

"How long do you stay for?" I asked the soup server.

"Normally we're packed up by seven-thirty, the food goes soon enough."

It certainly did. Once the cups of soup had all been served, he began pouring the remainder of the warm soup into empty plastic milk bottles, handing them out for those who wanted to take some home with them. The sandwiches, biscuits and coffee were also given out, and the crowd slowly dispersed with full pockets and bellies. I hadn't, however, discovered anything about the lives of those who had come for soup. This meant only one thing, I needed to return.

A few days later, the moon and stars were veiled by night-time clouds with a mist of drizzle in the air. It was nearing 7pm and I was leant against a lamppost on Walcott Street, on the edge of the car park. My notebook was open in my hands and I set about capturing the scene around me. Across the road I detailed the YMCA building with its gym on the second floor, where runners on treadmills were running endlessly towards the windows before them, with a view over the street-lit city and towards the dark hills on the horizon. The black tarmac road was varnished by an earlier shower, the light of the street lamps shimmering as though reflected on a lake's surface. I moved away from the lamppost and looked towards the end of the car park, a few down and outs had arrived, but still no soup stand.

No time like the present, I told myself.

I closed my notebook and walked down the road leading to the people who had come to receive hot soup. I couldn't help but gaze towards the hotel as I went. It felt wrong that something so ugly had been allowed to be built in a city deemed to be a World Heritage site.

I would normally have first introduced myself to the volunteers who oversaw the soup run, offering them my reason for being there. Seeing as how they were yet to show up, I was instead saying hello and smiling at the poor people around me. There was a middle-aged woman sat on her backpack against a metal wire fence, a group of twenty-somethings, smoking and standing in a small circle while talking loudly and somewhat vulgarly about how 'wet' one of them can make his girlfriend. I was already appearing out of place amongst the group, and silence was soon wrapped around me as I stood and tried to think about what I was going to say to these people. I was conscious that I could be seen as a writer looking to profit from their lives and strife, an outsider who thinks he can relate. I didn't want to offend but still I was seeking to witness what poverty means today and to do this I would have to write what I saw and experienced. Nevertheless I found it hard to find a way into engaging with those around me. I decided I needed to do something. I stood out anyway, so why not stand out a lot? I lifted my notebook before me, opened it and took my pen from inside. I began to write.

"What you writing?"

One of the women from the group broke away and approached me.

"I'm writing a book about people who are struggling. I've come down here to see what services are available."

"You're writing about homelessness?"

"That will form a part of it."

"You want to talk to her then," she pointed to a woman in a baseball cap, speaking to two young men who did not look very well in themselves or the world around them. I'm not an expert so I can't say for sure they were high. "She'll talk to you, tell you everything. Here Jackie (not her real name), he's writing about homelessness. Said he should talk to you."

Jackie approached and looked at me and the notebook in my hand.

"Yeah, I'll talk to you," she spoke furiously fast. "I've been in it all. On the streets, got a child, in and out all kinds of services. I'll talk to you."

"That would be great," I said, before trying to slow her down a bit as she was already offering me her number and telling me we could meet in the afternoons.

"I'm busy in the mornings," she added.

"No problem," I said, saving her number on my

phone. "I'm hoping to learn about what avenues are open to people who are in difficulty, or why people find it hard to get out of poverty."

"Well I'll tell you this straight away; they don't want us to be seen in this city. They go round and count the homeless. If there's more than fourteen then it's seen as a problem, and they don't want a problem. So they only go to the city centre, no one sleeps in the city centre. Last time they only counted two on the streets, but I reckon there were three hundred in all."

It's worth me stating here that this book is largely about the people I meet and giving a place for their voices, which means the factual reliability of what they say is not verified. However, this is what they believe to be true, and therefore informs us to their regard of the society and systems around them. To begin to understand something we have to be willing to give a space to different worldviews, even if some are inaccurate. I have nothing to say she was lying, just as I am equally unable to state her words to be the gospel truth.

"So you wanna meet or what?"

"I've got your number," I replied. (I bumped into Jackie a couple of weeks later and scheduled to meet the following afternoon. She didn't appear.)

She returned to her friends and they commenced a low conversation, an array of plastic bags at their feet, some containing food. Something struck me about this group as being different from the others who were sat at the fence, looking on and waiting for the church people to arrive. A tall man was pacing back and forth nearby. He wore a brown coat, jeans and his hands moved constantly to rival his feet. We made eye contact.

"Alright?" he said.

"Fine, thanks," I replied. "Just trying to learn about the services available to people who might be in difficulty in the city, learn about their stories. Are most of the people here homeless?"

He stopped pacing and looked at me, gesturing to the group standing together and speaking loudly again.

"Pisses me off in a way; most of them have their own houses. If I had a home then I'd be cooking in it, but all the junkies come down here and get fed. But then they (the charity) tell you it's for everyone."

By now, more people had joined us. An old man with an unlit pipe in his mouth was leaning on his bike, laden with plastic bags and perhaps his life's possessions, up against the wall, another held a guitar in a bag on his back and a woman wearing a grey hoodie was becoming increasingly verbal about the absence of any soup. This was followed by her swearing when it started to rain. (I passed this woman on the street a few days later; this time her cheeks were red with sorrow and tears fell from her eyes. She hurried past me sobbing and I turned to watch her disappear into the people crowding the pavements, never knowing what it was that had shattered the anger I had previously identified her by.)

"We'll have to go up," the stoic woman sat on her backpack by the fence said. "Won't set up here in the rain."

The group responded and soon we were a slow moving train of sorts walking back up the car park towards Walcott Street. I learned that when it rained the soup run operated under an overhang of the YMCA building. The October days were increasingly grey and cloudy so I guessed it would be set up under cover more and more from now on. I waited for a few minutes, observing the frustration boiling out of some after the rain promptly stopped and the church volunteers arrived and set up the stand in the car park. The soup sippers trudged back across Walcott Street, with the woman stalked by anger shouting at a car that failed to stop. I decided to make my way to the caravan, Steinbeck and an early night, but poverty, I was beginning to see, was never more than just another city street away.

VI

The river was black with night. I walked across the footbridge behind Bath Spa station, there was a train grumbling on the platform before continuing its journey to Cardiff Central. It was nearing 8pm and the impending winter nights were already closing in. The street lamps ahead led me towards Widcombe Parade, where I would then turn off at Prior Park Road and begin the slow trudge up Perrymead. Despite the sweat and becoming short of breath, I enjoyed my walk home to the caravan, always on the lookout for an urban fox, badger or deer. The wildlife used the darkness as an invitation to explore and scavenge.

I was tired. The writing of this book had stirred an uncomfortable feeling in me that I could never do poverty justice. I'd also worked until late the previous night, and I was beginning to run out of money – so this meant thoughts and energy went into questioning the real need of anything I set out to buy. Browsing the shelves in Waitrose for the reductions was laborious, those little red labels giving false hope that I might better afford the mixed bean salad with its 25 per cent reduction due to a shortened shelf life. My financial woe was temporary, I hoped; I had some money coming, but I was annoyed with myself that I had blown through all the money I had, especially considering I didn't even have bills to cover. I can't even recall where it went. I had been reckless, or I had simply lived. I continued walking.

Widcombe Parade was quiet. Parts of the road and

pavement had been ripped up with barriers erected as diggers stood still, the workmen now at home, resting after another hard day's labour. The only businesses still open were three drinking dens, a laundrette and a convenience store. I walked past with the strong strip lighting crawling out of the door to light the pavement before me. Tucked into the shadows ahead, a man was sat on the ground with a large bag beside him, a sleeping bag stuffed inside. He leaned into the light released from the convenience store; the book in his hands held close to his face. He was lost in it. The book was enough for me to identify him by, but the long hair, blue distressed and frayed jeans and red coat left me in no doubt.

"Hey, Dean."

I first saw Dean in the spring. I was walking out of Waitrose in the city centre, and was instantly met by Dean standing beneath a traffic light and offering me a *Big Issue*. At this point in time I was again in my own financial difficulties and had tried to stop buying things I didn't need, so I had also stopped buying the *Big Issue*. On this day however I had some change in my pocket and a man doing his best to help himself out of poverty before me. I gave him £2.50 and he gave me a magazine in return.

"Thanks," he had said. "That was my last one so I can go and read my book now."

Dean, given the amount of faces that pass him by at his pitch, would probably not recall this encounter. Some months later it saddened me to find him in Widcombe, sitting on the stone and clinging to light out of shadow. He had a head of long hair which fell to his shoulders with his eyebrows touching in the middle.

"What are you reading?" I asked.

The dark pavements and street were empty of people and cars. He turned the book over for me to see the cover. I was unable to make out the title in the low light.

"It's a sci-fi."

"You read a lot, don't you?"

"I love reading."

I told Dean that I was writing my own book about what it means to be on the street or in poverty. I asked if he would be happy for me to spend some time with him over the coming month.

"Yeah, that's alright."

The book laid waiting in his hands, his eyes flickering from me to it. I wondered if he'd eaten.

"I've just come from the soup run," I said. "Do you know about it? They give out some hot food."

"Yeah, I go sometimes but I'm not always keen on some of the people that go there. Prefer to stay here out the way."

"Cool, well I'll let you get back to your book. Perhaps we could catch up for tea one day?"

"Yeah, maybe," he said.

I walked away and Dean instantly fell back into science fiction. I crossed the street and turned down Prior Park Road. By the time I reached Perrymead and the steepest leg of my climb home, the heavens had opened. The rain hammered down. I was soaked in an instant. I climbed the hill in the dark and wet. I thought about Dean, doing all he could to protect the pages of his book.

The following weekend the city blushed in sunshine. I'd been sitting in the Abbey square watching my friend Amy staging her peaceful protest against the suppression of the Falun Gong in China; she performed her meditation sequence to the backdrop of Saturday shoppers and day-trippers, crisscrossing the Abbey square with a street performer playing for them.

Falun Gong is founded around the principles of Truthfulness, Compassion and Tolerance. I'd often sit on the steps at the edge of the Roman Baths watching the comings and goings in the square and writing my notes –

finding the principles of Falun Gong to be universal, fit for humanity although becoming somewhat lost on us at times.

I left the square and ambled through the streets, filling time as my shift in the inn didn't start for an hour or so. I saw Dean standing outside T.K. Maxx clothing store. The high street was one of the busiest roads in the city for traffic and people, coming to and from the Abbey square. Dean was stood offering his magazine to those who passed him. He was wearing his red *Big Issue* vest over his jumper with his bag, stuffed with sleeping bag, placed at his feet, his book closed and resting on top.

"Hey, Dean," I said, coming to stand beside him and noting the magazine. "How's your day going?"

"Alright," he replied. "Not great though. I could only afford one magazine this morning. I sold it and then bought two more. Now I've sold four. It's alright."

I couldn't help but look at the bag at his feet again; seeing the sleeping bag as futile against the deepening cold of night – I knew because I was finding it tougher each day in the caravan. I now slept in woolly socks, two jumpers, a sleeping bag and under a duvet, and still the cold found a way in to wake me in the early hours.

"Do you ever sleep in the night shelter?"

"Now and then; it's alright but you need £21 a week to stay there, and if you haven't got a *local connection* then they kick you out."

I had come to understand local connection to mean someone who had family in the city or had lived in the city for six months out of the previous twelve. I had also learned that if you didn't have this connection then your access to services was severely restricted; you would be directed back to the place from where you came. It was an added hindrance to those on the street that moved from city to city, finding people more willing to give to a new face. This often meant a person on the street might lose a connection to anywhere. Then what?

I didn't fancy spending £2.50 on a magazine as it would eat into my diminishing daily budget and I wanted to go for coffee before work, which I had chosen to pursue despite it becoming my second biggest weekly outgoing after food. I wrote well in the coffee shop so I would fund it as long as I could. I did have a packet of raisins and almonds on me, and knew I would be able to make a sandwich at the inn so I pulled them from my pocket.

"I've got these if you'd like them."

"Yeah, okay," said Dean. "Thanks."

He accepted the raisins and almonds and placed them beside his book on top of his sleeping bag.

"How you doing for books?"

"Okay."

"Do you need some?"

"Always."

"I'll see what I can dig out."

"Thanks."

I left Dean to try and sell the couple of magazines he had left. I walked back through the Abbey square, slowed by the sight of Amy sat crossed-legged in meditation on the stone. The day-trippers ebbed and swelled around her.

VII

Three nights previous to this, I was talking about poverty with a young woman who was doing a trial shift with me at the bar. Our conversation expanded after discovering she had recently finished her dissertation looking at the different services available to the poor in the city. "Charities are becoming businesses," she said. These words instantly took me back two years. I was staying with a friend in Paris and having dinner in her favourite Cambodian restaurant. She had been working for some years with a global charity that sought to end child poverty. She voiced her concerns about what charity was becoming driven by:

"We do an incredible amount of good, provide invaluable support," she said. "But it still feels strange that the office is really always waiting for the next crisis; that's when the donations flood in and we work at our best, it's when we thrive."

Two years later and standing behind an empty bar, I continued to listen as The Griffin's new recruit brought me back to the present with a measure of cold realisation. "The thing to think about when it comes to charities," she said, "is are they there to help people, or are they there to substitute something the government isn't doing?"

So, I decided to pay a visit to the Bath Bike Workshop, a social enterprise that was set up by Julian House. This means the profits from the bike shop go back into Julian House and help to fund the many services it provides in Bath and beyond. It's Tuesday and a day when the bike shop is home to more than just the sale and service of bikes; it is transformed into a space for 'meaningful opportunity'. I ran along Corn Street, hopping over puddles with their surfaces a wet bed of tiny explosions as the hard falling rain crashed down. I arrived at a whitewashed building with an old bike held high over the door beside a sign, Bath Bike Workshop. I wiped the raindrops from my brow with my sleeve and entered.

Rows of bikes filled the space inside, most of them second-hand and repaired with old bike parts, serviced instead of scrapped. Behind the sales counter was an area for repairs; it was busy with bikes lifted on stands and people attentively tightening bolts with spanners or spinning wheels while testing brakes. I was introduced to Vinnie, a member of Julian House who is usually based in one of their supportive houses but also helps out in the bike shop's day of meaningful opportunity. He was a man of bulging muscles and I thought him more suited to the bench press rather than assisting those in difficulty. I offered him my hand and unhelpfully imagined him crushing the bones in my fingers if he so wished.

"This is just one of many days of meaningful opportunities that Julian House offers," he said, leading me over to the computer. "I'll print you off a poster."

I have it beside me now and the list of activities is extensive and, I have to say, quite exciting: IT beginners course, indoor five-a-side football, bike maintenance, women's bakery, 50 Strong - a group for over fifties, women's craft, acupuncture and meditation, discussion and inspirational writing group, tennis and a class called Creativity Unleashed, exploring creative output using contemporary art. These are just some of the meaningful opportunities available to the clients throughout October.

"It's about filling time, taking their minds off their situation. Giving them something to concentrate on, a bit of escapism," said Vinnie.

I watched the five or so clients who were working

on the bikes, assisted by the bike shop staff and silently engaged with the task before them.

"It's also about giving them some training, acquiring skills which all help in forming pathways out of poverty."

"And do most people take advantage of these days?"

"Yeah, I think it's a real benefit to them. Take today for instance," he pointed to the glass panelled door and the curtain of rain that was falling on the other side. "Who would want to be out on the street in that?"

My feet were wet from the walk to the shop and that was bad enough.

"The trouble we have is when we take someone as far as our services can take them. We might provide someone with supported housing for two years, give them opportunities to train in something and learn skills, but when that time comes to go back out there, to move back into society, they're terrified they'll lose their benefits and support network. That's the real challenge to overcome. They think they'll be worse off; having to pay for rent, council tax and if they find work then it would likely be low paid. Some have real difficulty taking the needed step."

Julian House was one of the charities *The Bath Chronicle* listed as supporting the launch of Your Kindness Can Kill (I later found out the campaign was largely implemented by Julian House). I decided to ask Vinnie what he thought about the campaign.

"Kindness really can kill," he replied. "The campaign is about trying to help people out of that vicious cycle of poverty. If you're on the street busking and getting £15 in a day then the next day you're more likely to be out on the street doing the same. It won't help your situation. You're still going to be stuck on the street, relying on the hand-outs of others. So we give out cards to people which direct individuals to our services and then we can work with them to try and get them out of poverty."

I appreciated his response and it was good for me to

hear the rationale for the campaign from someone who works with the city's poor on a daily basis. I still didn't like the title, thinking its hard hitting approach unnecessary and unhelpful to guiding public perception on what it means to be poor.

I thanked him for taking the time to talk to me; a middle-aged man was working on a small yellow child's bike beside us, adjusting the stabilisers and making the most of this time to give energy to something, to not be merely poor and searching for something to do. Julian House is finding ways to strike back at some of the negative effects poverty has on an individual: lack of self-worth, confidence and purpose for being. Through meaningful opportunity, those in need and difficulty can get up on a morning and know that they have something to do that day; in this case it's fixing up a bike, but one thing really can lead to another. It is just one of the stepping stones on the run out of poverty. The five or so souls who were polishing frames and blowing up tyres had embraced this opportunity presented to them. They weren't sitting still. Poverty had not yet defined or defeated them. I left the workshop and entered the rain.

VIII

After a day of heavy rain it was pleasant to wake this morning and hear the crows chattering in the branches above the caravan, not drowned out by the beating of raindrops on the roof. I lay in my jumpers and under my blankets with my mind slowly rousing from the deep sleep I'd succumbed to after a few sleep-deprived nights. My caravan was modest and increasingly damp but it was homely enough, and I now had a desk where I could write. It was a simple desk; there was a pull out tray for a computer keyboard, which would have been useful had I a computer keyboard; there was space enough on it for my books, potted bamboo which was suffering the most from the cold and also my laptop. The desk had cost me £10; I thought this fair, especially as it included delivery. I had purchased it from the Genesis Furniture Project, a social enterprise that operated under the Genesis Trust, perhaps the largest organisation in the city that works with those experiencing personal and family problems, particularly as a result of poverty. The furniture is donated to the charity and the profits from its sale, as with the Bath Bike Workshop for Julian House, go back into funding the operational costs and continuation of Genesis.

Genesis reaches out in many different ways and I decided to line up a meeting with the project manager to learn more about what Genesis do; I was also still looking for a way into meeting people on the hard end of poverty. I first met Ian in the Genesis offices at the rear of St John's Church on South Parade, just off Manvers Street.

The church is a gothic styled brute amongst the otherwise Georgian delicacy to be found in the city, with its 222-foot spire towering over most and stealing one's vision when looking down on Bath from the surrounding hilltops. Ian was a kindly man who welcomed me into a large room, gesturing me to a table where a flip chart was stood at one end. It was a room fit for a conference: large windows, comfy chairs with paper and pens ready to sketch out ideas. I placed down my notebook and thanked him for taking the time to meet with me. I first asked him about the soup run, the founding project run by the Genesis Trust.

"I've heard it's been going years."

"It has, nearly twenty years now," said Ian. "Basically a couple of ladies from some of the local churches were in Bath and came across a homeless person. They brought some sandwiches. Next day they went back and brought some more sandwiches and it led to the realisation that there was a need so they started the soup run. It was coordinated through the local churches so that a different church took on a night when they would prepare soup and sandwiches and go to the same place. I don't know how frequently that was done initially, but eventually it was up and running. Sir Peter Haywood, who's a chairman of our trustees, belongs to a church over in Weston, Weston All Saints, and he decided to offer to go along just to see whether he could volunteer with them. He said he'd go for three times to see what he felt. He went the first time and was so shocked and overwhelmed by what he saw he said he was never going to do that again. And then he felt guilty because he had promised to go three times so he went back for the second and the third time, and by the end of the third time he was so committed that he then decided to found the charity which is the Genesis Trust. That's obviously a slightly shortened version of how the story goes but that's essentially what happened."

Ian took a breath and I remained sitting opposite him, my pen poised above my notebook.

"The soup run was subsumed into the Genesis," he continued. "Another project that started fairly early on was the furniture project, with the furniture warehouse and the collecting and donating of furniture and selling it to people in poverty. There's also the Lifeline centre in Bath Abbey, that's the drop-in centre for the homeless and vulnerable. There we have a team of staff and volunteers, a number of the volunteers were themselves at one point clients, and in a couple of cases were alcoholics and have come out the other side and are now helping down there. Once people begin to want to recover or begin to take the first steps of recovery they need help; if they're an alcoholic or they've had mental health issues, and those two often go together, it's estimated about 85 per cent of people who are addicted will have mental health issues. So if someone decides they're going to try to get their life together, they need help. They'll have lost confidence. They'll have lost the ability to work regular hours, to turn up on time. They'll have lost confidence in socialising with people, or many of them will have, even if not housebound, certainly lost lots of social skills. They're not confident in meeting with people. So the purpose of the Life Skills is to help people to get opportunities of working together in groups doing different activities like art, music, literacy, numeracy, computer skills, fun activities – things that get them together and rebuild confidence and skills. Through this we then help try to find people voluntary placements, either in Genesis or elsewhere."

"Like a stepping stone pathway out of poverty."

"That's exactly what it is. It's a bridge between the chaotic lifestyle of someone who is at Lifeline and someone who's being fully productive in society again."

The blue sky filled the tall windows behind Ian's chair and my attention flickered to the future before I pulled myself quickly back into the room, bringing the future with me.

"I'll be in London tomorrow," I said, "to follow a demonstration which is partly motivated in response to the way policies brought in after the financial crisis targeted the poor. Have you noticed an increase in people reaching out for your services in the last few years?"

"We've noticed a marked increase. There's been an increase in the need for the foodbank without a shadow of a doubt. Some of our foodbank demand has dropped but that's only because we used to cover the whole of the Bath area, but now there's a Somer Valley foodbank and a Keynsham foodbank, so they're picking up a lot of stuff. The issues over benefits are huge for us."

"Do you mean if people's benefits are cut?"

"They're slashed," Ian replied. "The way the benefit system is working now is that in order to maintain benefits, people have to have regular meetings with benefit agencies that are dealing with them. But in many cases the clients that we work with are chaotic in their lifestyles through mental health issues, through addiction problems, or they'll be called to do a work placement and then they'll be summoned to a meeting in the middle of a work placement and they can't be in both places. So they go to their work because they're required to do that, miss the meeting with their agency and their benefits are sanctioned. They then have to go through the process of appealing against the fact that their benefits have been cut by 35 per cent, 25 per cent, or whatever it may be."

"It takes time."

"Yes, it's time and in the meantime they're trying to live on something that is not sustainable, whereas they had a routine and they were keeping their head above water with the housing, food, rent, electricity, all those issues. Suddenly a whole chunk of that income is slashed and they fall into chaos again, crisis. It's then a cycle of constantly battling against the agencies or what seems to be sometimes very unsympathetic agencies. And I understand it, I mean sometimes our clients are their own worst enemies; they should be able to get to a meeting, but actually no they can't because of the mess they're in. So yes there are huge issues and the whole benefit system, sure it may well have needed a shake-up but it is having quite an impact on the most vulnerable. Hopefully there are people who have to go back to work who were otherwise skiving, but the people we work with aren't in that position. The people we work with have got chaotic lives or are struggling with addiction, mental health issues, and they're just holding it together. And it just needs something like that to tip them over the edge and then they're back onto the drugs, back onto the alcohol, or their mental health takes a tumble."

"I recently spoke to a member of Julian House at the Bath Bike Workshop, they also do a lot of work with taking people as far as they can go with them through meaningful opportunity, through training, and coming to the end of the supported houses. He told me that one of the hardest things is for people to then make the leap off benefits because they're often terrified of losing that support network. Do you find this to be the case with Genesis?"

"That's not something I personally have experience in because of the nature of my job, simply because I am less at the front-end of working with the clients, but I think that would fit. In some cases, particularly if you've got someone who has had a breakdown, or depression or mental health problems, to get from that place of dependency to becoming independent and working is a huge leap, it really is a huge leap. What's interesting is when you talk to a lot of the people who have become the most vulnerable, the rough sleepers or the ones on the streets, when you track back their family history it's unbelievably horrendous. And you think, there but for the grace of God go I; the idea that all of us are only six paychecks away from homelessness. You know it's a reality. One of our volunteers is a retired engineer; he was telling me the other day that he became vulnerably housed when his marriage broke down. He's got grandchildren, he's a really respectable guy, he does a lot of work for us, but he ended up sleeping on friends' sofas because he had nowhere else to go. It's so easy. And if someone had the propensity to drink, he didn't, but that's the time when alcohol becomes a solace. And for many of our people it has been that, it's an escape from the memories that have damaged them."

I nodded as Ian stopped speaking. I gazed down to my notebook not instantly picking out another question to ask. I sat for a moment, my thoughts racing.

"One thing I'm coming to realise," I said, "is the amount of Christian charities offering assistance to the poor in the city. I once believed it was done mainly as missionary work or conversion, but that doesn't seem to be the case. It seems primarily to be built on compassion."

"That is exactly what Genesis is about. The strapline is compassion in action. The best way to think of Genesis is as being the vehicle through which local churches can actually put that compassion in action. We coordinate the work of over five hundred volunteers, and we make it possible for people to donate time, money, food, clothing, furniture, and for it to get into the hands of the people who need it. Genesis is equally not just about Christian action; we also have a lot of volunteers who are not church members at all, but want to express their concern through the charity, which is fantastic."

"It's been really refreshing in that sense to learn about the amount of work that is being done, to see the soup run and other projects. I wasn't sure at first about researching poverty in Bath, thinking it to be a wealthy city, but now I'm beginning to see the amount of people who do need assistance and I think this takes people aback sometimes."

"Whiteway, Southdown, Twerton and Fox Hill are among the most deprived areas of the country," said Ian, "and then you've got pockets within wealthy wards. It's really quite scary. They're hidden because of the affluence around them."

"You walk around on a Saturday," I added, my pen still above my notebook, "and you see the amount of day visitors and the people on the street can be simply lost amongst them. But they're there if you walk slow enough and take time to see them."

"Very much so," Ian replied softly.

IX

I'm on a coach waiting to depart Bath bus station. My destination is London and Parliament Square where I will be following and standing with the latest social movement to take place in the UK, Occupy Democracy.

My understanding of the motivations behind the call to link arms and occupy the square before the Houses of Parliament for nine days is to bring many separate contentions the public has with the government into one movement. It is a chance to voice dissatisfaction with the failings of a system defined as being democratic.

The Occupy movement has mobilised in response to fracking, an unsound and unsustainable means of energy extraction which has already been shown to have poisoned and polluted large swathes of America, yet is still pushed through whole-heartedly by the UK government, despite the many grass root oppositions towards it. The Occupy movement has mobilised in response to the NHS being sold off to private companies. The movement has mobilised in response to the rise in tuition fees, putting the present graduates into a life already shackled by debt. The Occupy movement is a response to the secret trade deals which would give multi-national companies the right to sue governments if they are hindered from profiting from anything they see as fit for profit, no matter what this means on the ground or to local communities. The Occupy movement is a response to the estimated 2.33 million[2] souls living in fuel poverty as energy costs, as well as all other living costs, rise and rise while wages and pensions remain stagnant. The Occupy movement is a direct response to the massive rise in wealth inequality that exists in the UK; democracy, in its present manifestation, has safeguarded the wealthy and punished the poor. The movement uses a report published by Oxfam to convey the scale of this injustice:

Inequality is a growing problem in the UK. While austerity measures in Britain continue to hit the poorest families hardest, a wealthy elite has seen their incomes spiral upwards, exacerbating income inequality which has grown under successive governments over the last quarter of a century. Today, the five richest families in the UK are wealthier than the bottom 20 per cent of the entire population. That's just five households with more money than 12.6 million people – almost the same as the number of people living below the poverty line in the UK.[3]

I have to be honest, I'm still not convinced these movements can bring about the mass awakening needed to implement real change. The city workers who are made late to work by people who have come together in a common cause will likely be frustrated at the sight of tents and banners; the tourists, seeing a group of people shouting into megaphones will more than likely cross the road to distance themselves from the protestors, who must be dangerous because why else would the Metropolitan Police crowd round them like they're a ticking time bomb? I intend to go, to see and to write. I think a time to come together to stand in solidarity with those at the hard end of austerity can only be a good thing; it gives voice to civil dissatisfaction, and a space to contemplate how things could be different.

My bag is stowed in the coach's hull, containing a small tent, roll matt and sleeping bag. I have my notebook and pen and no end of woolly socks. I also have an umbrella which will provide the only shelter tonight. There is going to be an all-night vigil by candlelight to be, as best we can without ever being able to fully relate to what it must be like, at one with those on the streets or homeless. It's going to be a challenge, but together we can bring each other warmth. I'm also conscious that I only have around £25 left in my wallet. I hope the camp kitchen, if one is established, is cheap. The bus has left the city and is now pointing east; the embankments are green outside the window and sky heavy with rainclouds and a teasing sun that finds moments to shine down on the autumn brown earth below.

While walking to the bus station and being pulled to one side by the bag on my shoulder, I passed Dean on Stall Street. I waved as I approached and negotiated my way through the stream of pedestrians to stand beside him.

"How's it going?"

"It's alright, thanks."

"Good day?" I said gesturing to the magazine in his hand.

"I've just started," he replied. "I didn't have any money to buy any magazines so had to beg for a pound first. I've not earned much money over the past couple of days because of the rain. It's not been easy, I've had my jacket stolen three times and they make you buy a new one before you can sell."

"How much are they?"

"£15."

"Shit, it's tough to get ahead of things."

"Yeah, I need to sell this one before I can get some more. It's slow going some days."

"How long have you been on the streets now?"

"Since January this time."

I was conscious that I needed to get going as I didn't want to miss my coach. I pulled out my wallet and took out the remainder of my change.

"I'm just heading off to London and could do with something to read."

I gave him two £2 coins and said he could put the change towards an extra magazine. He thanked me and handed me a yellow magazine with a heavily bearded man on the front, arms outstretched and radiating divinity. The lead article was titled, *God Only Knows, or does he?* It was a debate between faith and fantasy. I folded the magazine and said goodbye to Dean. He leaned over and lifted his bag, his book resting on top of his sleeping bag and always waiting to be returned to. Dean left to buy some more magazines and I hurried to the bus station. I was soon on my way to Parliament Square and a long cold night outside.

X

I've been in London thirty minutes. After disembarking from the coach in Victoria Bus Station, I bumped and apologised my way through the stream of pedestrians on the pavements and decided to find a place to sit and eat the plain roll and apple I'd picked up before leaving Bath. I'm sat on the edge of a memorial in Grosvenor Gardens, opposite Victoria Station and The Shakespeare Inn with Buckingham Palace Road thick with car fumes and red buses. Pigeons are sitting on the edge of the monument above and I hope they don't shit on me. It doesn't comfort me when told that it's good luck. There's a quote inscribed on the side of the monument which must be ascribed to the guy sculptured in bronze riding on a war horse on top of the concrete plinth: *I am conscious of having served England as I served my own country.* (I later learned this to be Ferdinand Foch, a French soldier who became Commander in Chief of the Allied Forces in the First World War.)

People spot the wooden benches in the gardens and brown leaves form a crumpled carpet over the grass beneath the trees. I was sat here no more than two minutes when the sound of dragging footsteps approached; a small man in a black woolly hat leaned forward and close to me.

"Excuse me, sir," he said before his words joined into a mumble that I struggled to capture.

He held out his hand which I understood. I'd given the last of my change to Dean in Bath so apologised and instead pulled a packet of nuts from my bag.

"I've got these if you'd like them."

His hand retreated and he said nothing as he moved to the woman sat beside me, leaning over and unfurling his fingers. The pack of nuts remained in my palm.

It reminded me of a story I had been told in the bar over the weekend. Two regulars came in and we struck up a grand conversation about German beer, since they had recently returned from Oktoberfest and I had been in Munich in the spring. The conversation then led to poverty after they enquired into what I was presently working on. I told them about the difficulty of being able to know for certain the truth behind what I was told by those begging for money on the streets, and about the Your Kindness Can Kill Campaign and my search to see what I really thought about it. One of the regulars placed his pint glass down onto the bar.

"We have a friend," he said, "told us once that he was getting some money out of an ATM. There was a guy sat beside it asking for money. Our friend is quite flush but decided he didn't know the guy's story so thought he'd help him in some other way. He went to a nearby shop and returned with a bag of food and offered it to the man on the street. The man simply looked up at him and said, 'Sorry mate, I only accept cash.'"

The memory of listening to this story in the pub faded into the sound of the noisy capital. I looked on as the man in the black woolly hat scuffed his feet around the gardens, stopping at the benches, leaning over and reaching out his hand. The first woman he approached gave him some change, the woman sat beside her didn't even look up from the newspaper opened before her to register him. The next bench and two men waved him away. He scuffed on to the next bench, where a man instantly reached for the bag beside him, pulling it close.

Now Channel 4 is before me; two young women are interviewing a white haired man about his feelings about interest rates. The scouter for the interviews approached me too. I told him I was the wrong person to ask. I've a student debt to pay somewhere so that would be affected by interest rates, but in reality I'm ignorant to the financial ups and downs. I took the opportunity of this brief encounter with folk from Channel 4 to do some of my own research. I asked the cameraman if Channel 4 were planning to cover the Occupy movement in Parliament Square over the coming week. He told me that he had just seen it on the day's prospectus, but didn't know what coverage it would get.

"Depends what happens," he said.

He said that some new anti-protesting law had come in following the protests about the invasion of Iraq, so didn't see how the protest would be able to settle unless some sort of arrangement had been agreed with the police.

The demonstration is scheduled to remain for nine days. I was going to see how I felt about it and would return to the New Forest before its end for my grandmother's funeral. It's almost 4pm and Occupy Democracy is planned to start at 5pm. It's time to stand from this monument; the wars, whether for wealth or freedom, never seem to end.

Three or four hours later…
We've occupied Parliament Square; around two hundred of us circled by as many police in fluorescent jackets.

XI

My reason for joining a group of protestors in an all-night vigil was largely motivated out of my own despair for the workings of our democratic system, but also because I was sure it would bring about opportunities to meet people who had experienced periods of financial or personal hardship. I was on the hunt for tales of poverty. Around midnight, after a blow up mattress had been forcefully removed from beneath an aging woman by the police, a small circle formed and we began to share stories. This is when I first met Rosie. (Not her real name.)

She was a fire cracker ready to shout down any and all forms of authority; I quite enjoyed watching her give the Heritage Wardens (red ribbons around their hats and petty in their regard for a peaceful protest) what for; their little slips of paper fluttered pitifully to the damp stone after she refused to accept them – a tactic protestors employ to avoid laws imposed to silence them is to in turn drown out the authorities with songs and whistles, or by simply refusing to touch any written warnings handed out. It's effective, especially when Rosie's voice bellowed above all others, telling the police to sod off and police something worth policing.

She wore a beige woolly hat and a faded denim jacket over her baggy t-shirt; she drank from a can of cider and dominated the circle with her presence as soon as she sat down. I'd overhead her say that she'd experienced seven years of homelessness so I took the chance to enquire into her life a little. Tents were being erected on the strip of grass across the road, protestors who had travelled far that day from the anti-fracking camps up north needing to sleep, no matter the busy central London road they camped next to; the cars, buses and taxis streamed past them throughout the night. Rosie's voice easily lifted over the engines and occasional siren.

"It was a misunderstanding," she began. "My mum's a very strict Jehovah's Witness now and that obviously doesn't help. 'You're coming to church and must wear a skirt.'" Her voice raised in pitch when she mimicked her mother's. "And I'm like, a *skirt?* After all my life of having Christmas and birthdays and then suddenly I turn eleven and me mum goes, 'You know what, they don't exist anymore because I believe in a new religion.' And then wonders why I hate religion. But my mum's not that smart, and I have to go, 'Mum, stop preaching and then maybe I'll stop hating.' And she's like, 'What do you mean?' And I say, 'Well you're always preaching about God but you do not listen to anything I've got to say, about fracking, TTIP, NHS.' Cause her religion says she's not allowed to get involved in politics. 'Cause Armageddon's on its way and we're all going to die and after life we're all going to the second world!' Jehovah's Witnesses, you know, they're those knocker-door runners. Yeah man, they love me. 'Oh your mum, I know your mum, she speaks wonders of you.' I'm like, 'Yeah, about four years ago she wouldn't have done so fuck off.' It's absolutely fucking mad like, I can speak to anybody from any different religion and generally they'll understand where I'm coming from. If you'd got to eleven and then suddenly: no more Christmases! No more Birthdays! No more Easters! You'd be like, 'You what? You're mother-fucking robbing me of my presents. Mum, I want a new iPod!' You know what I mean? And my mum was like, 'Ah, you're eleven, you've got to understand my religious beliefs. I was like, 'I'm eleven. I'm sorry I'm like, you know, too clever.'

"Well I wasn't ever the brightest spark; I've got dyslexia, behaviour problems and fucking depression, who hasn't? They didn't understand it or register it in school. They were like, 'Oh she's just slow. She doesn't want to learn. She's just an idiot.' And then the last year of primary school, they went, 'Oh yeah yeah yeah, she's dyslexic, well we could have helped her but it's too late now.' And it's like, 'Thank you very fucking much.' So I went through high school with everybody thinking I was a fucking idiot, but the fact was, MSN, MySpace, and Facebook and all that bullshit, it's helped my English become tenfold now, and if it wasn't for social media and networking, and Google, and stuff like that, my English would be appalling. Literally I really couldn't spell many things. You know I struggle with everything."

A young woman sat beside Rosie interrupted her, "It's disgusting that you had to go to school and it didn't teach you nothing and then Google does, Google teaches you how to spell."

"I learnt myself," replied Rosie, the can in her hand buckling a little in her tightening grip. "It's fucked up man. I learnt myself after primary school. In primary school you're meant to learn your A, B, C… and you know what? I still don't know my A, B, C… and that's 'cause I'm dyslexic. Do you ever go into a job interview and they go, 'Do us your A, B, C… ?' Sorry mate, we're not in fucking primary or nursery now, this is fucking grown up shit.' You know what I mean? I want to know your values and your pros and your cons. The problem now is unless you've got *A* this, *B* that, whatever, and all these GCSEs you don't stand a fucking chance. And if you're someone like me who's never committed to school at all, because you can't do the classroom environment, you don't get anywhere. And I'm now registered as unfit to work, but they won't give me the sick note because I can walk."

"What's the sick note for?" I asked.

"For my mental health," replied Rosie. "And they're like, 'Oh well you can dress yourself and walk.' But the person who was diagnosing me was a nurse."

"I heard you say earlier that you went through seven years of homelessness."

"When I work it out realistically, it's been on and off for eight years, but I did six years' solid homelessness, where I was living in squats, peoples' couches, and there's literally only so many friends you can rely on before people start getting really pissed off with you. I literally used each and every one of my friends to my full advantage and they got to the point where they were really fed up with feeding me. They was like, 'Dude, look there's only so many brews I can make ya, there's only so many pieces of toast I can give ya before I'm out of pocket, and I can't eat for the week.' And I was like, 'Shit man, this is bullshit.' And I did nine months without any benefits. It was very hard times, a very very hard time in my life. But now I've got my caravan, yay!"

"Me too," I said.

"I love caravans. I'm trying to start up a self-sufficiency land organisation." Rosie's tone lightened with optimism. "Basically the self-sufficiency land organisation is for anybody who's a traveller who would like to come and graft for their keep. So basically if you want to come down, help pick out weeds round the vegetable grove, milk some cows, change out the shit and that, you can live there for as long as you want for free. And that's what I'm in the middle of setting up at the moment… "

Our conversation was broken by a young man with a goatee in a high-vis jacket with Legal Observer displayed on the back, handing out little green cards telling us what to do if the police questioned us, providing us with phone numbers to free legal advice if we were in turn arrested.

"We're now facing an overzealous Metropolitan Police," he said.

The small group pocketed the cards and surveyed the growing ring of police around us. Drizzle remained in the air and the first night of Occupy Democracy settled down on the cold stone at the rear of Parliament Square.

XII

We are four, four young souls sitting on plastic bin liners on the damp grass in Parliament Square. My new friends, three young women who live and work in London, are now my co-occupiers as we sit here before the Houses of Parliament, with Big Ben stabbing at the fresh morning sky and the bells chiming for 7.30am. It was a rough night. It was a cold night. I slept a fitful thirty minutes with my head rested against the trunk of a tree as the Heritage Wardens continued to make sure we weren't using any sleeping equipment. There are more of us but Occupy Democracy is going to have a tough time in Parliament Square.

I arrived yesterday evening to a square being observed by many police officers, aware of our arrival. I filtered into the growing crowd, waiting for the first speaker to announce our intentions for being here. I was soon aware of a Police Liaison Officer, identified by his blue vest, standing at my side and handing me a flyer.

"I see you have bags," he said. "You may not be aware but the laws regarding being able to use sleeping equipment in the square have changed."

In short, after the protests by figures such as Brian Haw, who lived in a peace camp in Parliament Square for almost ten years, protesting against the invasions of Afghanistan and Iraq, a new law has been passed that bans any structures or sleeping equipment in the square. If I was to take the tent out from my bag and erect it, then I would be breaking the law, but I soon learned that this law goes beyond merely tents and sleeping bags, it goes into the absurd.

It's one in the morning; a group of us had retreated to the concrete and under the trees at the rear of the square, sheltering from the rain. The night had passed by with guest speakers addressing some of the reasons underlying the need to protest: fracking, fuel poverty, international trade deals that bend us over a barrel for multi-nationals to shaft us from behind, and the difficult questions about whether this house, Parliament, was really democratic. I was beginning to tire. I had folded a jumper up and positioned it under my arse to stem the chill in the stone from entering me so easily. I used my bag to rest my head on. I was woken by a Heritage Warden surrounded by five police officers with another Heritage Warden filming us.

"I just need to remind you that no sleeping equipment may be used in Parliament Square."

We told the Heritage Warden that we were resting on bags, and he told us that we were using them to sleep. Fuck me, if you're homeless then don't seek shelter in Parliament Square. These guys in their pressed uniforms bear no compassion. We had sleeping bags we were not allowed to use; so instead we shivered. Our small group simply sat up and the wardens, cuddled into power by the police at their side, walked off. The four instead talked the night and cold away.

It was futile to try and have a rational debate with the Heritage Wardens; they were trying to impose a silly law in a serious tone. They were uniformed nonsense, better to let them have their time and self-important status. If we can't lie down then we can sit, come back to me with a new law Mr Heritage Warden.

The absurdity began early on. There was a suspicious sleeping bag before the first speaker had even got behind the microphone, then a parasol that was deemed to be a structure, a young chap rested his bike against a fence, unlit fire poi on the handle bars, and the police threatened to call the bomb squad; then the same young chap climbed a tree around 3am, which resulted in him being sectioned under the Mental Health Act, once, that is, the police figured out how to get him down. He made a break for it at dawn, sprinting past Parliament with two bobbies failing to catch him. All of this in the name of inspiring a new system of governance, one that serves the people of this land, not the elite. I have to be honest, we're fragile and too easily distracted from the core reasons for being here.

We are now seven. A few protestors who set up tents on a piece of grass opposite the square, free from sleeping laws, are stirring and stretching out their knotted bodies beside the busy road. The police presence is already large as three riot vans are parked at the rear of the square. There's a guy beside me digging a hole. I've told him that he is being silly as he's going to get kicked out, and perhaps take us with him. I'm a little frustrated as there were around two hundred people here when the protest started, but this has shrunk to around thirty who remained overnight. At the moment I don't see how the protest can hold out, considering the way we were stopped sleeping last night. I think the first glimpse of any tents going up will see the force roll in and the camp closed. Now there's a guy digging a fucking hole beside me and this is not what I want to watch after a night of no sleep (which I can only offer as an excuse for my bad language). I don't know why someone would choose to give them such an easy excuse to arrest you. Brilliant, the police and those jobsworth Heritage Wardens are walking this way…

They came over to tell us that my friend was not allowed to sleep in the square. I said thank you for informing us again and we put the sleeping bag she had snuggled into away. After some more people came to join us, I decided to take a walk beside the Thames to try to re-examine my own thoughts about what this protest was about. I returned just in time to hear a large cheer erupt from the square, I looked across to see the pale white cheeks of a man's bare backside bold against the green grass around him. His head was concealed in a hole in the ground as he did a headstand with his bits on show for the early morning tourists and his bottom facing towards the Houses of Parliament. He was quickly dragged away. I smiled with everyone else, but inside I was thinking how silly we looked, people trying to challenge the great struggles of our day, and all we could really do was to offer David Cameron the sight of a man's bare behind. He didn't even have to look at it; the police were doing a fine job of tidying us away like scraps of insignificant litter. There was a small bell chiming inside me: *Oh my God, we're living in a Police State.*

XIII

That night I left London. I had joined the large union march in the day and I was completely broken by tiredness and also a little frustration at how Occupy Democracy had begun, finding the speakers on the megaphones often driven by too much anger, which is an amazing force and at times a much needed rallying cry, but also too easily scares the general public on the street away. They don't hear a message, just rage.

The march, with the numbers in attendances rumoured to be over 100,000, walking from Embankment to Hyde Park was, in part, to demand an increase in minimum wage. I walked behind a large inflated banner swaying above a sea of heads and displaying the words, *Britain Needs a Pay Rise*. Leaving the camp, I chose to spend a few days collecting my thoughts and notes in Bath, but I continued to follow the protest, despite it being at the mercy of a media blackout and receiving little attention from the government. It was not only being silenced, it was being ignored. I watched shaky video footage on YouTube as a group of thirty or so protestors, sat in a circle on tarpaulin on the grass in Parliament Square, were surrounded by an army of Met officers, pulling at the tarpaulin beneath them and carrying unresisting bodies to vans parked around the square. I was disgusted and ashamed for having left this peaceful group who had not risen to the brutish tactics used against them. I knew then I would go back, stand with, and document this protest. I have decided to include the words I wrote in my diary and also published online during this time in this book. There is one view that poverty is built into the capitalist model that we are living under, and this means it's important to know what happens when people question the system. If a world without poverty is wanted then perhaps the system will have to be tackled, some say toppled, and yet if it bounds and inhibits a person's freedom of speech, how do those wanting change then mobilise?

Before returning to London I spent a day and night in the New Forest where I grew up. I was there to attend my grandmother's funeral, a woman I remembered most for her smile and gentle nature. I read one of my poems for her in the chapel, and thought about these words on the coach driving into nightfall and along the M3 back to London:

Nothing Left to Say

It's in the pictures we shared
In the memories we hold,
that help us to remember how did a life grow old.

In the music we danced to
in the drinks we drank
toasting those times we treasure and thank.

In the heart of each other
filled by the love of one another;
there is no ending that could take you forever.

Just here, in our chests, in our thoughts
you'll always remain near,
like a moment, fleeting but still dear.

So we shall keep those pictures on the wall,
along with the memories of your smile.
And that's it, there's nothing left to say
except you have helped us to smile today.

It's a beautiful thing. They took away our tents, our umbrellas, our sleeping bags, our tarpaulin, our right to converge on Parliament Square and voice our grievances with our democracy, and still we are here, and we are growing.

I arrived in Victoria Station and made a dash to the square, arriving to find a fence raised around the grass and fronted by a line of police officers, themselves faced by a ring of protestors. We've now made a gathering on a bank of grass to the eastern edge of the square. Churchill has his back to us, his statue instead facing Parliament; there is a prominent hunch on his back as he leans forward on his stick. When I arrived there were police dogs barking in the square. I thought of East Germany before the fall of the wall, patrolled and policed. Ah shit, it's starting to rain and I lost my rain coat in all the commotion. No doubt the police will now start sleep watch; conducting their rounds to wake us up. I will sit through the night and find somewhere to sleep in the morning. At one point the police tried to remove a woman with a megaphone; she was so versed in the law that they were defeated. They tried to apprehend her and the people swelled around her and the police pushed back. The group was stronger than them and acting through truth and compassion. The police withdrew.

We're now beginning to settle, most of the riot police have left. The last two hours have been spent cheering the passing cars, one banner being displayed to them with the words, *Honk for Democracy*. I can see my rain jacket; it's being torn into slim strips to make more emblems of this protest which are being worn at people's chests – it's become known as the Tarpaulin Revolution. I overheard a protestor saying how one of the police officers guarding the grass almost had tears in his eyes as he stood before him; the police know the protestors are speaking out for them too. It would be the grail of this week if the police acted to protect us instead of protecting the powers that feed off us all.

XIV

24th October 2014

I arrived back at Parliament Square last night. Following the removal and absurd arrests of protestors made earlier in the week, I wasn't sure what I would come back to. I hurried along the pavement, Big Ben towering over the buildings and trees ahead, before I rounded the corner and breathed out a silent, *Yes!*

The square had been surrounded by a steel fence; hundreds of police stood outside it, police dogs on leads barked on the grass inside, and then there were the people, hundreds of people standing hand in hand and surrounding the square. The Occupy Democracy movement is growing, helped by the injustices the protestors suffered at the start of the nine day peaceful protest. Despite the protestors' presence, not broken by the aggression used by the police, despite meeting them with peace, still the police remain in riot van after riot van, with cold wet officer stood next to cold wet officer.

Not long after I arrived a speaker from the Free Energy Party was almost forcefully taken away, I believe for speaking into a megaphone, but I think more likely because she was using it to help the Heritage Wardens to understand the law they appeared to know very little about. It was majestic; the Met tried to take her and bodies swelled like a breaking wave, "Shame on You… Shame on You" was sung as the Met were carried on the voice of reason back, and then, with them undone by peaceful defiance, we sang to them again, "We Forgive You… We Forgive You."

Moments later, and exhibiting a comic's perfect timing, Russell Brand arrived handing out sleeping bags and subsequently delivering a beautiful speech to the police. He left the square to go on *Newsnight*, helping the BBC to give the Tarpaulin Revolution the recognition it deserves.

The police have been wrong in the way they have handled Parliament Square, and they suffer more than us because of it. They are forced to stand for hours on end and watch a group of concerned citizens sleeping under plastic rain coats. The police are meant to exist to make communities safer, stronger, and I believe most of the officers with us in Parliament Square know they are not doing so in this instance. They are protecting government from hearing our calls. They have failed, we have not been silenced. And because of the way they tried to take away our right to protest our numbers and our cause have expanded.

It's a lovely morning in Parliament Square, well on the edge of Parliament Square – the protestors have occupied the embankment, the road running around the square, busy with traffic. I'm just starting to feel the effects of not having slept last night – there's a little blurring of my thoughts. I'm slowed. I am proud to detail how the protestors engaged and stayed loyal to their peaceful protest last night, because of this we had quite a calm night, or the police have simply come to the realisation that they can hound us with no more laws, they have already exhausted the weak ones they had. I'm now being filmed by some guys I've not seen before, perhaps they're a reinvented version of the Heritage Wardens, wearing their long jackets and maintaining folded arms, red ties at their necks. All the police and Heritage Wardens seem to do is stand with folded arms, quite pointless.

Two separate vehicles have driven past with the drivers yelling out their windows, "Get a job you losers!"

Of course if someone had no understanding of what the protest is about, they would just see a group of scruffy people sitting around with banners in their hands. I'm now being watched by the police, well a couple of officers. I'm writing so that's a certain case for suspicion. Big Ben is now letting us know that it's 10am.

25th October 2014

Saturday morning, it's a crisp beginning after a cold night. Some protestors are at the roadside with banners, others handing out leaflets to the cars waiting for the traffic lights to turn green. I'm now quite deprived of sleep, but I feel okay for it. It was just too cold to sleep last night, so I managed only an hour. The police were commanded to rouse us at 4am, which started around two hours of silliness, what with ponchos being defined as blankets. I'm tired of it now – any serious reason for being here is reduced to us name calling the Heritage Wardens, labelling them the 'Fashion Police'. Now there's another debate taking place between the police and the legal observers about the absurdity of a law that sees pizza boxes as sleeping equipment.

26th October 2014

It's Sunday morning, nearing 6.30am. I've just left Parliament Square to search out a cup of tea and a space to write. The Heritage Wardens and police have just woken those in sleeping bags; being able to control themselves until 6am is at least something, those desperate for sleep were able to find an hour or two, despite the cold.

I will leave the Tarpaulin Revolution today and reconcile my thoughts about the movement's aims and what nine days of occupying Parliament Square will do for democracy.

I know already that I have been inspired and encouraged to learn how many citizens not only want change but also believe change can happen. To have also received support from many Londoners is energising, through their interest and engagement with the banner holders or by the honking of their horns as they drove past, especially the fire engines and ambulances as Occupy rallies behind the invaluable work these men and women do, while continually abused by the government.

The question now remains, what does change look like and what can be done to bring it about? This is where divisions may start to appear as the debates tackle this dilemma. If the system is corrupt and broken, is it better to fix or abandon it?

Leaving these impassioned days and fragile nights held together by song and commitment to a cause, I believe the best thing we can do straight away is to stay true to the things that move us, and act in accordance with this compelling force. Occupy will no doubt evaluate its latest stand and now move forward in a pointed way, but for me Occupy will always be the needed rally call, helping to counter the media spun depiction of society, and helping to give the public a platform to question.

The way Occupy executed peaceful defiance is a testament to the change it foresees. Around 1am the Heritage Wardens, bringing the police with them, tried to stop the group from playing instruments, also being worked into the ever-changing legislation they kept presenting to the group. Bodies again wrapped and protected the musicians, and instead of accepting this attempt to silence, the group simply united and sang louder.

After one week the Heritage Wardens still failed to understand what the group was partly addressing, the right to freedom of speech, and there is no stronger exhibition of this than song. Every time they sought to suppress, the voices came together. This is what the system is waking to and afraid of, people are uniting. At the same time I still maintain we must stay true to the spirit inside us, and allow this to be the guiding force.

I will leave London today and carry my time here into my future words and will be stronger for three nights lying on a piece of cardboard while folding my arms to hold onto what little warmth I could. I also won't escape the image of a man sheltering in a doorway as I walked the streets this morning, his head hidden in his raised knees. His next taste of warmth is not known to him. Somehow he's found himself on the outside of society.

All experiences shape us and feed into our future, and I know my time with others in Parliament Square has reaffirmed to me that in Britain and the world today, too many are suffering and if that's a result of a controlled agenda by an untouchable few over the course of civilisation, then I will continue to question what I can do in my life to make a difference, no matter how great or small this might be.

XV

Back in Bath and Halloween filled the city with the walking dead; face-painted zombies and witches throwing up in doorways or staggering into the roads, not unlike someone having been resurrected from the underworld, as they sought out burgers and end of night kebabs. I can't judge as I ended the night in Opium, a cocktail bar known for its eclectic interior décor, well-made drinks and burning incense. I sat with friends and a toxic green glass of absinthe. I suffered for this dangerous little beverage with a hollow head the next day. I had been paid from the bar and also received my advance from the publisher so buying a round of cocktails, admittedly allured by the alcohol I'd already consumed, seemed like the best thing to do in that moment of time. Later, and especially if I'm penniless in India, I'll call myself a bloody idiot. Living the summer without having to worry about money means I tend not to worry about it full stop, I've a tendency to spend it when really I should be reinforcing the fact that I'm not going to have an income again from the end of November.

Arriving back in the city and inspired to press on with my notes after spending time in Parliament Square, passing hour after hour watching the police watching me, I contacted Bath FoodCycle and arranged to join them as a volunteer. On a sad Wednesday afternoon I headed into a faint drizzle and early dusk as I walked through Victoria Park and past the Royal Crescent, which was still being gazed upon by tourists despite the unflattering grey Bath stone becomes in the damp and low light. I walked until I arrived at Julian Road.

The FoodCycle operates in a hall behind St Mary's Catholic Church; the stone building was dark and foreboding as the night fell and the light from the street lamps strengthened, casting shadows on the wet paths. I entered the hall and met with Fiona, the session leader, who subsequently introduced me to the head chef and a kitchen with worktops laden with food. Every Wednesday, a team of around eight volunteers take these ingredients and come up with a three-course meal. People from the community then arrive at 7.30pm and are able to enjoy the spread. If they can afford to give a donation of £1 they are able to, if not they are invited to share in the feast all the same. I was given an apron and chef's hat and pointed to the basin where I could wash my hands. Before joining with the other volunteers who had already begun chopping the veg, Fiona outlined what the nationwide organisation sets out to achieve:

"FoodCycle was founded in 2009," she explained. "It's about four things: reducing food poverty, reducing food waste, inviting community participation, while offering valuable training."

I learned that FoodCycle relied on the participation of a supermarket in the city. When I was sixteen I stacked shelves in my local supermarket and was shocked by the amount of food that was thrown away, be it down to having gone past its best before date or because the packaging was damaged, or simply because the next delivery had to be put out on the shelves. It was abhorrent to watch perfectly edible food being put in the bins, especially when there are millions around the world going hungry.

In April 2014 I was in Sweden living with a community in a small town not far from the city of Växjö, in Kronoberg County. After having just spent two weeks strolling under glorious spring weather in Amsterdam, northern Europe was a chilling journey back into winter. In Sweden, I slept under four blankets in a red timber farmhouse, typically Swedish with its white window frames. The community was still trying to establish itself; shabby caravans and huts were scattered around the grounds and we were all short of money. At night we would take it in turns to drive into the nearest town, to a car park behind the only supermarket. Under the cover of darkness we would sift through the bins and take out anything we could find that appeared edible. This is known as Dumpster Diving. The following morning the community would inspect the night's haul and it was always amazing to see the amount of food we had retrieved, usually enough to feed the ten of us. We were never short of bananas, almost stale bread (but perfectly fine after a minute or two in the oven), yogurts, packaged meat, or ripened fruit and slightly shrivelled veg. While making dinner one night with the rescued food, I recalled a story I'd read in the news before leaving England, of an Iceland supermarket employee in Bridlington pouring bleach and toilet cleaner into the bins to stop the homeless from eating the wasted food inside. I've also friends who have worked in a coffee shop chain and they told me how they were instructed to cut open the unpurchased sandwiches at the end of the day, spoiling them before throwing them away to stop them from being taken from the bins. The chain was concerned they may be sued if someone fell ill.

Returning to Bath and a small kitchen in a hall behind St Mary's Catholic Church, I was staggered to see the four large trays of eggs that FoodCycle had picked up in the day from the supermarket. Fiona explained that if one egg in a box was broken then the supermarket, not having the facility to repackage them, will throw the entire box of eggs away, five good eggs wasted because of one spoiled. This is what comes when living in a society driven by profit over wellbeing; people die of hunger through lack of food yet society throws a stomach turning amount away every day. It should be a governmental imperative to tackle such foolish waste, and schemes like FoodCycle should be looked to as working models that can bring surplus food and those in need of food together.

Having partnered with FoodCycle, the supermarket, to its credit, now collects the good eggs in separate trays; it places broken packs of pasta or flour in bags and holds onto them, and it freely gives over any other products that would otherwise be destined for landfill. The supermarket benefits because its food wastage is decreased and FoodCycle are able to use the food to make a meal for vulnerable people in the community. It's a beautiful concept and, after having joined another volunteer to smash up bunches of bananas to make smoothies, a lot of fun.

The kitchen was a whisk swirling and chilli scented hub of activity; the volunteers worked in pairs on the separate courses and three hours quickly passed before the first diners began to arrive. I recognised some of the faces from the soup run, while there were others I had never seen before. There was one man that stood out, his long grey hair sometimes covering his face and eyes, his clothes or appearance not suggesting him to be in poverty. He sat alone at a small table, watching the noisy tables around him before returning to himself and sipping at the banana smoothie which had been served to the guests on entry. Fiona came to tell me that Peter, the name I shall give him, would be happy to talk to me. I left the kitchen as the volunteer from South America began to slice up her perfectly bronzed tortillas. I walked into the dining hall and made my way with Fiona towards Peter, noting the small chalk board placed on the table beside the salt and pepper, *Quiet table*.

I learned that Peter suffered from a poverty that went beyond finances, his poverty was isolation born out of an eating disorder and anxiety, and I quickly came to appreciate the position of trust I was in as he had agreed to speak openly with me. He didn't like the idea of me recording our meeting, not wanting me to have to suffer hearing his voice when I played it back, so I pulled my little notebook from my pocket and scribbled desperately as he spoke.

"Poverty can mean starving yourself," he said, his hands pressed together on the table and his voice soft. "Isolation was the word you used, and that was it for me. Before I came here I suffered from anxiety, I still do. Someone told me about FoodCycle, I thought why not give it a go to try and get out of the prison I was in."

"And what did coming here mean?" I asked.

"It made me feel valued and the love and care that is shown to me made me realise that there's a place in this world that you can reach out to. Between you and me, I questioned why I was here, as I'm okay financially, but then you don't have to be anything, there's no label."

A volunteer from Venezuela approached with a starter, smiling as she placed it on the table before Peter.

"Here we are, careful as the carrot is spicy."

"Oh, I love that," he replied lifting his knife and fork.

Not wanting the carrot dish to get cold, Peter started eating and I remained sat beside him, watching the front of house volunteers moving round the tables, serving food and engaging with the clients. I asked Peter why he sits alone.

"I'm not socialising," he said between bites. "People sometimes come here to meet others, but I just come here to be alone. I can't bear to be with noise, but I think that comes from being isolated. It's strange because I used to teach and always be around people, but now I can't be around noise."

He had no sooner placed the last forkful of carrot in his mouth when the volunteer returned, exchanging his plate for the one in her hand.

"Tortilla," she said.

"Oh, that is heaven."

Peter lovingly cut a small piece from the tortilla before bringing it to his mouth and chewing slowly, swallowing before becoming concerned that by my sitting with him I might miss on the chance to eat. I told him not to worry as plenty had been made and asked if he'd speak a little more about why he came to FoodCycle.

"If you want to be on your own, you can be on your own. That's what I love about it. I've been coming for a year, and I've missed only one evening because I was ill."

"And do you think it's helped you in any way?"

"Oh yes, I'm a different person. People used to say I looked like death and now look at me. I didn't socialise at home either. I would be terrified if someone came to my house. So for me to come here is huge. I once thought I can't go out of the house at night, but here I am. I've learned now to let go."

"Do you mind me asking what it was that triggered the troubles you've mentioned in the first place, especially as you said you used to teach?"

He placed the knife and fork down on the plate and turned to face me.

"I was wrongly diagnosed with Addison's disease and given steroids. This swelled my weight to fifteen and a half stone. I was out with my sister one day and someone later said to her, 'Who was that chubby person you were with?' This was the start of it. In my head I've always been fifteen and a half stone."

This experience led to Peter retreating into isolation, reinforced by an eating disorder, which was still a part of his life; he mentioned that he only has a slice of bread once a week. I noted how he ate around the sweet potato in the tortilla, purposefully avoiding taking in carbohydrates.

"I burned myself out," he continued. "I couldn't cope

and I'm still weak from the damage I've done to my body. You never think you're going to damage yourself. Now I could tell someone how I feel and for them not to do the same. I've really damaged myself, health wise. I keep getting stomach ulcers, infected ones."

I continued to write into Peter's silence, he watched my pen before speaking slowly for me.

"I've got so much to be thankful for, I'm so grateful for everything I've got. I haven't got cancer, I haven't got AIDS. Of course I'd like to go back to how I felt health-wise before this started… "

He was interrupted by the Venezuelan volunteer placing a mug of tea on the table.

"If I remember it's milk and no sugar," she said.

He turned to me, "Do you see why I can't stop coming? Everyone is so lovely. I like people, you see, really I do, but it takes me a while to trust that they're not going to make judgements, silly really. There's a side of me that wants to challenge myself, Matthew, but this is a step in the right direction. Who knows?"

The volunteers were now moving back between the tables collecting the plates in anticipation of the main course, a vegetable chilli made from food that would have been wasted if FoodCycle hadn't found a means to utilise it. It smelled wonderful. I decided to ask Peter what name he wanted me to use for him in the book. He sat back for a moment and peered into his tea. He again looked at me and spoke with a subtle smile.

"I have nothing left in this world, Matthew, except honesty. You see no one calls me by my name, it's been a year since I changed it and I'm now proud to be called by my name, Annunciata."

I later entered this name into a search engine. It means 'announced' in Italian, and refers to the New Testament in which the angel Gabriel informed Mary of the imminent birth of Jesus. The gender of the name is feminine.

The chilli arrived and I thanked Annunciata for speaking with me. I returned to the kitchen and stood beside the hatch, looking out at the many different faces and lives all enjoying the hot food and company of those sat beside them. Annunciata continued to eat alone but frequently spoke to the volunteers, thanking them for another delicious evening. Sarah, one of the longest serving volunteers, stood beside me and we watched the scene together.

"Are you targeting a certain type of person?" I asked.

"If you're here, you need to be here," she replied. "They're here for something."

XVI

3rd November 2014

Just bumped into Dean at the end of Barton Street; he was selling. It's cold today, especially so after an unseasonably hot few days. Winter is starting to make her presence known. Dean mentioned that he might be housed soon, which means he'll probably be in Bath for a while. I asked him if he was sleeping rough at the moment. He said he was and that last night was bad because his sleeping bag got wet. I realised then that it wasn't stuffed into his Sports Direct bag at his feet.

"I took it to a friend's to dry."

He then asked if it was me who had given him *The Grapes of Wrath*. I had and I'm wondering if he has difficulty remembering things, as he said he also has trouble remembering what it was that had most contributed to him ending up on the streets. We're going to try and meet up sometime soon and talk. He finished *The Grapes of Wrath* in two days.

"It was wonderful," he said, unconsciously moving the magazine in his hand into the vision of the pedestrians streaming by.

XVII

Something's gone wrong. It shouldn't have, but it has; the overriding sense of unknowing weighs heavy on your shoulders, pushing you down, stopping you from moving forward. What does moving forward even mean? Who defines it?

It was a long night, all your cards had been laid and lost already: friend's sofa – overused, night shelter – £3 you didn't have. The streets. The streets. You hid amongst the shadows pooled in a doorway, pulling the bottom of your sleeping bag onto your shoes, the pavement wet and emptied from the falling rain. The bells of Bath Abbey tolled in the distance. You brought your knees to your chest, rested your head against the hard doorframe, closed your eyes and found nowhere where your thoughts could take you. The rain fell; the puddles in the gutters deepened. You did not sleep.

Daybreak. A milk van pulled up, tyres rubbing against the curb. The milkman approached with two glass bottles, filled with fresh creamy milk. You hurriedly scrunched up your sleeping bag and stuffed it into the crinkled bag at your side, as the dawn light loosened the shadows around you. You stood knowing the milkman's eyes were on you. You moved away, turning to see him place the milk down before the door. His fingers remained on the necks of the bottles; you were still too close for him to let go. You walked, heading along Cheap Street with lights being turned on in shop windows. The morning sky was now a fragile blue; cloudless, empty, but new. The streets busied themselves with buses and cars, cyclists filtered through them and people began to claim the pavements. They walked to work. You just walked.

You found yourself on the path beside the river, watching the water flow beneath Pulteney Bridge before crashing down the city centre weir. It thundered and foamed. Across the water the Abbey dominated the view, towering over Parade Gardens, the beds spotted by petals of colour.

'The Abbey,' you whispered.

You've got no direction, so which way do you turn? You held onto the bag carrying your sleeping bag. It bumped against your leg as you walked again. You made your way slowly back along the path, across the bridge and towards the Abbey with only the quietness of your voice to follow, *Lifeline*.

At the rear of Bath Abbey, a statue of Christ resurrected stands at the top of a narrow stone stairwell leading down to the Abbey's vaults. I first visited Lifeline on a weekday afternoon in early November. It was a typical weekday in the city. The Abbey square was filled by tourists admiring the carvings shaped out of the high stone walls – angels, demons, crosses and more – while city workers sat on the benches eating their lunch. It was a warm day, the low sun being the crowning feature in the sky above. I walked to the rear of the Abbey and saw a man stood, small dog on a lead at his feet, leaning on the black railing. He was facing Christ. He was wearing a green jacket, had a messy beard and a weathered, perhaps tired, look in his eyes; Christ, on the contrary, had been sculpted in all magnificence, looking like a model from a hair conditioner advert with his hair flowing backwards in an eternal wind and for some reason being carved to look like a man from the West. I always found this strange, given that Jesus' biblical birth was set in the East. The man with the dog looked at me and I looked at Christ on my way down the steps.

I passed a young couple in hooded jumpers and scraggy trainers, walking up and sucking on lollipops.

At the bottom of the steps I was greeted by a man at the door, he wore a badge with the word *volunteer* on his chest. I explained my reason for visiting and asked if it would be okay to see a little of what Lifeline does. He said no problem. He stepped aside and gestured me in. I entered the vaults, surprised to find the busy goings-on underground. A number of down and outs were gathered around the hot water urn, making cups of tea; some sat at the tables nibbling biscuits, with others slouched on sofas talking. A man in a suit and silver-painted jacket, a feather pointing up on his brimmed hat, talked on a phone, while two men were sitting at computers squinting as they focused on the screen. Volunteers moved amongst the clients, conversing with them. One was logging their names in a black book at the door, over thirty names had been recorded so far.

Lifeline operates in the vaults every Monday to Friday between 1.30pm and 3.30pm, it is often the first point of contact for anyone who has fallen into crisis, whatever that may mean to them with a universal definition being unhelpful and unrepresentative to real life. In the vaults the reason for one's being there will be taken into consideration and assistance can be offered, but by simply being there means you are welcome to the services and kindness offered by a team of volunteers. A hairdresser is available for those who need a haircut but can't afford one; there's a desk where you can sit and discuss your troubles with an experienced advisor; there is a clothes bank as well as an emergency foodbank able to provide a day's worth of food, or vouchers which can then be taken to Manvers Street Baptist Church and the Bath Foodbank.

I walked through the vaults, again seeing the familiar faces of the long termers who I had seen at the soup run and the FoodCycle. It was a noisy and chaotic hive of activity; two clients crowded the advice desk wanting to make sure they were next to be seen, others jeered each other and made lurid jokes at each other's expense while one man simply sat in silence drinking his polystyrene cup of instant soup.

I spoke to an elderly woman who was responsible for logging the names on entry. She had silver hair and a biro pen poised in her wrinkled fingers. She tapped the nib on the open book and closed her eyes when she couldn't recall the name of a long termer when one entered, too embarrassed to ask them for it again.

"My memory's terrible," she said.

I stood beside her for a time, watching the list of names grow while learning that the busiest day of the year had seen sixty people making use of Lifeline, sixty souls in need of a little warmth and support. As I continue to pursue my notes I'm beginning to realise the underbelly of poverty that exists in the city, and yet on the earth above you see splendour, wealth and life, occasionally tainted by a man or woman sitting on the street, suffering. Underground, however, poverty comes together and treatment begins. I see Lifeline as a social club and treatment centre, only there is no magic pill that can be prescribed to cure the ills of poverty, just self-belief and the compassion of others to help you on the way. If others refuse to give up on you then you'll be less likely to give up on yourself.

XVIII

It was not quite mid-morning. I walked across the Abbey churchyard, past the Roman Baths. A man was stood in a black suit at the entrance, waiting for the first coachload of day-trippers to arrive. He will arrange them into a queue and smile as they ready the cameras at their necks after he permits them inside. The Baths remain to be one of the city's top attractions. On the stone slabs before the Abbey, a cross, shaped out of large concrete curbstones, was stood over by an elderly couple. They looked down at the green grass the curbstones contained, reading the names on the little wooden crosses which had been pressed into the soil, dressed in red paper poppies. The war dead honoured in the heart of the city. The 'Ode of Remembrance' was framed at the head of the cross:

> *They Shall Grow Not Old*
> *as we that are left grow old*
> *Age Shall not weary them*
> *nor the years condemn*
> *At the going down of the sun*
> *and in the morning*
> *We Will Remember Them*

Near to the cross, a street performer was setting up his stool and small amplification system, the sound of him playing Spanish guitar music will soon echo off the stone walls, enchanting the tourists as they filter out of the handmade fudge shop or sip their coffees at tables outside the restaurant, nearby café or pasty shop. The Abbey churchyard, to me, is the heartbeat from which all life in the city flows out and away from. I come here often to watch, to imagine and to write.

Walking away from the Abbey, I headed towards the colonnade that spans the entrance of the square, leading out onto Stall Street and also providing shelter to the street performers and those caught out without umbrellas in an unexpected shower. In the spring and summer months hanging baskets, overflowing with bell shaped flowers of varying colours, hang between the columns. They are taken down in winter, the days and nights too cold for flowers to flourish. The late autumn sunshine was shielded by the yellow stone structure, a curtain of shade instead pulled across the length of the colonnade. The windows of the small corner café were laden with cakes. Opposite the café a man was sat on the steps that lead up to a fire exit door to the Pump Rooms. He held a newspaper opened before him. He wore a long silver-painted jacket over a corduroy suit and tie. There was a silver-painted bucket at his feet, containing birdseed and loose change. On his head was a narrow brimmed silver hat with an orange feather standing out within the shade trapped beneath the colonnade. On the lip of the hat's brim, a pigeon was perched and looking down at the bucket of birdseed. The Pigeon Man continued to read, flicking the pages of the newspaper and frequently looking up to examine the people passing by. Five or so pigeons swooped down beneath the roof of the colonnade, landing on him and the steps. He didn't flinch or react to the birds now on his shoulders and feet. He read the day's headlines. I approached.

I'd often seen the Pigeon Man inviting tourists to hold out their arms for him to dress them with pigeons. I thought it a strange thing for the Asian tourists (in fact any tourists) to want to experience, especially given the masks I'd seen over the mouths and noses of Japanese people while living there for a brief time, much of the population perpetually concerned about the germs they might be breathing in. Yet I'd all too often see tourists, predominantly Chinese, with big smiles and uncontrollable giggles holding out their arms for pigeons to perch on them, while their friends took pictures before placing some money into the plastic bucket. I like and respect all animals, but this still doesn't mean I want to be up close and personal with a pigeon. God knows what their beaks have been pecking. The pigeons however failed to recognise my coldness towards them and I soon had one flapping on my shoulder; I flinched as its feathers brushed against my ear. Moments before becoming a bird stand I had sat beside the Pigeon Man and mentioned to him that I was writing a book about poverty and the personal stories behind it. I asked him how he came to work with the birds. He closed his newspaper and turned to speak to me.

"I started off by being a statue," he said, with more and more pigeons landing on and beside us. "I figured that if I got the birds to land on me I'd do a bit better. I was watching the birds while I was stood there and thinking they're all starving. You could tell they were really fighting. I thought I'd bring a bit of birdseed along with me and try and get the birds to land on me and whatever. I used to stand underneath where the birds sit, put a bit of birdseed on me hat and I got the birds to come and land on me. Then they started to want to land on my hand because that's where the food was coming from. Everyone just started asking me to hold the pigeons and I just became known as the Pigeon Man."

"I saw you in the Abbey vaults the other day," I said. "What takes you to Lifeline?"

"I go there for a cup of tea. It's good to get a free cup of tea."

"How long have you been in Bath?"

"I came here in April 2010. I've got an evening job that I do three hours a day, just like a minimum wage thing. I do that and I do this. I make more money off this in the summer and probably the same as my evening job off doing this in the winter. It's not brilliantly paid in the winter. Although I might make the same I'm probably doing more hours."

"Do you find it's difficult to exist on minimum wage?"

"No, not at all. I find Bath is a really easy place to get by and you'd have a hard job to go without anything here."

I found this surprising given the findings by the Joseph Rowntree Foundation at the end of 2013 that 6.7 million[4] families were living in poverty in the UK despite also being in employment, and today, nearing the end of 2014, the foundation has just disclosed that the number of people from working families in poverty is as many as people from workless ones.[5] My own experience of seeing my wages evaporating into the cost of living after every wage slip also made me feel that it wasn't easy for all to exist on their incomes alone. The minimum wage in the UK at the time of writing is £6.50 and yet the living wage, based on what is actually needed to cover the cost of living, is calculated at £7.95, rising to £9.15 in London. This means millions of low wage workers are struggling to get by and meet the cost of living, it means millions are bound in poverty and in a system that makes those in work as poor as those who are not. I didn't know what expenses the Pigeon Man had so cannot say how he found himself able to buck the trend and find minimum wage tolerable.

"Is it because of the services that are available?" I asked.

"That as well, yeah. Compared to some places where I've lived and where I've been, I think you're pretty lucky if you're in Bath."

"Does that mean in the past you've had periods of poverty or difficulty?"

"Yeah, I have, yeah."

"And when you were in that situation, what was the thing preventing you most from getting out of it? You often hear people say it's like a trap."

"I think most people when they get caught in the poverty trap it's because they go on benefits, or they go on sickness benefits and they can't get off it. Once you're on it, you're kind of stuck on it and it's really hard to find any employment or anyone wanting to take you."

"And how about the future, do you want to keep working with the birds?"

"No, I don't want to be doing this forever. I used to run a construction company but don't know if I could go back into that now. I'll keep working with the birds for the time being. I'm doing okay."

A stream of small children suddenly passed by in a long line, flanked by anxious adults whose primary thought was not to let one slip away into the busyness of the square and out of sight. The Pigeon Man instinctively stood and lifted his arms for the pigeons on the ground to in turn instinctively slap their wings and fly up to him. The children passed by with their faces a diverse mix of horror, amazement and bewilderment. The teacher, holding the rear of the line and collecting any stragglers, on seeing the Pigeon Man shouted over and over: "Keep Moving Children!" Pigeons had clearly not been included in the disclaimer their parents had to sign before the trip into the city. "Come on children, keep moving!"

I stood and watched the Pigeon Man, undeterred, place one hand into his silver-painted jacket and pull out a handful of birdseed; he sprinkled it onto his hat and then moved into the crowd. Two birds, feathers in motion as they rode on the hat, fed on the seed while others rode on his open hands.

"Thanks for speaking with me," I said.

"You're welcome." He then nodded to the silver-painted bucket at the foot of the steps. "I've a pot for a little money."

I didn't even have a pound in change on me, but I dropped what I had onto the seed and the money already in the bucket. I moved out of the shade and into sunshine, into the mass of bodies flowing up and down Stall Street; there was a sudden flurry of screams and laughter behind. I turned to see the Pigeon Man crowning a young Asian woman with a grey feathered bird. The pigeons that had remained perched on the roof of the colonnade looked down on the show from above. I held my notebook in my hand and walked away.

XIX

It's November 24th and today saw the first real frost of winter, my partner's car was covered by a thick layer of ice which we used as the excuse after she reversed into her father's car in the drive. He's an understanding man. Making the most of the short time V and I have left together before I leave for Asia has meant I've not stayed in the caravan for a couple of weeks. Before the weekend, I visited Clare, my landlady, to thank her and to pick up the remainder of my things; some books, the duvet and pillows my parents had given me and my sleeping bag. The bedding was damp to touch. I folded it up and scrunched it into a bag, the caravan had become one big cool box and I don't know how I would have fared if I had been sleeping in it.

After parking in the long stay car park this morning, V and I again inspected the scratches on the rear bumper of her car. We said goodbye; V went to work and I decided to walk around Bath's busying streets, my coat buttoned up and hands cold as I held onto my notebook. Wooden huts, or better sheds, had been erected in the churchyard and around the Abbey; traders were filling them with their wares in anticipation of the crazed consumerism that is the yearly Christmas market. The city's infrastructure strains to welcome and host the thousands of extra visitors the market brings to Bath. It's a small city after all. I walked along Manvers Street and watched the down and outs on the steps outside the Baptist Church and the steps that lead down to the Julian House night shelter. They moved from foot to foot to ward off the cold and socialised with each other. Almost three months had passed since I arrived back in Bath and many of the faces I had seen outside the church then were still standing there now. Would they be out on the steps when I returned to Bath again in three months' time? Is this it for them, life's lot? I walked away.

Passing the Abbey and the Guildhall I saw Dean ahead; his long hair draped over parts of his face with fingerless gloves on his hands.

"You didn't sleep outside last night, did you?" I asked, standing beside him and back a bit so he could still tempt the passers-by with the magazine he had held up before him.

"Yeah," he replied. "It was alright, I had to use extra blankets."

I looked down to his feet. His Sports Direct bag had been replaced by a bigger bag, it was blue and the sleeping bags stuffed inside it were almost falling out of the top. It must have been between minus one and minus three degrees in the depths of the night. It wasn't a nice thought to imagine him curled up under these layers of fabric. He looked anxious to sell the magazine, perhaps hoping to make enough to cover the cost of a night in the shelter.

"It's hard now because they're £3, lots of people run away from the price," he reflected.

The release of the *Big Issue Christmas Special* meant 50p extra was added onto the price. I had once tried to pitch a story to the magazine and, still new to the game at the time, got frustrated after being avoided by the editor, almost at the expense of losing the timeliness of the feature. Pressed and stressed, I managed to find another home for the article that chronicled the suffering of an ex-Falklands veteran living in Trowbridge. He had experienced twenty years of homelessness due to his Post Traumatic Stress Disorder not being dealt with well enough by the military, society and health practitioners. It was only diagnosed as one of the major factors in his troubles five years ago and long after the first nightmares of falling bombs and burning bodies had first ravaged his mind. It was a harrowing story that resulted in addiction and, ultimately, will lead to his death which he explained was a result of his last round of treatment failing to cure the hepatitis he had caught from a dirty needle. His experiences in war had led to terrors, inability to adjust back into society, the breakdown of his marriage, the loss of his home and loved ones, which led to a deepening drug dependence and poverty.

War can impoverish a region through destruction and fear, but it can also impoverish those in battle through the mental scars of service it leaves behind. Yet in 2013, Britain spent over £56 billion on military expenditure.[6] War, despite the great costs, is something the government sees as worth shelling out for, profit must be made in it somewhere amongst all the bloodshed and helplessness. I find it strange that this doesn't anger tax-paying citizens more than it appears to, remembering the austerity of late, and especially those struggling by on £6.50 an hour with their hard earned money chipped away at by tax which is then partly invested in bombs and fear. Wasted.

A *Big Issue* vendor, what with so much free content available through the internet, must compete in a saturated world of words. Selling a slim magazine for £2.50 means they have to be creative in their sales pitch, although I've frequently been around sellers who have been given money by passers-by who refuse to accept a magazine and simply wish to give to someone in need. The *Big Issue* operates on the premise of a 'hand up, not a hand out' and it certainly was an inspiring and empowering venture when it was launched in 1991, and has undoubtedly helped many vulnerable citizens find a way back into society. I can't help but wonder though if it can also paradoxically maintain those in the poverty trap as they battle the elements to sell enough magazines to get by while also reinvesting in more magazines for tomorrow. *Big Issue* sellers, having purchased the magazines for half the price they sell them for, make £1.25 for every magazine they sell. Therefore to make minimum wage, a seller would have to sell just over five magazines an hour, based on the £1.25 they keep after the cost of the magazine is accounted for. This means to make £50 a seller would need to sell forty magazines. Remembering that the living cost, not the legally enforced minimum wage, is calculated to be £7.95, on an eight-hour day a *Big Issue* seller needs to sell fifty magazines. This seems like a tall order. My doubts over how effective the *Big Issue* is at personal empowerment also comes after passing the same faces at the pitches in Bath year after year. Is it that these sellers wish to keep selling magazines on the streets or is it because they're trapped in a low paid job dressed up as an opportunity?

I was still to interview Dean in-depth and every time I thought I was close to getting him to commit to coming for a tea, he had to dash off and purchase some more magazines. I wondered if he was really willing to share his story with me after all. I had only one full day left in Bath and I felt it would be wasted if I couldn't at least learn a little of his history after having made this small connection. I was curious to know why I had never seen him around any of the services in the city: Lifeline, the Food bank, FoodCycle or the soup run. How did he get by on what he earned from the magazines? What did he see for the future? I had questions and unfortunately it was looking like they would go unanswered.

That afternoon, and after reading back through my previous chapters introducing Lifeline and the Pigeon Man in the central library, I went to the dentist. I arrived at 2pm and was in the hygienist's chair at 2.10pm. She talked and I, silenced by the suction gun in my lower gum, listened as my teeth were polished. Fifteen minutes later I was in the dentist's chair, she looked over my teeth and recommended flossing and maintaining a healthy diet and in less than five minutes I was back at the front desk, sliding my debit card into the card reader. The hygienist, privately operated, cost £49. The dental check-up, NHS provided, cost £18.50. I was back out the door at 2.38pm with my bank account £67.50 the poorer. I had had to work for nearly ten hours in the pub to earn this amount. I gritted my stain free teeth and swore under my breath. At least the pigeons posed for a picture as they sat in a long line on the rooftops of the shops spanning Pulteney Bridge, the sky above a perfect blue.

XX

The day before leaving Bath rain fell continuously over the city and the cover of grey clouds brought an early dusk. I walked down Milsom Street with V, the raindrops pattering on her umbrella. I had invited her along to the annual event by one of the groups in the city that worked with vulnerable people. We were early so decided to go for coffee and dry off a little beforehand. On the pavement ahead, a line of umbrellas waited at the bus stop, the faces beneath them dry but still somewhat soggy. Dean stood outside the entrance of a bank near to the bus stop, displaying the magazines he was holding towards the waiting passengers. The magazines were inside a plastic cover, keeping them dry. Dean was wet through. We still had an hour before the event started; I turned to V and gave her my best *I know I've invited you for an evening out, but please don't think too ill of me if I leave you for a bit to talk to Dean* look.

"Do you mind?"

"It's fine."

We were getting nearer to where Dean was stood.

"Thank you," I said. "I'll try not to be too long."

"It's really fine."

Dean saw us and smiled. He had three magazines left to sell so I said that if I came back in thirty minutes and he'd still not sold them, I would buy them and maybe he would be happy to come for that tea. He said he would.

I walked with V to the coffee shop where I had an espresso and turned over some questions in my head while

V read her book. I apologised for abandoning her again.

"I said it was fine," she replied, her certainty pushing me out the door and on my way.

I ran in the rain along the bottom of Queen Square with the evening commuter traffic moving slowly round it; I then passed down Quiet Street with the shop doors being locked before skipping between the stationary traffic on Milsom Street. Dean was still standing outside the bank. People walked with long strides past him, wanting to get out of the rain. He'd sold one magazine in the time I'd been gone.

"I'll buy the remaining two," I said. "Want to get out of the rain for a bit?"

"Yeah, alright."

Dean placed the magazines in the big blue bag at his feet; part of his sleeping bag had not been sheltered from the rain and was visibly wet. We walked side by side, turning down Green Street, a pedestrian street and home to a run of independent shops and an old inn. We crossed the busy road at its end, passing St Michael's Church, the spire hidden behind a blanket of rain. We pushed open the doors to the Podium centre, Dean's bag thumping down on the escalator as we headed for the café on the first floor.

"The zip to my sleeping bag broke last night," he said as we stood still and travelled up. "Woke up about two in the morning, soaking wet."

Dean reflected on this as though it was nothing big or important, just what had passed as he slept outside. Something else would likely pass tonight, tomorrow night and the night after. He saw no need to accentuate his situation. We went to the counter and ordered two teas and two slices of flapjack; I pointed to a table on the edge of all the other tables. It was a supermarket café with the overlapping conversations creating a heavy drone and I feared I would miss much of what Dean had to say. We sat and both poured our teas; Dean then hurried off to find sugar. I waited and noticed a group of adults with learning difficulties being encouraged by their carers to eat their slices of cake and drink their drinks on the table next to ours. One of the men was striking out at his carer; the carer gently restrained him and placed the man's hands back on his knees. The man looked lost as the carer then placed his hand onto his shoulder. He struck out again. The carer again caught the fists coming his way and resettled them upon the man's lap.

"Got some," Dean said, sitting back down and instantly scooping some sugar into his cup, stirring it. "You want some?"

"No, I'm good thanks."

He placed down the teaspoon and warmed his hands on the warm cup; he still had his red *Big Issue* jacket on and raindrops clung to the long strands of his hair. He'd lost some of his teeth and the ones that remained were stained by tobacco. We had a little to drink and ate some of our flapjacks before I asked Dean how long he'd been living on the streets.

"About two years this time, I think. I was in Weston when I first moved here and, after staying with friends for a bit, I got a room. It was £108 a week rent. When this coalition (government) got in they put a cap on housing benefits for under-thirty-fives, so there was a big deficit. I managed to hang on in there for a while without paying the extra rent. I was thirty-five a couple of weeks ago so now I can get full rent. I didn't manage to hang on until then. I lost my place in January. I only had to wait like nine more months and I would have been okay."

"Is this the first time you found yourself on the street?"

"No, few years ago I was also on the street in Cardiff. It was summer. It was Mardi Gras so I just went there and stayed there, and that got me into not caring about being on the street really."

"What about in the long run, is there a point when

you'd look to find a way off the street?"

"Yeah definitely, I'm pretty much involved in it now, trying to get a place. I got to stay in Julian House for six months."

"Is that because you need to have a local connection in Bath?"

"I've got local connections. It's just the rules they have, you know. You got to stay there and adhere to all their rules, to prove that you can keep to the rules and that."

"I've heard mixed feelings from the people I've met about Julian House. One *Big Issue* seller told me he was paying £119 a week in one of their homes."

"It is yeah if you haven't got housing benefits or you work then you have to pay that, yeah. Everyone's got to pay three pound a night for the night shelter. I'm more free now than when I've had places to live. You've got to make sure you can pay the bills, make sure you can do this, can do that, you know. So I'm pretty free at the moment."

"But now we're in winter, will that not be more of an issue?"

"I just get on with it, don't really think about it. Last night was tough, what with my broken sleeping bag. I got to sort that out really."

"What about your evenings, do you have a place where you tend to go?"

"I usually just read. Just sit somewhere and read. I've got a few places where I go, that I know are safe and in the open, cameras up and stuff. I'd rather sleep right in the open on the street than go hide somewhere out of sight. A lot of people would feel safer hidden out the way, but I feel safer right in the open."

"Do you have any fear while sleeping on the street?"

"No, not really. I'd probably feel more uncomfortable in a house than I do out on the street really."

"Because of the bills to pay?"

"I don't like it indoors, like at three o'clock, four o'clock in the morning; it just feels a bit weird on my own. But outside it don't bother me, I could be in a churchyard and I'll be fine."

"Do you feel let down by anything or anyone for being out on the street?"

"This government, this coalition has been a bit shit for capping the housing benefit. You know, you have to be over thirty-five to get anything over £65 a week. You can't get anything for £65 a week. It's impossible. I'm thirty-five now so maybe I'll be okay."

Dean lifted the edge of flapjack from his plate, placed it in his mouth and chewed. He then returned for the crumbs, pinching them between his fingers. I drank some of my tea, silently searching for my next question.

"Have you always had a love of reading?"

He swallowed. "I'm getting more into fiction now, whereas when I was younger I used to read more non-fiction. But as I got older I realised non-fiction turns into fiction and sometimes you find there's more truth in fiction than there is in non-fiction."

"Isn't there something you would like to work towards?"

He poured the last of the tea into his cup, placing the pot down and lifting the teaspoon to stir in some sugar. The liquid swirled as he spoke.

"I was doing the ECL before the coalition got in, a computer course. And when this government got in they slashed the budget on funding and that lost my IT qualification. There was seven exams a module and I'd passed three already, four more to go. I was going through the module and then it's gone. That's the first thing this government done and then the second was a few years later when they brought in the housing benefit reforms."

"So do you see yourself selling the *Big Issue* for a while?"

"Yeah, well I imagine until I've got a proper job, yeah. They only give you benefits when you've got a placement or a job and I never manage to keep benefits for very long you know, keep claiming for a few weeks and then I lose them."

"Is that due to the amount of things to go through to maintain them, applications for instance?"

"I usually have to end up signing off for something you know. I was getting bored of doing it. I can survive without it anyway."

"I've noticed that you also don't seem to use the services in the city, like Lifeline and the soup run."

"Yeah, I don't use them. I don't want to mix with the people that's there."

"I learned from one guy at the soup run that some of them have houses."

"At all the services they do, at Genesis they do, at Lifeline they do. It's not homeless people using it, it's pretend homeless people you know."

"What about the *Big Issue*? I was thinking about it and questioning its effectiveness for combating poverty. Have you found it's been of benefit to you?"

"Yeah, definitely. I don't really need a lot you know, so as long as I can get food and stuff, it's okay."

"So you can get by on the magazines you sell?"

"I just sell what I need to survive. I don't own anything; I don't need anything so much. I don't aspire to own anything or save up for anything."

"Do you see yourself as being in poverty?"

"I don't, no. There are a lot of people who have got things and they are really minus graph, aren't they, or just in credit because they owe it. They got to go head over heel. Technically I'm better off than people what've got houses and cars, and even when the house is full up of stuff you know. They don't really have that anyway. They're slaves to that, aren't they? They've got to go to work every day to pay for all that and it will all fall down if they don't go to work, keep paying for it all. I wouldn't see myself as poverty stricken, although technically I probably am. Anything I get is just disposable income, 100 per cent disposable income. It's got to be the degree of what poverty is. If you've got disposable income then you can't be so poor. You see some people with a big manor house and that, and yet they're in some sort of poverty, everything they do is to maintain the building."

"So what makes a day a good day for you?"

"If I've got a good book, really. If I've got a good book then I keep reading that and I don't get round to doing anything."

"I thought this after you read *The Grapes of Wrath* in two days."

"Oh yeah, I really like that book, it's great. I'd read *Of Mice and Men* a few weeks before too."

"He was prolific."

"Yeah, that's what he got the Nobel Prize for, wasn't it? Cause he never actually did anything that was poor."

A smile had dressed Dean's lips after we had begun talking about books. He finished his tea and then looked across the table at me.

"You know, I haven't got no big sad story about being abused or nothing."

"I'm pleased you haven't," I said, before mentioning how humbling it is to see so many out on the streets in the city in the days, asking for help.

"A lot of people it's their day job as well you know," replied Dean. "They all got flats and that and they're on the street all day begging, pretending to be homeless, and then they go back to their flat at the end of the night. Every single one you see begging round town, every single one of them has got a flat. All the ones sat there crossed legged all day have got flats. Being homeless is just their day job, they go back to their flats at the end of the night, which is sad. You know what I mean? And that's what puts all the stigma on homeless people, it's the people pretending to be homeless. They shouldn't make begging illegal; they should make making money by false pretences illegal. You know, when they're asking money for this and that, they should get done for that. But they're trying harder to stop people from giving money to homeless people."

"The trouble is what happens when you've got people in genuine need who haven't got £3 to go down to the night shelter, where do they get the money from? This is what I thought; when you have to buy magazines, if you haven't got money to start with, what do you do?"

"Exactly, I've had that a few times as well."

"What do you do?"

"Even if I'm just reading I'll get money eventually. But now it's half day closing for the *Big Issue*, it's got to be before one o'clock if I'm going to work."

"Do you have a set target each day of how many magazines you want to sell?"

"I used to when the office was open all day every day, I used to try to sell seventy-five magazines a week (making Dean £93.75 after the cost of the magazine is accounted for) so I could start a pitch, so I could reserve it as mine. Now it's half day closing I've given up on it, totally. It's like everything else; I've given up trying to get a place, I've given up with the *Big Issue* now, because I can only get magazines by one o'clock, and I haven't got the funds to get the stock in. You know you've got to get that many magazines every day to get that target. It was enough for me just thinking about it let alone trying to do it, bring myself down you know."

"Do you think you'll be housed by the spring?"

Dean shook his head.

"So you're going to spend the whole winter outside?"

"I might get in the night shelter some times, but not resting my hopes on it, or I might stay at my friend's place. I got places I could stay at but I don't like to stay at my friend's place for too long."

"I met a young woman at a protest in London," I said. "She told me how she would stay with her friends' for a while and then at some point her friends would say to her you can't stay here all the time because they were struggling to fund themselves, let alone her too."

"I got friends who say I could stay at their place but I don't take them up on it just for that fact. Besides I don't like being in people's spaces; when there are silences and having to have conversations and all that, and having to do all the emotional things as well, you know; having to be around them when they're maybe not at their best all the time. Can't be doing with it. I guess it's pretty selfish but I'd rather be out in the freezing cold."

"Well at least you're honest."

I still had half a cup of tea left so offered Dean the remainder of my pot.

"Yeah, go on then yeah, I'll have a bit."

I poured it for him.

"Nice one."

I placed down the now empty pot and Dean added milk and sugar.

"What happens when it gets to say minus five in the winter?" I asked. "What do you do?"

"There'll be compulsory letting people in then, at minus three. It's got to be by law, if it's minus three the government have got to do something about it."

"And when you're on the street do you find you're moved on or left alone?"

"I was but they know now that I'm not begging so the police will leave me alone, they'll pass me by. I'm one of the only people homeless on a Friday or Saturday night who is sat in a doorway reading, and not moved on. They know I'm only sat there reading, waiting to go to sleep."

We finished our drinks and over Dean's shoulder I saw the male carer now resting his hand on top of the young man's, keeping it still while maintaining a soft tone in his voice. "Don't hit," he said. "There's no need to hit." I see people who can maintain such patience, understanding and love for those they care for to be the angels of the earth. Dean and I began collecting our things, pushing back our chairs and standing. We walked between the tables, him holding his big bag before him so as not to bump into those sat over their coffees. We stood still as the escalator took us down.

"So when you writing this book then?" he asked.

"I'm writing it now."

We walked out into the rain. Lots of people were leaving the supermarket around us with plastic bags, some hemp, at their sides and filled with their evening dinner. I shook Dean's hand and wished him well over the winter. I also gave him some money to cover his time away from selling. It would give him a bit of a head start in the mornings as he could invest in a few magazines if he so wished, or buy a small pouch of tobacco to have a smoke while out in the cold that night. I won't judge him poorly for it if he does.

XXI

Departures. A middle-aged man and woman are sitting opposite each other, sipping at their coffees and nibbling on their pastries. The glass windows they sit before look out over Heathrow airport, the winter sunshine reflecting on the runways still wet from last night's rain. Planes line up and wait at the end of the tarmac; soon accelerating, their engines roaring and sucking up air as they speed along the runways, their noses lifting and pointing up and into blue sky and patchy clouds. On the table next to mine, a man in a blue suit with polished black shoes holds a smart phone to his ear as he talks into it; occasionally he lifts the ball point pen on the table and jots down notes on a piece of paper, a pair of sunglasses are open and rest on the page, his scribbled notes framing them.

Around twelve other tables are occupied around mine; all but two of the people sat at them are staring into the phones in their hands. The digital age is never more present than in a departure lounge as a final farewell is sent to loved ones, while so many of the practicalities of life can now be addressed through the little instruments held in the palms of the waiting passengers' hands. I've already sent a message to my good friend in Japan, called V in Bath to tell her I'll miss her once again, and researched the currency exchange for sterling to Indian rupees. My flight to Mumbai leaves in just over an hour. V, born in the States, wished me a Happy Thanksgiving over the phone. It's the first time I've had this said to me, so I've never really thought about the meaning of Thanksgiving.

I wonder what most people, if brought together around a table, would give thanks for. Would they be thankful for the iPhone in their pocket, the television, the car on the drive, the roof over their head, the wage slip at the end of the month, the salary at the end of the year, the job, the security, the warmth of another to sit beside and carve out roast turkey with, sharing stories and being together? Would they be thankful for life? If they are healthy, would they be thankful for this? To have sight, to process movement, physical freedom?

I sit here and watch the planes take off and wonder what if someone didn't have some or any of these things. What then would they be thankful for? Would they instead be thankful to those who do not look down at them and see a bum or an outcast? Would they be thankful for those who crouch down beside them and say, *Good morning?* Perhaps they would give thanks for the morning sun bringing light, or the summer nights for being warm. What if they had a home but could not afford to keep it or to put food on the table? How would they then celebrate Thanksgiving? Would their children ask them what it means? How do they respond? *It means to be grateful for the things we have, children.* There are those much worse off than us. There are always those who are worse off, but we should not then accept being impoverished in any form as our lot. *It was the hand life dealt me.* No. I think Thanksgiving should be a time to remember the power of the human spirit, to give thanks for it because it can lift us to the realms the religions tell us are only accessible through God. I say this is not true. Without human consciousness, what would the world know of God? Very little. So much better to see God as a creative force inside us all; there is no greater power than the power we harness in our hearts and minds. Poverty persists due to many external forces, but poverty is strongest when it has broken the hearts of those that it ensnares, weakening the mind into submission. It is hardest when the society on large refuses to see it.

Over the past three months I've sought to see what poverty means in the English city of Bath. I'm now leaving feeling it is a word that can hold no universal definition. One person's poverty is not the same as another's. One person's way out of it may not work for another; it has to be tailored to the individual. There are also those I would have seen and did see as living in abject poverty, like Dean for instance, but through engagement and taking time to listen, to share a cup of tea and slice of flapjack, I learned that he is poor only in terms of financial wealth and material possessions. His spirit is no poorer than mine. His spirit is perhaps far richer than many millions who are stuck in the new poverty trap of merely living in the UK, where housing costs, food, fuel, taxes, targeted cuts to those on low incomes, has resulted in people battling to spread their wages thin enough to cover it all, to pay for life. Never has being alive cost so much. This would be tolerable if only it didn't cripple us spiritually. Slavery was abolished, we're told, but I look at contemporary British society and ask myself was it really? All those sitting on the tables around me on their phones, drinking their warm drinks and eating their expensive pastries, are they doing okay? Are they free, really? Or are they the face of what poverty means today; the generation of seemingly longer working hours and yet ever decreasing disposable incomes?

A Christmas jingle is now playing in the background. It might be the first and last one I hear this winter. My gate is about to be opened. In one hour I depart for India.

INDIA and NEPAL
November 2014 to late February 2015

I

The plane landed at 4am local time. I tried to get a couple of hours' sleep after I arrived at Seashore, my hotel located in Fort, an affluent and touristic region in Mumbai, and also home to The Gateway of India, an arch monument built during the British Raj that would have impressed majesty upon those having made long voyages by ship before reaching the Arabian Sea and finally docking in the harbour. Close to The Gateway and along the seafront, the traffic is often slow and stationary as cars are stopped before entering the Taj Mahal Palace Hotel for their undercarriages to be searched by men holding mirrors on the end of poles. The hotel was a target during a wave of attacks that occurred in Mumbai in 2008, perpetrated by Lashkar-e-Taiba, an Islamist terrorist group. Thirty-one civilians, both staff and guests, were killed. The Taj is regarded as one of the finest hotels in the country, red-domed roofs crown its four corners with many of its white-framed windows looking out on The Gateway and down on the street sellers, beggars and tourists that busy the pavement running alongside the sea wall. The hotel's renowned stature, with rooms starting around 13,000 rupees (roughly £130) per night and ranging up to The Grande Luxury Suite which was listed for 102,000 rupees (over £1,000), helps Mumbai to exemplify its place as India's wealthiest city.

From my room in Seashore, 700 rupees per night (about £7), I had a view to the sea and a noisy fan spinning over my bed. It was a beautiful beginning to the day, the sky above the water a varying palette of pinks – I lay on my bed and was asleep before the sun had even peaked above the hazy/polluted horizon.

I'm writing this now in Welcome Restaurant, fifteen minutes' walk from The Gateway of India, and off Mahatma Gandhi Road. Beside my notebook I have a clay cup of chai; it's still too hot to drink (or my lips are simply still tingling from the tomato based vegetable curry I had for lunch, picked from the plate with pieces of buttered naan). The fans on the ceiling spin furiously, causing the stack of paper napkins on my table to shake in the downward flow of air. There are twelve waiters that I can count, along with two water boys circling the tables and exchanging empty steel cups of water for full ones; there are also two clearers, collecting the finished plates in the steel baskets held on their arms. The surrounding tables are predominantly occupied by men, although two women in suits are sitting opposite each other on a table in the middle of the restaurant. I will finish this later as the waiter has just put the bill on the table, held down by a small dish containing fennel seeds to chew and freshen the breath. They're a little dry on the tongue. It's the busy type of restaurant where they want you to move on so they can reuse the table. I should go.

After lunch I walked for some time around the surrounding area. Fort is home to some of the best known museums and galleries the city has to offer. The old colonial buildings have maintained their magnificence, despite many of them being blackened and often the foothold of ivy and other vines. The roads are a chaotic mix of buses, cars, taxis, rickshaws, cows, along with mule-drawn, as well as people-drawn, wagons. It's a little like a game of chance when traversing them but soon enough you're following the locals' lead and crossing no matter the speed of the vehicles bearing down upon you. The sound of beeping horns is by far the most dominant noise permeating the city.

At Wellington Fountain, a large roundabout, with Apollo Pier Road leading back to the seafront and The Gateway, I stopped and decided on my next street to explore. I sidestepped my way up Colaba Causeway, the pavement lined by jewellery and clothes stands to tempt the many tourists, with familiar clothing brands being sold for incredibly cheap prices, their authenticity the compromise. I picked up a pair of sandals for 350 rupees, more comfortable than the rest so more expensive. Converted back to my own currency the sandals had cost £3.55. This, I believe, was the tourist price; an Indian would be able to purchase them much cheaper. Doing my best to avoid bumping into the many people on the pavement I decided to make my way back to the hotel, the heat and my lack of sleep was slowing me and I found it hard to take everything in, the noise and bustle was dizzying. Stopping again to rub my eyes and brow, a large laminated map of India was suddenly unfolded before me. A young man with a moustache and smile stood behind it, holding it on display.

"Map for you, I make you good price."

"No, thank you," I said, smiling and going on my way.

He followed, rolling up the map and running a little before walking beside me.

"What's your name?"

"Matthew, or Matt if you like."

"Matt," he repeated.

"And your name?" I asked.

"Vijay." (Not his real name.)

"Nice to meet you, Vijay."

I continued walking, thinking the course of our introduction would now be over as Colaba Causeway is not a great place to have a conversation, anything distracting you from the people heading back and forth was one distraction too many.

"What brings you to Mumbai?" Vijay asked.

"I'm travelling."

"Ah, travelling. Good idea." Vijay then grabbed my arm and stopped me. "Hey, Mac, you want to go for a chai. I talk to you about my city and you tell me about your city."

Vijay now had his maps folded under his arm and waited excitedly for my answer. A taxi pulled up beside us and the driver beeped and waved his hand from inside, gesturing for us to get in. I waved him off and turned back to the first friend I'd made in Mumbai.

"Yes, Vijay, a chai would be nice."

Vijay took me to a restaurant where we sat opposite each other and drank chai, learning a little about each other's lives. He was from Jaipur, the capital city of the state of Rajasthan in the north of India. He had come to Mumbai believing the city would be the home of opportunity, and, being fit and healthy, he thought he would have no problem finding work. He was wrong. The city was also the home of many thousands if not millions just like him, all following an illusion of a better life. Vijay was also the provider for his younger brother and sister whom he had cared for since the death of his parents. He relied on his wits and intuition to earn rupees where he could, and the tourists in Fort seemed like as good a source as any. His maps were rolled up on the seat beside him.

The chai was served in cups which contained about two mouthfuls, so they didn't take us long to finish. Vijay offered to take me on a small tour of Fort, to the section where the Indian people shop. I was happy for the insight. We visited the fish market where Vijay said that much of the catch was caught off the coast of the city, or brought into Mumbai harbour from further afield. We then went into a tailor's and Vijay convinced me that it was in my interest to buy some traditional clothing, explaining how

I'd appear like I'd been in India for a long time and was less likely to be overcharged for items I subsequently wished to purchase. Finally he took me to the Oval Maiden, the large public cricket ground which first appeared like an ocean of grass and relief after having spent the morning walking around the hectic city streets. We walked to the boundary of a game that was taking place and sat down. Vijay was, as are most Indians, a diehard cricket fan. He told me he came to Oval Maiden every Sunday to bat for his team. Quickly relaxing and now in a better place to talk, I again asked Vijay what had brought him to Mumbai.

"I come here to Mumbai to find job but it's difficult to find job here. You know Mumbai is a big city, everybody think like that, *Mumbai is a big city, we find easy job*. But not easy, it's very hard. Many people they struggling, many people in Mumbai."

A cheer erupted amongst the fielders.

"They're out," said Vijay pointing to the fielder who had just caught the ball. The sight of the fielding team then coming together to slap hands and pat backs made him smile. It stretched before disappearing as he continued speaking, "You know many people in Mumbai they struggle in work, in office, in many things, struggle. Many people doing hard work in Mumbai. In Mumbai, you can't stay here long time. You have to move from here. You have to go in some good place. So go there. Mumbai is just this: it's like a busy place, it's like a rush place, busy parts. Mumbai life is a very hard life. If you want to stay in Mumbai you need a lot of money. You need more money and you need good contact in Mumbai. Because in Mumbai there is many many different happenings, many people they're doing wrong with you; they beat you, they get your money, they get your wallet, get your camera, many places it's like that happening in Mumbai. I come here one and half year ago, I see many many happenings here in Mumbai. If I find some tourist I give advice like

that; *you go there, you go there, you do this, you do this,* because
I give the right advice. I'm not trying to make money, if I
try to make money I not make building. You understand,
Mac, I not make building, so I give the good advice, do
good karma. I just think like that. I just do karma for the
back for me karma. I'm not think like that, *If I get money I
make building.* If I get 2,000, 5,000, 10,000, what I'm going
to do with that. It's nothing. After some days we spend
this money. Nothing we have. If I do right things, step by
step, one day we go good life. We go in success life. You
understand?'

"When you say *make building,* do you mean a home?"

"Yes."

"When I was in the taxi travelling to my hotel this
morning, I was amazed to see how many people were
sleeping outside."

"On the street," said Vijay, nodding his head. "On the
street. That is a life here. In India many people they think
like that, *We go in Mumbai, we don't find job, no problem we can
sleep anywhere.* So that's why people sleeping on the street. I
tell you one thing, on the street life is like that, woman and
man, as in like girlfriend and boyfriend, like wife and man,
marriage life, they do this, just doing sex on the street
and they make a pregnant and they make children. Then
after two years they're put out on the street, 'Go and do
yourself begging.' I see many peoples here in Mumbai do
this."

"So do you think you'll stay in Mumbai for a long
time?"

"No. I have to move from here. I don't want to stay
here long time. If I come to good life, if one day I come to
good life, I go back in Jaipur. I don't want to stay here; I go
back to where I'm from. I don't want to stay here because
I know it is like a crowd place, it's like a rush place, it's
like a busy part. It's not like good part. If you have good
money you have a good house, you have good contact, so

you stay in Mumbai. You have no good contact, you have no money, you have no house, you can't stay here. You know, Mac, if I get a rent house, I get agreement paper. That agreement paper I show somewhere and I find an easy job. With the agreement paper, but it is very difficult for me. Why? Because first I have to give the money for deposit, about 20,000 rupees (£200) I have to give. And then monthly I pay 1,000, 2,000, 3,000 rupees. But first we need deposit money, like 20,000 rupees. And that 20,000 nobody helped me. That is the main point."

"So you haven't got the money to start with."

"Yes."

"In Britain," I said, "young people have the same trouble of not being able to buy houses or afford rental deposits because they're too expensive… "

"Oh yeah wow," Vijay said clapping his hands and no longer listening to me as he focused on the cricket. "Oh what a catch! Did you see that? He just jumped. What a jump. Nice cricket. Cricket is a very very interesting game."

Vijay was clearly happy when watching cricket and I decided to ask if he was happy in general with his life.

"Happy in myself?" he asked.

"In yourself, or… "

"No," he cut me short. "I don't feel in myself happy. I need two things, just success in one thing and I'm happy, so if I get a shoe box I'm happy. If I get a rent house I'm happy that also. You know in Mumbai many people just give me hope, but nobody help me. Everybody give me hope. *Yeah, one day you'll be success.* But nobody help me that. Life is very hard life in Mumbai, very very hard life. If you struggle so much then one day you be success, but first you have to struggle in your life. Then after you'll be success in your life. You know, direct you can't go success in your life."

"That's why it's hard to see those who have struggled all their life and never appear to have found a life without

125

struggle, because that can happen too."

"Yes. That's why I come to play and watch cricket," said Vijay. "I feel I'm happy when I'm playing cricket, because that's national game and if I'm playing cricket I feel happy in myself, otherwise... Oww, shot that!" The cricket ball scuttled across the grass towards the boundary and the batsmen ran back and forth between the stumps. "I'm a batsman too, not a bowler. You know, Mac, many people think if I was a rich man life would be easy, but they also troubled, they also struggle. Their life is that you think it's easy, but it's not easy. You think rich man pay money and he get everything very easy, he can't get easy. They have also problem, much problems. You know the poor guy also have a different life, and rich man also have a different life. Like you and me; we'll talk about you and me: we are together. We are same. We have hands the same. We have a leg, you also have two legs and you also have two hands. Same face. Same eyes. Same everything. But what is the difference? What is the difference?"

I didn't answer.

"We have a different mind," Vijay declared. "That's why we say: *Five fingers is not the same, everybody is not the same.* Everybody has a different mind; woman also has a different mind, and child also has a different mind, old man has a different mind. Everybody has a different mind. That is the main point, *five fingers is not the same, everybody is not the same.* Everybody has a different life; hard life, easy life. How you use your life, you know very well about that, your life. How I'm using my life, I know about that in my life. Other lives are not easier. We just think life is easy but it's not easy, it's very hard. We have to do hard work. You know Indian people they just rush so much and they just hurry and it is very busy and they hope so much – that's not easy. In America, London, in many places, there also is everybody busy, everybody do hard work. In world country also everybody do hard work. In your country also it's not easy life, it's difficult life. They have a life that's good but it's difficult life. In my country, in India, the government they don't pay you nothing. Just pay you in the municipality hospitals. In municipality hospitals and in municipality schools, they are two places they spend money. In your country, in English country, they give you all support. They help you in school, they help you in hospitals, they help you work. You have no work, so they give you work also. In your country from your government, they give you good life, you have no house they give you personal house also. They do all for you. You can't afford for your child in the school, so your government they help you. In India people making sex and making children on the street, then father and mother think, *Now they do themselves in begging.* So they send it to beg. It's very very bad here, very bad."

"It's a culture."

"Culture. Real Indian culture and it's a bullshit culture. You have to understand in our life, you understand in everything. Don't lose in anything because life is not come again, buddy. Life you just find one time in life. When you're lost in your life you don't know where you come to, how you're raised. Life you get one time, so use your life careful. Don't be lost in your life. Life is not come again, buddy. Life is very beautiful. Just you see and you just feel in your heart, how is life. So you think, *Yeah, life is very interesting.*"

"Yet many seem to forget this."

"Right. They forget because they drink and they smoke, and they use cocaine, brown sugar, and then they lose the life. I also could do everything but now I don't have mother or father so if I want to do anything, smoking, drinking, if I want to go junkie, I can go junkie, if I want to go drink people, I can go drink people, but you know I have to look at myself in my life. I don't want to lose my life. I want to go step by step to the good life. I have to look after my brother and sister. I don't want to lose my life. I want success in my life. Life is not come again. Life is very interesting. So you have to use your life. You have to love your life. You have to love yourself; don't love your girlfriend; don't love anyone. Just you love in yourself then you understand how is life. That's true, buddy." Vijay leaned back on his hands and faced the cricketers, before he smiled and gestured with his head. "See there is a woman playing cricket over there with the boys, tourist. Hey Mac, are you happy? Are you enjoying?"

"Yes, I'm enjoying being here."

"It's nice to talk, Mac."

"Likewise, Vijay."

We rested on the grass and watched the game play out.

II

Hey,

So I've had my shower and no longer do I have beads of sweat trickling down my body... How you doing, V? Knowing I'm going to be out of touch for some time over the coming month I thought I would write while I can, and share with you a little of my journey so far...

The flight was relatively pain-free except the first movie I watched very nearly had me in tears and left me thinking about you for the remainder of the flight, despite watching two more films... Damn Hollywood for playing on our weak spots. The film was called *The Fault in Our Stars*, released this year, and told the tale of two late teens who meet at a support group for those suffering from cancer; they fall in love, take a trip to Amsterdam and... well, you'll have to watch it with Sugar (the cat) one night...

I arrived in Mumbai at four this morning and took a cab, still in the dark, to my hotel. I know people always say to prepare yourself for what you'll see, but I thought it was an old depiction of what India was, and over-exaggerated. I was very wrong. Sitting in the cab we passed down streets where family after family slept only on mats on the roadside. I saw babies asleep next to street dogs, and men washing themselves with buckets of water in the gutters. The journey was around thirty minutes to the hotel and I couldn't have counted the street dwellers even if I had tried, there were hundreds.

Due to the time difference I didn't have any sleep last night so after checking in I opened my window with a view to the sea, and then lay down as the sun came up; a tree beneath my window is full of crows chattering away. After waking I decided to take a stroll, one minute of walking and a woman was at my side, baby in her hands. "Please help," she said. I replied, "I'm sorry." She asked for milk for the child. I said, "Okay, I will get some milk." We stopped at the first shop and I bought a can of milk powder which seemed expensive, tourist price I thought but I was still too new to know any better. I gave it to her and a guy, also a local tour operator, caught up with me outside and told me to be smarter. He said she'll go back to the shop and return the milk, they split the cash and then she'll return again with another compassionate tourist. Everyone's a loser really, except the shop owner, as the woman will be on the street tomorrow, which is the likely destiny of the child in her arms too. I learned this two minutes later; a little girl, probably five years old, at my side and asking for rice, pointing me to the shop where I'd bought the milk, this time I refused but she wouldn't leave me, even after a policeman, knowing what she was doing, ran at her with a stick. I calmed him with a smile and said, "It's fine". The child walked with me for two blocks. I asked her about school and she said she can't go, "No money."

I think there's state education in India, so maybe she means that her parents see her as more valuable on the street, earning. I have to harden quickly because it's impossible to go anywhere otherwise.

I then met Vijay, he tried to sell me a laminated map of India and I refused. He continued to walk with me and spoke a little about his life in Mumbai and I have decided to trust him. We went for chai and he told me about some of the ways tourists are exploited, telling me to buy some traditional clothes as then it looks like I've been here for a while and know the prices. We went to the wholesaler and I did buy some, cheap in comparison to the UK but not so cheap for me. We then went to the public cricket ground and I'm going to go there again Sunday morning to watch him play; it's a spot of tranquillity in the city. While we were sat on the grass I asked him some questions about his life in Mumbai. Tomorrow he's going to take me on a tour of a slum. He says he doesn't want money but if ever I found it in my heart to help him then he would love a shoe polishing box because then he could work for himself and earn a living. I hope it's not like the milk powder trick. There's no point pretending otherwise, I'm going to buy the shoe box. If he's lying then he's lying, if he's not then I've really helped him out.

It's just gone five and the light is changing, the sea darkening as we move into evening; car horns are honking at each other on the street below, and the crows continue to caw. I'll try to write again before leaving Mumbai on Monday, as long as I can charge my stuff. The adaptors you gave fit the sockets great but I think the sockets are broken.

Have a lovely evening and weekend, do you have many plans? x

That same evening…

I'm back at Welcome Restaurant. I like it here as I enjoy the way the waiters and the water boys so attentively care for the tables, they are reading them always. The waiter suggested I try the *bahji*; it is being made fresh at the entrance of the restaurant where there is a hatch so it can also be easily ordered by those on the street too. It's been quite the day. I'm frustrated I was so easily convinced to buy clothes which, despite being nice, I don't need as much as the rupees I gave for them. After leaving Vijay, who I have arranged to meet in Oval Maiden in the morning so he can take me to a slum, I returned to the hotel and emailed V. The waiter is approaching with my food…

… So the dish was a vegetable mix, tomato based, which is continually crushed on a hotplate, served with chopped raw onion and white rolls. I think *pav* means bread or roll as I ordered 'Butter Pav Bahji' and the roll that came was soggy from melted butter – a *clatter clatter* is again echoing through the restaurant as the chef is crushing some more *bahji*, while the continual drone of the overhead fans is heard above. After finishing my meal I asked the waiter for a chai which he has since brought and placed down on my table, I now know to ask for 'Marsala chai' to get spiced tea, because chai on its own simply means a cup of milky tea. The spiced is far nicer.

I won't stay here long as the waiters get the bill on the table as soon as you've finished your chai. I think I'll head back to the hotel and try to get to sleep as my body clock has still to adjust to the time difference. I can't get the electrical sockets to work in the room and my laptop is out of battery, otherwise I would have liked to write up my notes. Before I finish my chai I should capture a little more of Mumbai; it's a patchwork city of wealth and deprivation, but rarely do you see desolation – the poorest of the city are suffering but not all of them appear stricken, although plenty do as they forage the overcrowded streets for a new way of making money; shoe shiners, balloon sellers, one moment a city guide and the next moment a map seller, like Vijay. I am however in Fort, a wealthy part of the city which beggars are drawn to because of the tourists. What will my impression of poverty be tomorrow after Vijay takes me to a slum?

III

I met Vijay in the Oval Maiden. It was 10am on a clammy thirty-something Saturday morning in Mumbai. We walked away from the cricket ground, crossing the busy streets and having to hurry out of the way of the many taxis, rickshaws and buses speeding towards us.

"Here, Churchgate," Vijay said, pointing to a large building and the entrance of the train station.

We entered. The horns continued to beep in the background as I followed Vijay to the ticket booth. We purchased two return tickets for the city train, costing 40 rupees (around 50p). We then ran to the train sounding its horn and already beginning to move away from the platform, we jumped into a carriage. The train rattled to speed; passengers hung out of the open doors, while the overhead handles for standing passengers to hold onto swayed rhythmically. The train exited the station. The sights outside the window quickly passed by, too quick to capture them all although Vijay did his best to point them out all the same.

"This is cricket stadium; India play England here, Pakistan, Australia, big games played here," he said. "And this is football pitch."

I looked out the window and towards the football pitch but my vision quickly fell back on the people sat on the edge of the tracks, watching the trains trundle by with banks of rubbish around them. Mumbai, like most if not all cities, is home to rich and poor, but unlike most cities, there is rarely much space between them. Street sellers, beggars and cricket fans are the most prominent characters that stand out in Mumbai. There are of course the millions of inhabitants who have jobs, homes and other struggles, still financial no doubt, but less a question of survival – they can get up in the morning and not have to think about where they will find food and water, or shelter. The city workers form the moving backdrop of the city as they chase after their busy lives. It also means the people sitting still are all the more discernible; clothes dirty, often shoeless, faces sunken by hunger, or lying down on the edge of the railway tracks, looking to be wasting away.

"Bandra is two stops after Mumbai Central," said Vijay sat beside me. "We'll go for tour of slum, you'll enjoy."

I looked away from the window and towards him. "I don't think enjoy is the right word, Vijay," I replied.

Vijay looked distressed by this, thinking I was questioning his ability of today being a tour guide instead of a map seller.

"No, Mac," he'd begun to call me 'Mac' instead of 'Matt' since the previous afternoon and I felt unable to correct him as I'd left it too long. "I do good tours, you'll enjoy. I promise."

I didn't respond. Another stop and with some more railway line behind us, the train traversed a bridge over a river – the air was suddenly saturated in a scent so foul I could have placed us to be passing through a sewage plant. It stank. The train continued, now passing small tin houses. The rubbish on the ground increased until the earth beneath it was fully covered and the waste grew into mounds. This was the second time I'd seen what had become an open air dumping ground in the heart of the city. It wasn't a landfill site; it was just where the waste of thousands, hundreds of thousands, of impoverished souls was dumped. The city must have waste collection and disposal but to implement it on a scale that included the slums and at the same time keep up with the waste created by Mumbai's twenty million or so inhabitants was, from the rubbish I saw strewn all around, not enough; to also educate the city's inhabitants, both poor and non-poor alike, to discard waste responsibly is a lesson in social responsibility that has so far not overcome the negligence of the culture. I later learned that for many Indians, rubbish just gets thrown on the ground. Besides, what do the poorest of the poor owe society? If the infrastructure is not in place for them to be environmentally concerned citizens, then what priority does someone give to searching out waste bins and recycling points? Life is about food, water, shelter and human warmth – everything beyond this, unless addiction is present, is just extraneous matter to existence. The result is painful to observe; plastic bottles bobbing beside the boats on the surface of the sea in the harbour off Fort, and the tainted air always lingering, circulated by the fans suspended from the roof of the carriage, chopping and changing the foulness of the scents second by second. The train began to slow.

"Come, Mac, Bandra now."

I followed Vijay to the open door which he leaned out of feeling the warm wind in his face before the train slowed to a stop and we disembarked at Bandra station. The platform was busy; snack stands selling bottled drinks were crowded around by passengers, while others climbed the steps to a bridge that spanned the tracks and led out of the station.

Bandra is a suburb located in West Mumbai and the slum is only a small part of it. Bandra is commonly regarded as being a sought after and 'trendy' region of Mumbai, home to Bollywood stars, cosmopolitan living beside the sea, and as such often called, 'The Queen of the Suburbs'. I wondered how the slum appeared on the queen's dress.

The biggest slum in Mumbai is Dharavi and, being

home to more than a million people, it is also the biggest slum in Asia. The World Bank claims that over half of Mumbai's population now live in slums[7], and projects that by 2025 over 22 million of the city's inhabitants will be slum dwellers[8]. Dharavi was further away than Vijay had in mind for the morning, so he instead led me across the bridge and down into a narrow street skirting the outer edge of the slum built beside Bandra station.

A Muslim market was in motion and the produce was abundant: fresh fruit, vegetables, skinned chickens hung up to tempt the passer-by and small fish lined up on upturned plastic boxes on the ground, a man sat beside them on a stool with a knife in his hand, chopping off the fish heads as they were sold. I followed Vijay as we walked away from the traders and began to follow a train track which passed through the middle of the slum and out into a barren dry landscape. Beside the railway lines fabric houses had been erected side by side, the walls made of carpet and held up on sticks. Those who arrive in the city seeking better lives are sometimes so poor they can go no further than where they disembark. They begin to build homes beside the tracks, their hope of finding a better existence in the city perhaps still not diminished, or they simply have nothing left to return to. These tent-like structures will one day likely become tin huts, or wooden shacks; one day they might have a satellite dish pointing upwards from the roof, even a water tap, but the poor inside them will still be desperately poor – the walls around them will simply be a little more solid, while the sheets of metal above them could be called a roof. This is how slums are born. Four children run behind us, wanting me to take a picture of them so they can see themselves on the screen of my camera; they stand in a line together, the train tracks behind them and litter at their feet. I kneel down and capture them, their arms around each other, their faces all smiles and innocence.

"Mac, are you enjoying?"

"I'm pleased I came, Vijay," I replied.

I felt uncomfortable with the question, as though this picture of children growing up in a place interspersed by festering waste would bring me some kind of contentment. I felt ill. I chose not to challenge him on it as it was only a misuse of language. We followed the track back to the station and the concrete high-rise slum that would have perhaps once been a tent village in its infancy. The tracks passed between the buildings and beneath balconies; the spaces between the railway ties were filled by bags of excrement, festering puddles of waste and rubbish.

"We can't go down there," said Vijay. "Smell too bad."

"That's okay," I replied. "Can we walk back through the market?"

"You enjoy market, Mac?"

"Yes, Vijay, I enjoy the market."

After walking back through the market we crossed the tracks; we passed six beggars on the bridge, they all brought their hands to their mouths as we passed. We descended into Bandra Central and were soon amongst city folk a few rungs up the financial ladder than the slum dwellers. The roads were clogged, the shop doors open and people were chasing money left, right and centre. I took Vijay for lunch in a Punjabi restaurant. I had a dhal dish and roti. Vijay enjoyed a chicken dish, followed by rice and curry sauce which he ate with his right hand, as is Indian custom. Over lunch he told me that he hadn't gone to school, but had cleaned a church when still in Jaipur and 'the Christians' had educated him, which explained his good level of English.

"I didn't like all of it," he said. "I have my own culture and religion but I do believe in Jesus, and I like to think about him."

After lunch I walked with Vijay back to the station, he was going one way and me the other. He missed two trains heading away from the city to wait and make sure I got onto the right train back to Churchgate. As we said goodbye I gave him enough money to buy a shoe polishing box, with a bit to spare to stock up on polish.

"Ah, Mac," he beamed. "Thank you. I go now and buy from shop."

"Good, Vijay. I hope it helps."

I have no idea if Vijay had been playing me for two days with this story of having a better life if he could afford a shoe box and make a living. He talked a lot about karma, but then so do the taxi drivers when negotiating a fare; Vijay said he will do right in his life and one day that will repay him. I took him by his word. If he was lying then he has deceived me out of a relatively insignificant amount of money, but if he was being truthful then he will have the means to try and make a daily wage in the city that is unforgiving to the poor – where they have little or nothing to rely on except their lust and ingenuity to survive. My train appeared around a bend in the distance and Vijay slapped my back.

"Hey, Mac, give me 10 rupees. I don't want to be seen with these big notes. I need to get rickshaw to shop where I buy shoe box. You know what I mean? Have to be smart, Mac."

I took some change from my wallet. "Here. Take care."

"Thanks, Mac. You wait and one day you come back to Mumbai and see me with my shoe box."

"I'm happy I could help you out, and thank you for showing me around and for the company."

The train slowed and the sea of passengers on the platform swelled towards it like a breaking wave. I was swept forward with them.

"Bye, Vijay," I called.

"Goodbye, Mac."

Vijay put his hand up in the air and smiled. I turned within the bodies now tightening around me in the carriage and struggled to lift my hand to wave back. I will never see him again amongst the millions of faces to be seen in the Indian city of Mumbai.

IV

The following evening, my final in Mumbai, I went for dinner with a friend who was going to be travelling with me to Somnath, a jungle community on the edge of the Tadoba Andhari Tiger Reserve in northeast Maharashtra. Once there we will join a group of internationals for a week of silence and meditation, followed by a work retreat in Anandwan, a community dedicated, like Somnath, to the caring for and empowering of the socially outcast. Both projects were founded by a man that for now I know only as Baba Amte.

Our bellies full of Indian delicacies, Sian and I walked back to our hotel, stopping at The Gateway of India to admire the stillness of the dark ocean against the busy backdrop of Mumbai. The seafront was noisy with taxis pulling up at The Taj Mahal Palace Hotel to drop off its wealthy guests while the pavements were thick with both Indian and foreign tourists enjoying an evening stroll with the sea air doing its best to cleanse the city's polluted breath. Street sellers and beggars moved amongst the disinterested faces.

We walked to the end of the promenade and took a moment to look across a narrow stretch of water to watch a wedding celebration taking place on a pier, lit by many lights and alive with jubilant cheers and music. Distracted by the festivities, we almost stepped on two children at our feet, a little girl and baby boy. The girl lay asleep on the pavement, her head rested on a make-shift pillow, the plastic bag dirty against her cheek. The baby beside her was playing with a scrap of paper he had found on the pavement, making it into a cone and then fondling and putting it into his gums with his childlike curiosity of touch and taste. The baby wore only a torn and threadbare t-shirt over his body, his bare bum cheeks pressed against the concrete where he sat. His sister, I presumed, slept sweetly beside him, her long black hair tracing her small back, with her feet also bare. It was dark. There were no guardians watching over them. They could be taken. Anything could happen to them. Yet the baby smiled as he folded the paper into a new shape, and the girl appeared so at peace she may well have been dreaming. It was harrowing. Sian and I looked at each other, unable to keep the sadness of what we were stood over from our faces. It was the first time in writing this book that I had wanted or needed to look away. Ten minutes later and back in the hotel I sent an email back to England, confiding in V:

30th November 2014
… I went for dinner with Sian. It was another terrific spread; cottage cheese pieces in a Northern Indian sauce, chickpea dish, rice dish, and not forgetting buttered roti to eat it off the plate with. After the meal we walked back to the harbour, past The Gate and Taj Hotel. At the end of the promenade there was a lavish wedding taking place on a pier; we stood by the sea wall to look across the water and watch. This is when I saw a small girl, perhaps four years old, lying asleep with a plastic bag full of fabric for a pillow. Next to her a baby sat bare bummed on the pavement making a cone out of paper. It's night. A group of Indian tourists were stood near to them, also watching the festivities on the pier. I looked along the pavement, trying to see anyone that might be the children's parents. I saw no one of such description. It was the worst of all the sights I've

seen so far. The child slept and the baby played with the paper, so vulnerable yet so worthless that they went unnoticed by the world around them. I can try not to see but day by day Mumbai would break my heart. Sian was also struggling with what we were witnessing. The only thing we could do was walk away. A baby knows nothing of rupees; it would not even be able to fend off the rats if given food. The children were safer having nothing. I can pretend to be around such stuff for a time but in the end you can't hide anything. I had just eaten plenty and the £4 it had cost seemed like nothing, then you walk home and feel guilty for having a full belly and refusing to give money to the beggars because there are so many you just can't...

V

Sitting on platform 17 at Mumbai Chhatrapati Shivaji Terminus; Eva, a German who joined us late last night and is also travelling to Somnath, and Sian's backpacks, are resting against mine by my feet. They've gone to pick up some food for the fifteen-hour journey to Nagpur, a city in the northeast of Maharashtra State. Once there we will see what transport options are available to take us to the jungle. A group of teenage boys are sat on the benches beside me; the platform's tin roof is providing needed shelter from the early afternoon sun. It's hot, mid-thirties. The slight breeze also brings mild relief despite the occasional pong it carries. I'm being watched as I write by one of the lads sat next to me; Westerners quickly become cause for attention and curiosity. Indian music, sounding like something from a Bollywood film, has just started playing out of the announcement system; I think it is to signal that people can start boarding the train. Now two men are heading this way along the platform, one pulling and the other pushing a trolley stacked with boxes, they wobble from side to side and appear on the edge of toppling but never do. I read the labels displayed on their sides:

⬆ This box contains ice cream
stored in dry ice.
Do not sleep near this box. ⬆

Parliament Square: Day one of Occupy Democracy

Naked protest in Parliament Square

Thousands march through London to demand an end to austerity

A banner calling for increased wages is pulled through the streets of the capital

Bath Food Cycle volunteers serve the main course

A Big Issue seller at his pitch on Union Street

The Pigeon Man at work in the Abbey square

A family of monkeys at Somnath

A woman sifts rice, Somnath

A sweeper, Somnath

Thread makers, Somnath

Indian woman, Somnath

A girl from Anandwan on her way to school

A community member working a loom in Anandwan

Specially designed hand crank bicycles for those unable to walk

This man is having a wound dressed before he goes to work

A woman on her bed in the old people's home

Shama enjoying the New Year's celebration

A man in the old people's home for those who have lived with leprosy

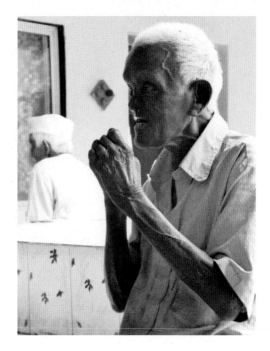

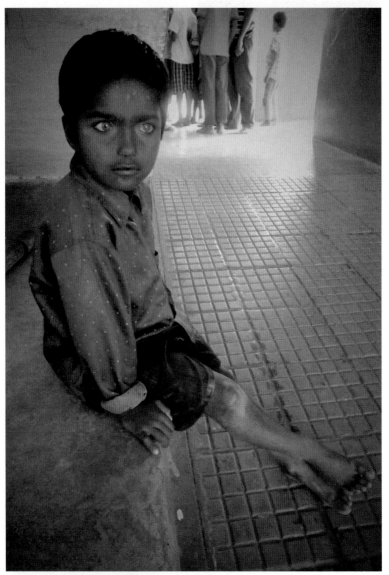

A hearing impaired boy in the hostel at Anandwan

Tulsiram was a regular for a massage in the morning

A woman sits for her photograph to be taken in the old people's home

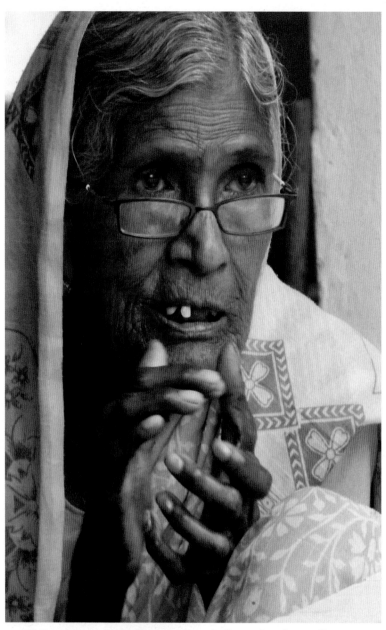

This woman claps along as SanghaSeva sing farewell songs to the community

Billboard in Kolkata: "If you can't feed a hundred people, then feed just one." Mother Teresa

Waiting before Mother Teresa's door. Nirmal Hirdy, Kolkata

Living Dead on Howrah Bridge, Kolkata

Ducks on the banks of the River Punyamati, Nepal

Life in the shadow of the MSJ, Kolkata

View of market sellers from Howrah Bridge, Kolkata

Babo tests the feel of a Buffalo's ear on his cheek. Sauraha, Nepal

Brown seascape of farmland. Panauti, Nepal

A Sadhu sits on the steps of Kedar Ghat, Varanasi, India

18th March 2015: Tents now house the community of down-and-outs living on the iron bridge just north of Gare du Nord, Paris

I'm enjoying being on my own for a bit; time to digest the coconut *uttapam* I had for lunch (a savoury pancake is the closest thing I can compare it to), and time to digest being here and what that means. The chap beside me is still watching my pen move; I don't think he can make out my scribbled hand. I asked him some questions but it frustrated him when he couldn't answer, his English is limited. I did learn that he's from Chandrapur, a smaller city also in northeast Maharashtra.

"Where you going?" he asked.

"Nagpur," I said.

He nodded and our conversation quickly ended.

The damn flies are now flocking around me; I think the two bananas resting on top of my backpack are enticing them, or my sweaty body. If I look to my right and up, there is a big digital clock with a crow perched above it in the rafters. The seconds quickly pass; *13.36 42, 13.36 43, 13.36 44…* Time goes by. Another trolley is being pulled this way, this time loaded with boxes containing *Tablets*.

The chap sat beside me just asked my name.

"Matthew," I said.

"What are you doing here?" he asked directly.

"I travel," I replied. "What is your name?"

"Brirar."

I then asked Brirar why he was in Mumbai and he said for an exam.

"Did it go well?"

"Railway. I will work railway."

He's wearing black polished leather shoes, jeans and a shirt, pretty much the standard dress for men in Mumbai, except many wear sandals on their feet due to the heat. I look back up at the clock; *13.44 44, 13.44 45…* Time goes by.

Another trolley creaks as it passes, the boxes wobble like jelly; *Cynterac K50, 50mg.* They're not full of computerised tablets as I first thought but medicine. The crow caws as it flies from its perch, drawing my vision back to the clock. The train departs at 15.00. I wave the flies away from my bananas again. I sit and I wait.

VI

I'm not in Mumbai anymore, far from it. I've re-joined SanghaSeva, a group that seeks to serve different communities with the practice of meditation at its core – the fruits of which are harvested from a greater inner and outer awareness. We are in Somnath, a jungle community in West India. It's day one of seven days of silence and I'm curious to see what presents itself now the chitter-chatter of daily life has been removed. I'm surrounded by plentiful birdsong as two birds sing to each other from opposing treetops, along with the sound of stiff straw bristles sweeping stone and the hum of human voices as two Indian men talk at the entrance of where we are staying.

Over the coming month to be spent with SanghaSeva, led by Nathan Glyde and Zohar Lavie, we will be exploring ways to engage with different types of suffering, supporting ourselves through our meditation practice. Meditation, in this context, could be said to be like a window opened by the heart that looks out on all with compassion, with ears that will listen and a mind that is present and fostering a capacity to be able to look beyond judgement. I see it as love in action. In one of her opening talks to the group, Zohar introduced the Tibetan word for meditation, *Gom*. Simply, 'to become familiar'. It's an invitation to become familiar with myself, to know my being in its purest manifestation, stripped of all that I have adorned myself with and wear when out in society.

My experience with the group in Israel and Palestine led

me to writing a book entitled, *The Wall Between Us*. It should really be 'The Walls' as there are many, from physical to mental, and equally applicable to many different conflicts and divisions found within one society or between many. The social exclusion of those for reason of a physical or mental impediment is one such example. Anandwan was established in the early 1950s, a place where those afflicted by leprosy could find care and treatment, but it also served as a place where they could be without the aversion of others and, importantly, it was somewhere where they could find a purpose for being. They were given an opportunity despite many bearing the physical loss of limbs and mobility that leprosy can lead to. Anandwan today serves many different community members; the one thing that unites them all is their social exclusion from mainstream society, whether through a total or partial loss of sight or hearing, old age, or a mental illness. Exclusion can often lead to poverty, both financial and emotional, but in Anandwan potential is seen in all.

Somnath took seed from Anandwan, establishing itself two and half hours' drive away in the forested heartland of India. It is a farming community and the produce it grows is used by both Somnath and Anandwan with any surplus being sold locally. If I look up now from these words and across the courtyard before me, with a mighty and wise old tree growing in the middle, there is a small home belonging to one of the community members. On the wall a passage has been written in English and is credited to a man named, Bill Bernbach*[1]. I've asked around but no one has been able to tell me who Bill Bernbach is or was, but nevertheless the wall tells me that he once said:

*[1] The internet later informed me that Bill Bernbach (1911 to 1982) was an American and inspirational in the modern day standard of advertising, and a leading figure in the creative revolution of the 1950s and 60s.

If you stand for something,
you will always find some people
for you and some against.
If you stand for nothing,
you will find no one against you
and nobody for you.

VII

Day two of silence. Ants are busying themselves on the concrete beside the step I am sat on. The bells are being chimed to signal the start of the 9am work period. I'm the chai *wallah*, responsible for making afternoon chai, which means I can now spend an hour writing in the morning sun.

I woke up at 6.30am. After dressing, I took my camera to seek out the community of black-faced langur monkeys that can easily be found in the trees or on the rooftops. Yesterday they were all sat on the roof of a barn, basking in the first light and warmth of the rising sun. I'm captivated by the monkeys' daily rhythms, quickly seeing hierarchy amongst them as mothers claim children while one monkey picks the flees from another. The monkey being groomed was stood with arms folded on a branch, clearly relaxed while two infants raced around the tree, not sure if I was a threat. The adults show no fear of humans after having lived so close to the community at Somnath over the years.

I think about the similarities between our kinds; if a monkey's natural habitat, the jungle, is destroyed and unable to sustain the monkey, then it will begin to search out food. This might lead it to populated regions, concrete jungles, where it can scavenge. Many of the desperately poor in Mumbai have come from rural areas, their seemingly simple lives and old traditions having been placed low down on the ladder of what a good life means today. Their lifestyles are devalued or the environment around them exploited for a quick profit, pillaged and left worthless, if not toxic. Like the monkey whose jungle is destroyed, the rural communities will abandon their lives, customs and traditions and be drawn to the city in need of money and survival. Many of them will arrive and be forced to scavenge.

I once stayed in a rural village amongst the stunningly green mountains of Wakayama Prefecture in Japan. I was inspired to learn about the urban to rural migration of the young who made up the communities and largely maintained them. I spoke to some of the young farmers and many expressed how they had become disillusioned by life in the city, returning to the countryside for a richer life, not in terms of financial wealth but both inner wellbeing and overall happiness. In the decades prior to this migratory switch, the old among the village had watched the young hurriedly and excitedly leave for the cities. This abandoning had led them to believe that their traditions and community living was of little value. It took the returning young, having seen life out of office block windows and with days broken up into giving your time for other people to profit, to convey to the old that their way of life was important and something worth holding onto. I will never forget what my host, Fuki Jo, said to me one evening after I asked her why it was important for her and her friends to learn and continue such practices as growing rice in the terraces: 'The culture of the countryside, like how you grow rice,' Fuki explained, 'passing this onto the next generation is important, because once it stops, people will forget it.'[9]

For a long time there has been a steady and increasing migration of people from rural areas to the cities and industry. The city is seen to be a place of opportunity, a better life perhaps, but there is also great poverty, not just for those who don't find a way in and end up on the streets and searching, but also for those who find their lives enslaved in order to simply get by in the city. This is not to say that rural life is easy; crops need to be tended to, backs can become pained and misshapen after years of labour, and Nature demands to be heard and listened to. The survival of any rural community is dependent on their ability to work together, and there can be great contentment to be found in a life lived in sowing the seeds that maintain just that, life.

After visiting a city such as Mumbai, where I walk and see great mounds of rubbish and people visibly hungry in the street, I say to myself this can't go on, humanity is unsustainable – too many people and not enough earth when so many are addled by greed. When that time comes (if it's not here already) when the human race is consuming too much for the one earth to provide, when food is scarce and water in shortage, and not just for those in an unfortunate geography, but for all, then we really will need those who can tend to seeds and make them grow. We will be forced to look at finding innovative ways of launching small scale farming on a global scale – not left to rural areas but incorporated everywhere including right in the hearts of the cities.

Meditation is an ongoing practice to ground us in the present moment, the only moment we can ever directly know and experience. We sit and bring our attention to the breath as a way of embodying ourselves, for the body remains rooted in the present even if our minds dwell on the past or run away into the future. In the moment we can open our eyes and better see the world around us. We can project and predict how the way we live today will shape and impact on tomorrow. Some pockets of the earth, Sonmath for instance, exhibit a flourishing of life as a collective of people tend to life. Other parts, densely populated cities such as Mumbai, Beijing and London, suggest a sustainable future to be incomprehensible. The question is, could the weight of humanity be balanced, its strain on the earth lessened, if city and countryside were better coupled?

An old woman is brushing at the fallen leaves around me, her pink sari wrapping her head and her back hunched forward as she sweeps with hard straw tied into a brush. The strands scratch against the concrete as she sweeps. On those few occasions when she stands up to see what's left to sweep, I see there is a curvature of her lower spine. She has been a sweeper for many years, it has shaped her body. Vijay was right – life, be it in the countryside or in the city, is not easy.

VIII

Day four of silence. I have picked up a cold which has already taken hold of four other members of the group, I'm seeing it off with vitamin C and sunshine, although it's a little cooler today with a spritely breeze teasing the green leaves on the trees.

Yesterday afternoon was the first time when I started to soften around such deep practice – I appreciated sitting despite the aches in my legs and back. I appreciated being able to observe the grasping nature of Mind, and, through first recognising this tendency to cling onto abstract thought, I was able to find a stillness I hadn't felt on the previous days. During a talk Nathan mentioned how, in a one-to-one interview, a member of the group had found it strange why 'we're always focusing on the problematic'.

Hearing this I instantly registered my own journey into meeting with different aspects of poverty. Some of my chapters before leaving England now seem bleak and despairing about what has become of Britain. I don't think this is a fair reflection of the British people, who, and for the most part to their own detriment, put up with the government's bullshit with a stiff upper lip and old fashioned spirit of riding through the tough times. 'The good times will come,' I hear as the national prayer.

As I write, three Indian women dressed in colourful saris are busy before me; one is crouched down using her hands to dig up dry and dead plants from a small bed around the trunk of a tree. Another is washing clothes at the water tap next to the tree. The tap is on and water is flowing into a metal bucket placed beneath the spout; she sinks an item of clothing into the water and then brings it to a rock placed beside the tap. Using her left foot to hold the fabric on the stone's surface, she can then use both her hands to pull it back and forth, rubbing it against the stone. She turns it over, repeats the process, dunking it into the water before returning it to the stone and rubbing it down. She then lifts it and begins smacking it down against the hard stone, before finally wringing the excess water out. She'll now hang it to dry in the sun. There are no washing machines here. There are no pre-packed and washed salad leaves; a gathering of women sit in the shade under a tin roof outside the kitchen and pick the dirty stems from the small green leaves. It's an hour's work or more. There are no vacuum cleaners either; instead strands of hard straw are tied together and used to sweep everything that needs sweeping, inside and out. These brushes are no longer than a cricket bat and the reason why many of the older women's backs are terribly bowed. I can hear it now; a woman is sweeping the concrete before the entrance to the dining hall. The men, for the most part, are out in the rice fields, spending long days gathering the now dry straw and collecting it into large piles, some are so big that from a distance they look like small thatched cottages; for some reason they are finished with two pointy bundles at their tops, giving the impression of chimneys.

I wanted to use today's reflection to touch on the spirit of the Indian people. So far, and of course I can only write in generalities as no two people are the same, the Indians are a friendly, reserved, proud and playful people… I've just seen the time and I have to chime the bells to let people know there will be a sitting meditation in the hall. I wish to return here and capture an encounter we made in a rural dusty village which we travelled through on the journey here. I will pen my beginning now so I can find my way back into it: the journey to Somnath was a bumpy trip on roads dotted by potholes and occasionally clogged by cows and goats…

There. I also want to make note of this moving line in a book of many moving letters that Etty Hillesum, a young Dutch Jew who lived in Amsterdam, wrote to loved ones while she was in a camp in Holland before her transportation to Auschwitz in 1943: 'From my bunk I can see gulls in the distance moving across the flat grey sky. They are like free thoughts in an open mind.'[10]

IX

So the journey to Somnath was a bumpy trip on roads often dotted by potholes and occasionally clogged by cows and goats being herded by men with sticks. We travelled in a 4x4, six internationals including myself, and two Indians, the driver and a young chap with a mobile phone who had done some fine work in Nagpur to find a taxi willing to take us the 180 kilometres to Somnath. It turned out that the driver didn't even know the way to Mull, the closest city to our destination, so he subsequently employed the young chap with the mobile phone to be a human satellite navigation system. After having simply been hanging around the chai stand outside Nagpur bus station, he seemed very happy with his new employment. We began the arrangement of eight people, along with six backpacks, into and on top of one 4x4. I sat in the front next to the human sat nav. I asked him his name and he said it was Naresh.

"I born Nagpur. My home," he added.

Both Naresh, smartly dressed with his shirt tucked into his jeans and black hair freshly gelled to one side, and the driver, a not so well groomed older man in a leather jacket, spoke little English. The 4x4's engine and honking horn filled the silence. The internationals, with the overnight journey by train affording us little sleep, were also quiet. We gazed out of the windows, watching the buildings on the edge of Nagpur thin out before open land – rice fields and orange groves mostly – began to fill the windscreen and stretched far into the hazy horizon. The morning sunbeams streaked through the haze in a fabulous light display.

Naresh and the driver appeared keen to break up the journey; we stopped first to fill up the tank with diesel, then for snacks from a roadside stand, and finally to put air into the tyres from another stand a few kilometres along the road. The wooden framed and tin roofed hut housed a compressor unit and the man operating it and nothing else. I wish I hadn't watched him inflate one of our rear tires as seeing the large chunk missing from the rim of the rubber was worrying to say the least. He pointed it out to the driver who replied with the customary Indian head shake. Every time I think I've pinned this movement down to one meaning, it always ends up being used for another situation entirely. It's just done. The head stays straight and moves from shoulder to shoulder. It seemed too casual a response to the heightened risk of a blow-out and death. The tyre was inflated all the same and everyone got back in, dust was blown into the air behind us as we pulled away. It was getting hot and still only 10am. With 100 kilometres now behind us we began to pass wide fields of rice shoots with small figures moving amongst them, all carrying piles of straw on their backs and adding them to growing piles. Naresh suddenly turned towards me and pointed towards the straw carriers.

"Look," he said. "Hungry people."

This caused Naresh and the driver to chuckle. I watched them deeply amused by the sight of the 'hungry people'.

"Do you mean they are poor?" I asked.

Our shared language was too little and Naresh, now searching for his tobacco on the dashboard, pointed to the fields again.

"Lots of hungry people," he said.

We drove on and Naresh rolled a cigarette between his fingers, anticipating our next stop. The driver, hands loosely holding the steering wheel, said: "Here, agriculture."

We were in a region where farming was the mainstay

of life with little else to choose between. Wooden and concrete buildings began to trace the roadside as we drove into a village.

"Here, snacks and smoke," Naresh announced.

The driver pulled off the road and onto the dusty verge before a run of food, drink and cigarette stands. We got out of the vehicle; six Westerners standing together and surveying the bemused faces staring at us. I soon realised just how rural we were. The villagers had not seen the likes of us for some time and we quickly became an attraction. First middle-aged men who had been sitting before a chai stand came towards us, looking at us at length. Then school children ran across the road, girls and boys in clean and smart uniforms; a group of women in traditional dress followed the children's lead, also crossing the road to join the growing ring of Indians around us, a silent circle of stares. We looked back at them, smiled and said, "Namaste."

The villagers must have been from the same community as the 'hungry people' who Naresh had pointed out in the fields, but up close they didn't seem hungry in the slightest. The market stands around them were full of fresh produce; the children full of smiles and clearly receiving an education. The men stood straight as did the women and I didn't see a single drawn face to identify malnutrition. These people may have been poor in terms of financial wealth, but they certainly did not appear hungry. This led me to believe that Naresh associated a livelihood such as farming to one of being poor; this perception is not in all ways wrong or unique to India. In the UK, farming has always been associated with hard work for little gain, exacerbated further as small scale farmers struggle to compete with mass production in what has become a global marketplace. Despite the hard work they endure, tending to rice fields or labouring over stone all day, the Indians of this remote town nevertheless radiated a certain amount of wellbeing.

Not one of the villagers outstretched their hands towards us, to then raise them to their mouths as so many had done on the streets of Mumbai. Not one of the villagers asked for a single thing from us; they just stood still before us and showed interest. Sometimes it can feel uncomfortable being a Westerner in India and other developing countries, often being asked to have pictures taken with people you pass when out and about. I used to be really tense around such engagement, thinking they were idolising me as a Westerner. I wanted to tell them I'm nothing special, just human, like you. However, I've softened to this recently, often their interest is motivated out of a deeper intrigue. During my trip I have already stopped and stared many times as Indians go about their daily lives, a culture so different to my own that I am fascinated by it. I want to get closer to it, to feel and understand it. The villagers simply wanted to see who we were, to know why these strangers had stopped in their town and to know where we ourselves were from. If I find an Indian of interest, then there is no reason why an Indian shouldn't feel the same about me. Our curiosity always draws us towards the unknown and that has always underpinned my love of travelling. After a group photo with the people from the town, we got back into the 4x4 and said goodbye to the Indians who had stepped forward to now peer at us through the windows.

We pulled away and I looked back to see the diminishing huddle of people in the dust behind; was I looking at poor people? On the surface they appeared happy and nourished, connected to each other by the many hands I saw rested on shoulders, and filled by intrigue – some staples of a good life. At the same time I realise that many of them would be poor financially, most probably earning very little each day. Naresh had therefore seen them as hungry, but it was a different hunger from what I had seen in the stunted bodies of the beggars in Mumbai. On the platform at Bandra station, for instance, and before visiting the slum with Vijay, I'd seen a man hunched up on the ground with a little bowl before him, a scattering of rupees inside it. His body was the size of a six-year-old boy's, and a malnourished boy at that; his arms no bigger than the bones beneath his skin and his spine terribly disfigured and twisted. This man was hungry beyond belief, and alone on a station platform as the world walked around him, his body broken and his future, like his present, weak and uncertain. Driving away from the village, I found it increasingly hard to know what to define as poverty. After meeting with so many different forms in Bath and now India it was becoming clearer all the time – I was lost in it.

Sat back in the front of the 4x4 and resuming my silent prayer that our rear tyre didn't blow as we hit yet another cluster of potholes, I shared in some of the *pakora* that Naresh had picked up from the town. He ate the battered vegetables and I bit into what turned out to be a green chili. My eyes squinted, lips on fire, as Naresh tapped my arm and chuckled again, "They very hungry people, yes?"

X

Day seven of silence. Sitting in the low light of dawn. It's just after 6am and the first bell chime of the day to wake us for personal practice. I like to think of writing as a practice, it means I can always work at it and hopefully get better at conveying life and my experience of it through words. In the courtyard before me there is a flowerbed, its radiance muted while waiting for the sunlight. The courtyard is enclosed by a concrete wall and beyond it there is a bank of trees; the deep and resounding *Whooo...* *Whooo* of the monkeys erupts from inside their dark body of leaves. The branches reach out over the lake, there is a blanket of mist resting over the water which distorts and blurs the view over the rice fields to the edge of the jungle in the distance. The sky at the horizon is beginning to turn a tender tone of pink and the white of this page and the lines I am writing on are becoming increasingly visible, second by second. Both dawn and dusk come and go quickly here; darkness exchanged for light before light is strained into darkness once again. The birdsong stays strong and true from daybreak into a flourishing finale for the moon's arrival. The sun will kiss the horizon in around twenty minutes...

... *Une petite pause*. My trip to the bathroom – a quick tense walk, a frantic search for the spot where I choose to hide my precious sheets of paper, before praying another wasn't already locked away in the communal toilet – has successfully broken my train of thought so I'll write about a talk that moved me yesterday, about compassion.

I have always understood compassion to be about helping those, human and non-human, who are suffering. Therefore in order to be compassionate we first have to recognise suffering. Yesterday I learned that the word itself, *compassion*, identifies just such a meaning. In the Pali texts which capture a lot of the Buddhist tradition, the word for compassion is *karuna*, which is sometimes translated: *The quivering of the heart in response to a being suffering*, or something that makes the heart tremble. And if the English word, compassion, is broken down into its Latin constituents we find that 'con' stands for *with* and 'passion' means *suffering*. Compassion rightly means *with suffering*. This shifted my understanding of compassion as something I must strive to be, compassionate and giving, to something that I must strive to see in order to understand another's, or even my own, suffering. It's a practice of the heart.

But the world is so full of strife and woe, so full of desperation, insurmountable sorrow and wasted life; how then can I, with just one heart, look upon all the suffering of life? Partly in the acceptance that suffering, in the present state of humanity, does exist and that some form of suffering, like the grief of losing a loved one, will always exist. The question is how we as individuals and a community respond. It is clear to me that our community is global, our humanity is one, far away borders and lands are affected by market shares thousands of miles away, livelihoods are affected by local and international policy. If we see suffering over there, it's quite possible it can be alleviated by actions taken right here. Compassion. *With suffering*.

I have sought to see poverty but I will be honest, in the beginning I found myself not wanting to engage with all that I saw. Some of the faces on the street in Bath seemed too hardened and others too inebriated. I walked past them. In doing so I do not now understand their suffering, and I am unable to share it for others to read and see also.

If I am compassionate to myself and to others, meaning I recognise the suffering in myself and others, I am already in a better place to begin to care for my own or another's needs. My actions will be motivated and guided by the heart and this is a source of love like no other. This is perhaps something I have learned from my notes so far: be compassionate with love, and love out of compassion.

It's now approaching seven o'clock; a South Korean born Parisian from the group is practicing qigong in the courtyard, moving her body slowly and purposefully though the sequence of movements. I can also see another group member performing yoga down by the lake, the great orange sun showering the water in sunbeams; they ripple and stretch over the surface towards her. She salutes the sun again, her arms reaching up before she bends at her waist for her fingers to touch the tips of her toes. The mist has lifted or been burned away and the daylight has arrived; it is to be our last morning in silence.

XI

It was early evening and dark already. I sat on the steps
leading up to Rest House, our new sleeping quarters,
after having travelled the 100 kilometre journey from
Somnath to Anandwan. Rest House is where we will be
sleeping, relaxing and meditating during our three weeks
in this community made up of 2,500 people, the majority
having once had and been cured of leprosy. In front of
the building the slim stretch of land up to the gate and
road has been separated into different beds, salad leaves
and papaya trees growing amongst them. When we first
pulled up and began untying our bags from the roofs
of the 4x4s, there was an elderly man and two women
tending to the crops. Their wrinkled faces beamed as we
opened the gate.

"Namaste. Namaste," they all said, bringing their
hands, some missing fingers, to their chests and smiling.

"Namaste," we greeted them back.

Namaste is a most beautiful greeting, commonly
translated: *I bow to the divine in you*. We found our rooms,
dumped down our bags and quickly made our way to the
canteen where our lunch had been kindly kept warm for
us.

It is difficult to know where to begin when outlining the
amount of things that take place on this once barren land
which was home to snakes, scorpions and long hot months
during the dry season. Today a forest runs along one
edge of the area given to Baba Amte by the Maharashtra
government in 1951 for him to seed his ambition of

empowering leprosy suffers. The lakes that now break up and feed the land were dug by human hands, and often hands missing fingers or bodies missing limbs. If a person was unable to work with one part of their body, then Baba was keen to help them find the many things they could still do with the rest of their body. Abandoned by loved ones and society, often through fear of contracting the disease, Baba instead sought to change the debilitating perception they had of themselves. Today Anandwan has its own industries, which generate income to support its high cost of being home to so many, from farming, to handloom weaving, to crafts, shoe repair and even mattress making. The people here work and they work hard. Despite the revenues raised from these ventures, Anandwan still relies on donations from both home and abroad. The hospital, with thirty-one patients currently being treated for leprosy, was itself constructed by the generous funding of others. Leprosy is a fully curable disease, although I have heard whispers of there being certain strains becoming resilient to the drugs.

If caught in its early stages, normally when patches of light skin are found on the body, leprosy can be treated through a course of medication and the patient should have no lasting scars, even the patches will first darken and then return to normal skin colour. It is when the virus is left untreated that it will begin attacking the nerves, usually at the extremities of the body – hands and feet – then the bones inside, and this is why the majority of those left untreated are recognisable by the loss of fingers and toes, as well as other forms of disfigurement. There are many here who have had legs and arms amputated, others with limbs having been twisted as the disease took hold. Again, once receiving the drugs, they are fully cured and no longer able to pass the disease to others, but the lasting disfigurement is something they now have to live with, along with the stigma associated with having had leprosy.

Anandwan serves leprosy patients and in turn they serve Anandwan, without their hard labour the community would not be able to do the amount it does.

I sat on the steps and picked up a book which I was told would give me a good insight into the life of the man first named Murlidhar Amte, later known simply as Baba. I opened the cover of the hardback and began to read when my attention was stolen by the *tip, tap, tip, tap* passing by the gate. I looked up and saw two figures moving along the road in the dark. The sticks in their hands helped to support them as they slowly limped on their way, their steps ruptured by the disease that had once attacked their body… *tip, tap, tip, tap, tip, tap*… They faded into the night. Mosquitoes flew in from the light on the walls, searching for an exposed piece of skin. I fanned them away and returned my gaze to the open book on my lap. I read and cursed those mosquitoes whose persistence had paid off. I scratched the angry red bumps they left behind. Rest House slowly quietened down for the night.

XII

Is an individual disabled by a loss of physical mobility, or are they in fact disabled by a society that has reduced them to an invalid? Baba Amte sought to enable those who had been cast out of society. All around Anandwan there are signs displaying some of Baba's favourite quotes, such as the Bill Bernbach passage I noted at Somnath, but there are also plenty of Baba's most memorable sayings. I am drawn to one in particular: *Give them a chance, not charity.*

If I'm honest I feel that many of the charities operating today, although out of the best intentions, merely put plasters over the wounds of poverty. In doing so they can bring much relief to the impoverished, support them and more importantly let them know that at least someone is thinking about their suffering, but all the while the wound is still there, just a little more hidden. Baba believed that the best way to empower someone was for them to empower themselves, to be able to engage with and contribute to the society around them, and not be left, wounds gaping, on the fringes of society's indifference or occasional handouts.

It was our first morning in Anandwan and we made our way from our rooms to the meditation hall at one end of Rest House. The hall was, when we first arrived, merely a large concrete room filled with dust and mosquitoes. We swept the dust away and put rugs on the floor, before placing mattresses and cushions for people to sit on (all made right here by the community, as are the steel bed frames in our rooms); we draped nets across the windows and placed a small run of books onto a shelf in one corner. Our space to meditate and share our experiences together was ready. We sat on our cushions in a circle facing Nathan and Zohar, eager to learn more about Baba Amte and this community maintained by those who, without it, would very likely have remained down, out, and dying on the streets. I wish to include the brief history we were told about Anandwan because it reflects the power of one person's vision to do things differently. If something is broken in society then Anandwan shows that a replacement can be introduced and be of immense benefit not only to those it serves but, through reaching back out to society and finding a place to operate within it, to all.

The morning light shone through the nets over the windows; the sound of construction could be heard outside, as more brick buildings are made to house the additional projects and people. Zohar, an Israeli with long black hair and a beautiful spirit, cleared her throat and began to speak, introducing us to Baba's life and legacy:

"In many ways the story of Anandwan starts with one person, Baba Amte," she said, sat crossed legged on her cushion before us. "Baba was actually his love name here. His real name was Murlidhar Dievidas Amte. He was born in this area to a very privileged family, land owners. They say that even as a young child he was outside the system; he used to play with the children of the servants; he didn't want to conform to the caste ideas of who he could touch, not touch, play with, share food with. As he grew up he had, as I said, a privileged upbringing. This was the days of the British Raj here. He hunted, drove fast cars and had correspondence with movie stars. There's all this mythology around him. At the same time he was also always interested in seeing more deeply into life. He hung out with people like Gandhi, Tagore, inspirations and teachers for him. Also Sane Guruji, who is not famous internationally, a spiritual teacher and social activist. Baba also spent some years as a *sadhu*, which we see here in India as someone who left his home and practised (spiritually) and spent time in nature, begging for food. Even though that's a period he never spoke about. He became very interested in social causes; he was involved in the struggle against the British colonisation and he became interested in social issues. He was also educated and practised as a lawyer. He was using his training to give legal aid to underprivileged groups and at the same time doing social experiments. With his wife, Sadhana Tai, who is as important as he is to the story and also came from a privileged family, they both renounced their money, the land, and they set up a small community in Warora town here, where they were living together with untouchables, low caste people, people from different backgrounds.

"During this period, Baba was representing the sweepers' union in a struggle about salaries with the local municipality. The sweepers, who actually still exist in India, were a people, a caste, whose job is to clear the night's soil, basically the poo and the pee. It was a municipal job and also a private job to clear the night's soil and dispose of it, to collect it from each home and bring it to some area where it was being collected. He was representing them and, in order to really understand their needs and their issues, he followed Gandhi's advice which was you'll never be able to help someone unless you walk in their shoes. So for several weeks he worked with them, and working with them meant actually carrying baskets of shit on your head. That was what the work entailed. There were not even plastic buckets in those days. He was doing this for several weeks and the story goes that:

"One rainy evening as he was returning from this work, it was already twilight or just dark, he chanced across what he thought was a bundle of rags on the road, and when he looked more closely he saw that it wasn't a bundle of rags but it was actually a human being. It was a man called Tulshiram who was very severely affected by leprosy, actually dying from infection of untreated leprosy wounds. Baba Amte saw this and his reaction was to run away, which I think is something we can all really understand. The way he told this is that he ran away back home and he spent the whole night unable to sleep, facing his own demons. One really important thing that he saw about himself was that he was afraid. You'll see photographs of him around, most of them are from later on in his years but even then, even when he was in his nineties when we met him, he was a tall strong man. He had incredible physical strength and you could feel his inner strength as well. So he had this image of himself as someone that was not afraid; he hunted tigers, he stood up to the British, Gandhi's name for him was *The Fearless One*. A real strong image of someone for whom fear didn't play a part in his life. In meeting Tulshiram he met his own fear. It's really important when I tell this to say that at that point of time (1940s) there was no cure for leprosy. It's not that the fear wasn't rational. The fear was rational; there was a high chance of infection. He spent that whole night looking at his own fear thinking, *I've not only got myself, I've got a wife and two very young children. What if I bring the infection to them?* The real interest for him was, *I am experiencing fear and now what do I do with it?* His strong conviction was that he was interested in facing that fear. This is the way he used to say it right until his death. He'd say: *People call me a sage. People call me a saint. I'm just a human being. I saw my fear and what drove me was that interest to look at my own fear. That was my motivation.*

"He went back the next morning. He built a shelter over Tulshiram and he nursed him for several days until he died in his arms. Baba Amte said that that was when he found his calling, his true calling, and that was to serve leprosy patients. He went and spoke to his wife, to Sadhana Tai, and together they decided to shift their focus and dedicate their life to working with people with leprosy. One of the first things that Baba did was that he wanted to receive training to know how to treat the leprosy, which was only treating the wounds at that time. That was all they could do. So he went to Kolkata where there was special training, usually for doctors but he was such a strong-willed man that he managed to convince them to train him anyway. He got the training on the basic treatments that were available. During that time he also offered himself as a human guinea pig. Part of the reason it's difficult to understand leprosy, and it's still difficult, is because it only affects human beings. They couldn't do that horrible practice that we have of experimenting on animals or using animal research in order to learn more about the disease. He was actually injected with the bacteria, I think several times. It didn't take. One of the things they now know about leprosy is that not everyone is susceptible to it, and it's to do with some genetic susceptibility and also connected to how strong your body is, how strong your immune system is. Again, it's a story that reflects the kind of person that we're talking about, and what he was willing to do.

"He came back here to Warora and started a mobile clinic and they would go around to the surrounding villages and treat people's wounds, also give them some nourishment and look after their needs. They realised that this wasn't anything like enough that was actually needed. Firstly, more care was needed; secondly, these people were outcasts and needed to find a home and a place, and thirdly, their emotional needs needed to be looked after as well as a change in society's attitude – bringing them back to the centre of life instead of just leaving them as outcasts. They decided to start a community and although Baba and Tai had renounced their own money, and as a result their families weren't very happy with them, they were still very well connected. They applied to the government and they received this land that we're now on from the Maharashtra government to start a leprosy project. I think this was a hunting reserve. It was scrubland. There wasn't any water. There weren't any trees. Baba Amte used to say, *Outcast land for outcast people.*

"They came here in the month of June which is the hottest month of the year. The temperatures get to forty-eight degrees. It's extremely hot. They came, Baba and Tai and their two young boys, six leprosy patients, a cow and a dog – one of them was lame and I don't remember if it was the cow or the dog – and I think like 6 rupees or something, they had a tiny amount of money. One of the first things they wanted to do was to give a name to the place. Baba turned to the leprosy patients and he asked them: 'This is your place, what would you like to call it?' And they said, 'Anandwan.' *Ananda* is happiness or bliss and *wan* is forest. So it means *the forest of bliss* or *the forest of joy*. When Baba told us this he said: 'You know I looked around and I thought, what are they talking about? It's like forty-eight degrees heat. There's no trees. No shade. There's nothing to be happy about.' He thought it right that they should give the name so he said okay. When he told us this story he said: 'Now I look around and see how wise they were. There is a forest now, they've planted so many trees, and there is so much joy.' He used to say: 'The joy in Anandwan is much more infectious than the disease.' Somehow those first six people, so ill, saw the potential of what this place was going to become.

"They started off by digging a well, because water was really needed. They dug a well by hand, and in the extreme heat. I think it took them six weeks to dig the well. The well is still here. Eventually they found water and that was the first great success and from there they gradually grew, more and more people joined the community. They had a lot of difficulty with the surrounding population

173

who didn't want anything to do with them. There is so much fear around the disease. Leprosy is considered, in Indian culture, as a sign of past sins or your past karma. It means that you're bad. Of course there's the real fear of contracting the disease; even when the treatments were found in the early fifties there was still a lot of fear around it. When the community got to a stage when they were growing enough food that they had a surplus, the local people from Warora didn't want to buy their produce because they were afraid of infection. Even though there was a lot of progress, growing food, having water, building a sense of community, there was still this great gap between the community here and the people around. I think in the late fifties one of the things that started to bridge that gap was that there was a group of international volunteers that were spending time in one of Gandhi's ashrams which is about two and a half hours away. They heard about the difficulties that were going on here so they came to Anandwan and helped build the first houses, the first permanent buildings. Up until then they were living in huts. Somehow that arrival of internationals started to shift a little of the stigma and the prejudice. There was also one Greek nun who spent a few years here in the beginning, and a nurse, and they were working to treat the patients. The stigma was gradually shifting. The community was growing. They were building more. They were transforming the land… "

Zohar paused as the room trembled with the heavy engine of a tractor passing along the road. We sat and waited for it to splutter and cough on its way. The room regained its silence.

"By the mid-sixties," she continued, "the community was almost self-sufficient in food, except for sugar, salt and oil, I think. They were making their own clothes. They were building their own homes. It was incredibly vibrant and successful, and they were actually starting to have a

174

surplus of funds. They started to look around and said: 'What else can we do?' Which was always Baba Amte's way, it was never enough. So they started looking at the needs of the larger community here, and realised there was no opportunity for education in the area beyond school. There were no colleges or universities anywhere in this area of India. The leprosy patients built two colleges for the general community; the colleges are still there, they're still functioning at the Crossing (1 kilometre away). That was really the final step in the integration, the movement of Anandwan actually providing a service for the general community. I remember when we first came in 2004 and we were doing some shopping in the town. The shopkeepers were saying to us: 'Ah, you're in Anandwan.' We'd say: 'Yes.' And they replied: 'I went to college there.' They would say this with a lot of pride, an example of the shift that happened from the generosity, from the giving of the community here.

"At that point, more projects were being created; Somnath where we just were was created in those years, in the late sixties. The original vision of Somnath was also an educational vision, it was going to be an experimental agriculture training college where the students would be given an acre of land each where they could actually grow things and experiment, as well as learn techniques but also to really be creative. Because the local community there was against the amount of land that had been given to the Anandwan group, eventually they had to go to mediation and only ended up with half the land that they were supposed to have. So instead of this vison of an agricultural training place it became just an agricultural community. It still grows a lot of food for the whole association.

"Another thing that was happening in the late sixties was an awareness of the plight of people with visual disabilities in the rural areas. They had no form of education, no form of training. They were isolated. They were alone and considered a burden on their families. So in the late sixties the community founded a school for the blind. They're not politically correct here, so they say school for the blind when it's actually visually impaired. You'll see when you meet the children that a lot of them still have some sight, just different capacities of sight. Some of them are completely blind. If they were in the West, the situation for a lot of them would be completely different. They founded the school for the blind and started having visually impaired children coming; it's a boarding school because the children come from low income families from a large area around and there wouldn't be the time or the finances to get them back and forth. They live here. They study here. They have two holidays a year when they go home, and sometimes you see their families visiting.

"Then the Anandwan primary school was founded because there were more and more children being born here. Warora was expanding and getting nearer, so now it's a joint school. There are children from the town and children from the community learning together. A really radical and special thing about Anandwan, which was Sadhana Tai's passion, is the right to have families for the leprosy patients. She called it: 'Right to sexuality.' When they originally founded the place it was like an ashram, so the men lived together and the women lived together. Many people that came here and come here have families, they are married and have children but they've had to leave their families and are alone. Sadhana Tai said: 'They also have a right to sexuality. They have the right to family. So let's support that to happen.' People started marrying, second marriages and first marriages and having children. There was another thing that Baba and Tai did from the beginning, they had a tendency to collect orphans and children whose parents couldn't look after them, and they themselves looked after many. They had two adopted daughters and I don't know how many other children that they looked after for different periods in their lives. They actually created an orphanage in the late sixties, and that still also exists. There are both orphans there and children whose families can't look after them for a certain period of time or not at all for various reasons. They have a home here.

"In the early seventies, Baba became aware of another area that drew his attention. It's a tribal area about four and a half hours' drive from here. It was an area that as a young man he used to hike in. It's very wild. The tribes there live really deep in the forest, and are very traditional. There was no health care, no education, no farming – they were hunter-gatherers. At that period in the seventies the modern world was starting to arrive in that area, and what was happening was that it was arriving in its negative impact. It wasn't medical care or education that was getting there, it was businessmen and people that were trying to get whatever the forest had to offer. The rights of the local tribal people were being violated. Baba decided to start a project there called, Hemalkasa. Baba and Tai physically started it so they went there and left the community here to be run by their eldest son, Vikas Amte. He had graduated from medical school at that time. He was the first doctor here, because up until then, no doctor was willing to come and work here.

"Baba and Tai were going back and forth between here and Hemalkasa. During the monsoon and after the monsoon the river water would go up and Hemalkasa was actually cut off for six months of the year. You couldn't get anything in or out. They started the project and then their second son, Prakash, who had also graduated a year or two after his brother from medical school where he met his wife, Manda, took on the project. On Baba's birthday they came and told him: 'We have a special gift for you, we will dedicate our life to Hemalkasa.' So they moved there and have lived there since. Hemalkasa is probably now the most famous of the projects of Anandwan; there's recently been a Bollywood film made about Prakash and Manda Amte so there are a lot of people going to see the project after seeing the film. They founded a hospital, that was the first thing they did, and for years they were the only medical care there, performing everything from birth to very complex surgery. Prakash Amte is an incredible person. They also founded a school for the tribal children; they have five hundred children studying there. They also did a lot of agricultural training, teaching them how to have small food gardens and things they could do within their lifestyle that could give a source of food. They provided education about nutrition and hygiene, very basic things. I think about ten or fifteen years ago one of the first students of the school graduated from medical school and went back as a doctor to Hemalkasa, so that was a big achievement in seeing that wheel going around. Now Prakash and Manda's two sons and their wives are running the project, one of the sons is a doctor and married a doctor again so they're looking after the medical side and the other son is looking after the administration. It's continuing through the generations.

"Coming to the eighties, Baba Amte's attention was drawn to the violence between communities in India. There was a lot of violence between Muslims and Hindus, and between Sikhs and Hindus. Indira Gandhi's (Indian Prime Minister 1980 - 1984) assassination by Sikhs sparked off a lot of violence and before that there were a few cycles of extreme violence between Muslims and Hindus. So Baba started a movement which he called, Knit India. He did a few journeys across India, one from the south to the north, from the southern tip of India to Kashmir, and one from east to west. He was travelling in a convoy of buses, trucks, cycles and walkers; stopping in places and having meetings with people and talking about things, and just bringing that spirit of non-violence and community, and of being one whole and of not dealing with our issues through violence. He spent a large chunk of the eighties doing that, on these massive trips that you can imagine, with the size of India, took a long time.

"And then I think he spent all of the nineties actually on the Narmada River in an ecological struggle against the mega dams. In India there has been an ongoing process of creating mega dams which cause a lot of environmental damage as well as displacement of tribal and low caste people, again always the weak, and for very little gain except for the people who are building them. Baba was always against these mega dams; in the eighties they had a successful struggle against a dam like that in the Hemalkasa area. The Narmada was already an ongoing struggle and already quite established when he joined, but he was a very well-known man in India at that time, and he basically made his home in a little temple on the banks of the Narmada, and he said: 'If you build this dam I will die here.' He had that kind of impact; he lived there for ten years, and during those ten years there was a legal battle going on and he was one of the leaders of that struggle against the big dam there. At the end of those ten years, Baba was already in his eighties and Sadhana in her seventies. She said to him: 'I really want to go home.' Baba, recounting this period, said: 'All our lives she's followed me, now it's time I follow her.' They came back to Anandwan for their last years here.

"They were deeply deeply loved by the people here. Baba knew everyone, from the youngest child in the school to the eldest person in the old people's home. Something I haven't mentioned yet is that he had a degenerative spine condition, which meant for the last thirty years of his life he couldn't bend his spine. He was either standing or lying down. He couldn't sit and he would have had a lot of physical pain. I know for myself that I would consider myself pretty disabled if I had a condition like that but for as long as he had strength he would stand for hours. When we first came here in 2004 he was still walking. He would do a long walk twice a day, one early and one in the afternoon. At about five-thirty in the morning and five-thirty in the afternoon he would walk around the community. When he could no longer walk those distances, the people here built him a bed on wheels, and he would be pushed on this bed on that same route, or some of that same route, so that he could still see the place and meet the people, be in contact. His door was always open for as long as he had control over it. It was always open for anyone to come and see him. During the first years when we were here and would meet him while he was lying in his simple room, just a bed and a little space along with a *thangka* from the Dali Lama on the wall, they were very good friends; he would say: 'I look out the window and I feel in every moment that I'm ready to die happy, because I see what's here.'"

XIII

Our service in the community commenced. We were given a choice of where we would like to work: in the schools for the visually and hearing impaired children; in the production of the many crafts for sale; chopping onion after onion in the kitchen which is then cooked with other ingredients to feed the many hundreds of hungry bellies each day; the wound dressing clinic which cleans and bandages community members' wounds, often on the feet, early each morning before they set out to work; or the hospital where the sombre faces of those having suffered an accident or illness sit or lie in their beds in two large rooms, one for men and one for women. I decided to spend my mornings at the old people's home, offering the old chaps massages and later expanding into cutting their finger or toe nails. Some of the nails grew out of what had become stumps where fingers and toes had been lost or disfigured; some of the nails were so long I presumed they hadn't been cut since SanghaSeva last served in the community, one year ago. They were brittle and yellow and hard as crustaceans. In the afternoons I would walk with Peter, an Englishman and fine whistle player, back to the old people's home, this time to the women's section.

On our initial tour we had been led into a large rectangular room home to fourteen beds, seven along each wall, with thirteen old ladies, most of them sat on their beds in their colourful saris. They all smiled as we entered. "Namaste," they said. "Namaste," we replied, following their lead and pressing our palms together before our chests. The room echoed of a smell I had grown familiar with over the past few years, after visiting my grandmother in her care home, and where she lay bedbound for the majority of her time there. It was a smell not easy to liken to anything else, one of stuffiness, rigid bones, a tired stench of old skin and dusty lives. I can't help but smell it to be the end of life. Among these beds holding women with an average age touching eighty, there was one bed different to the others, lower to the floor. Under a thin cotton blanket a woman was lying on her back, staring at the ceiling with her knees raised towards her chest, fixed in this position by the chronic arthritis that had taken hold of her body before she had turned twenty. Her name was Jyotie. She is twenty-six years old, a youngster compared to the women around her. We were introduced to her and she smiled and laughed like someone who knew no sorrow or pain. Her head poked out of the blanket, her short black hair shiny, and her teeth slightly discoloured (which I soon learned was partly a result of her love for all things containing sugar). I looked down at her and saw my grandmother; simply less wrinkled and without my grandmother's bushy white hair, which I used to see resting like a peaceful cloud on her head. My grandmother's body had also been riddled by arthritis, and my heart ached seeing Jyotie immobile within this warren of a building initially constructed to house those who had been afflicted by leprosy. I had always struggled to see my grandmother diminished and pained by such a thing, and to now see it in a young woman, bedbound in her early twenties, was cruel.

The old people's home in Anandwan is something you will not see in the UK; it is a barrack-like operation where a chain of command is filtered down from a matron, overworked and toughened because of it, to those that clean and dress wounds. There are also the visiting nurses and doctors, and then the rooms themselves are left in the charge of one of the old inhabitants who resides in them, normally the most mobile and mentally aware of the bunch. Jyotie's main carer is a woman in her seventies, perhaps even her eighties, and someone who Jyotie loves deeply. Agee Bai walks bent forward with one hand coming behind her to support her back as she does so. She takes care of overseeing the cleaning of the room and also tends to the other women's needs, from helping to change their saris to distributing food. She changes Jyotie's cloth nappies when SanghaSeva is not in town, cleans them and feeds her; she also looks after the biscuits we bring Jyotie which will often be the first thing she asks for after we arrive to sit beside her for a couple of hours in the afternoon. Jyotie is a ray of sunshine in a room of diminishing light, and yet life remains. Anandwan is a place of such remarkable joy, and all too often it is because this joy has been born out of deep sorrow.

I believe it would be wrong of me to capture Anandwan as a place knowing only happiness, because, as the Buddha taught, life is suffering. So anywhere we find life I find it hard to entertain that some form of suffering will not also exist. Anandwan is not a utopia, it is a community made up of people once broken by a disease and society's ill-informed regard of them. I was first surprised (myself blinded by the wonder that has transpired here) to listen as one group member, working in the hospital, discovered there to be some community members on anti-depressants. The scars on their bodies have deepened to leave scars on their minds. This is not a culture where inner feelings are expressed and worked through. There is no emotional therapy; the drugs simply numb the pain, but the scars don't go away. The UK is no better in such things, despite the talking therapies and deeper regard of psychology. I read just yesterday that the amount of children, and before school age, being prescribed ADHD drugs to treat hyper-activity is increasing.[11] It's another example of where society tries to fix a mind to operate within a predefined system, yet the system itself is never looked at as potentially being the thing that's broken. Society instead drugs, numbs and – I can't help but feel – destroys.

Over 4,500 miles away in Anandwan, another group member reinforced the growing awareness of an undercurrent of despair beneath the forest of joy; working in the wound clinic she conveyed the shame that she saw in the faces of some of the women she bandaged, they were suffering silently as a result of their deformities. So this is Anandwan, a place where the seeds of an inspiring vision have grown into amazing beauty, which is spellbinding even, but it is a place home to humans. I walk around it and thus will capture the smiles along with the suffering. Yesterday afternoon I saw suffering most of all.

Peter and I walked into Jyotie's room; she lay there in the same positon as we had found her to be in over the previous week of coming to sit with her, to subsequently share the small conversation we could share. Her English vocabulary for sweet things, like ice cream, cake and all the brands of biscuits the general shop stocked was second to none. We made our way to her bed, first turning to all the old women sat on their beds and offering them a customary, 'Namaste.'

I saw it instantly on their faces that something was not right. One of them, a big and often severe woman (yet I'd seen her succumb to tears after one of the group members had massaged her legs before rubbing coconut oil into her long grey hair) pointed to a bed on the far wall. It was empty. I knew the bed belonged to a woman who had just been moved into the room the previous day. She hadn't looked well when I'd seen her then, almost collapsing as she tried to get out of bed. The woman pointed again, her finger lowering. I looked to where she indicated and saw her on the cold tiled floor between two beds. *She's dead*, I thought, preparing myself to crouch beside her and find her chest and pulse still. They were not; her chest was rising and falling. I pressed the saris back from her face and her wrinkled fingers slowly found my hand and pinched it, her eyes closed.

"Come on," I said gently, "this is no place for sleeping."

Another group member came in and we lifted her back onto the bed. It was then I felt my hand becoming wet; she had wet herself and a small puddle remained on the floor where she had been. I don't know how long she had been down there. We placed her back in bed and tried to get her as close to the wall as possible. Fortunately, Grace, another group member from Bristol and an experienced nurse, was spending the afternoon in the home. She instantly put on her rubber gloves and took charge of taking off the woman's wet saris and cleaning her. I went to Jyotie and sat beside her; in her limited English, she explained that the other women in the room were cross with the new arrival, because she didn't sleep at night and had kept them all awake. Agee Bai, in her bed next to Jyotie's, was trying to sleep under her blanket. She was roused by the matron to put a clean sari on the new arrival. Agee Bai moved wearily to assist Grace. It made Jyotie sad, although she didn't convey so in words, to see her tired and wanting to sleep. The human warmth in Jyotie's life was nourished by this old woman who has taken charge of being her loving caregiver.

Relaxing a little to see Grace now nursing the woman I had found on the floor, Jyotie and I began discussing our favourite snacks again, she managed to find new ones each day. Peter had returned to Rest House to wash out the urine and dry the sari. American David, who Jyotie affectionately calls *Father,* arrived and we sat with her and watched a film on his laptop. David is an aging California-dreaming type of guy, long hair and watchful eyes, a very slow moving and gentle man; he has given much time and love to Jyotie over the past four years of his coming to

Anandwan to serve with SanghaSeva. Her affection for him is like no other. The previous day was a celebration as we succeeded in seducing Jyotie to the idea of a walk; David, Peter and I pushed her in a wheelchair and walked beside her as we visited Baba and Tai's tended grave, before sitting at the chai stand with David feeding her a butterscotch ice cream. It was the first time she had been outside since her birthday in May, over six months had passed by with her lying in bed, day and night. The sun shone on her ice cream painted smile.

Back in the room and a day later, I looked upon her silently watching the laptop and film which we'd positioned on a stool beside her bed. Her hands, fingers locked into crooked positions, were rested over her heart. The film followed the latest Bollywood hunk's adventure to Manali, a renowned beauty spot for mountains and hiking in the northeastern state of Himachal Pradesh. A book-bound and sheltered girl joins the trip on which she breaks out of her shy self and, amongst snowy mountain ridges and innocent embraces, falls in love with the hunk, named Bunny in the film. The trip over and mountains conquered, Bunny leaves abruptly for a university in the States and… Dinner time so we were forced to stop the film. I imagined the love she found in the mountains was also born in him and he crosses back over land and water to return to her and make it known. I wondered what Jyotie thought and felt as she watched the young lovers finding freedom in the wide world, falling in love and pursuing their dreams. She lay in a low bed in a room of eighty-something's who would frequently erupt into separate arguments and disputes; these would then spread out the door and into the internal courtyard and neighbouring rooms. Did Jyotie ever think of such things as falling in love, or running in the mountains or forests? In that moment I felt so much for her, I wanted to write her into her own fairy tale, give her everything in fiction that she will not have in life. But it would be contrived, and perhaps painful for her to read. She will be, for the majority of her days, confined to a low bed, her small body not as it should be. This is her reality.

The new arrival and worry in the corner, having been left by Grace to sleep and after having been given two cups of water, suddenly raised herself to the edge of the bed and shakily came to her feet. My heart dropped thinking I was about to watch her fall. She didn't. She walked slowly past us, muttering as she went. She left the room, followed by many angry and poor sighted eyes; the other women crossly sat on their beds, muttering also. She was disorientated but had somewhere to be, a place only her mind was certain existed. We said goodbye to Jyotie and left the room too. Walking along the corridor and towards the weakening daylight outside, I stopped and turned to watch the new arrival simply walk in a circle around the internal courtyard, occasionally stopping to peer into the other rooms. The matron, sat with a group of some of the more mobile old women, watched her too. I was amazed to observe what a cup or two of water could do, I'd found this woman in a wet crinkled heap no more than an hour ago.

I returned to Rest House and sat in the depth of my room, where I'm sat now writing this, wanting to be alone and think for a moment. I wanted to reflect on the poverty of being infirm or in an environment where the care needed is not provided or available. It was dusk and the strip lighting in the room hummed. Peter's whistle sadly sung through the open door as he played on the roof. I just sat silently on my garden plastic chair which I had put a pillow on to soften the hours spent capturing my notes. My phone vibrated on the shelf beside me. It was an email from V, and came shortly after I had received news of her excitement at having received a large donation for a campaign she was working on to fund a befriender service for old people suffering from loneliness in the Bath area:

Dear Matt,

I just heard something horrible.

Today we went to take a photo of that amazing guy who got his company to give us the large donation (and who personally shelled out when I met with him on top of it). Speaking to him originally he'd alluded to something really terrible that had happened recently that spurred him and his wife even more to help, beyond their time caring for an elderly neighbour in recent months, but he wouldn't elaborate. This morning he told us.

About six weeks ago an old man was found in a bathroom at a hospital with a bag over his head. They tried to resuscitate him, but it was too late. Beside the body they found a note. In it he apologised for doing this to them. He said he was just so lonely he couldn't take it anymore, and although he regretted one of their staff finding him or worse yet a patient or their family, he couldn't face being left in his house for weeks or months without anyone coming to find the body.

I wish we'd been able to reach him, to tell him he wasn't all alone. I wish he hadn't died by himself, suffocating in a bag in a hospital toilet. That he hadn't suffered a horrendous indignity of a death just so he wasn't alone in his end too. But more even than the sadness, I feel so mad. If he'd been younger, if he'd been a teenager or a kid or a twenty something or a young parent or a professional, his unconscionable desperation would have been all over local media. No newspapers covered it. No one at the hospital even thought to tell his story. No one reached out so that we could help put something in place to reach more people like him. He is simply another dead old person. We don't even know his name.

As I write this there's Christmas music on the square outside my window, and I'm due to leave early to start my holiday. I still need to buy gifts, still need to wrap things, still need to stress about the food we'll be eating and how I'm going to get it all from Waitrose. Someone just gave me some homemade fudge, and I'm just sitting here trying not to cry for that poor man who no one is missing today, who no one has missed for the last six weeks. Who no one missed for I don't know how long before he was really gone.

I honestly don't know how we blindly keep going. I suppose we just always do. x

The motivation driving the charity V works for to raise money for the service came after statistics were released finding that one in four households in the region has a lonely older person in it, and that the south west of England is the loneliest place to be for an old person in the UK.[12] I had wanted to document this in some way before leaving Bath, to meet with someone who would relate their story of being old and lonely, a deep and despairing poverty. I failed to find such a person; the loneliest of people are for that very reason the hardest to see in society. I wanted to be with V then, so we could sit and be sad together. There were thousands of miles, mountains, oceans and cities between us, but in that moment we were inseparable by the human suffering we each saw around us.

XIV

Our time in the community quickly became scheduled and a following of routine. I enjoyed giving massages to the old boys in the morning, even when some of the limbs my hands cupped were nothing more than skin and bones. I worked my thumbs and fingers up and down to try and find any muscles amongst them. One morning I crouched before a pair of legs thick as tree trunks, I gripped them hard and looked up at the man sat before me, his white vest stained and head short of hair, his cheeks plump like his belly.

"Accha," I said, the Hindi for *good* as I began to work my thumbs around the stiff muscles, tight as guitar strings, in the backs of his legs.

The men I massaged liked a hard going over, I was also informed by those working with the women that they too appreciated firm fingers, anything lighter and you can lose their interest. I think it helps to relieve the hard life they've lived which has shaped and made their bodies rugged and weary. When I arrived to a bed and the man upon it was missing a leg, hand, or arm, then I would gently massage his stumps. I quickly stopped seeing the stump on entering a room and instead saw the person moving themselves in anticipation of the massage and human touch to come. When it comes to tenderness, Indian culture is a polarised one. At some points I saw it as cold and unforgiving; observing the old men, and the few young found residing amongst them, often working not only against the immobility old age brings, but also the immobility the loss of limbs, or the use of them, from the leprosy they had suffered at one point in their lives. Some push themselves round the tiled internal courtyards on square planks of wood which have four small wheels on the bottom; others lean on a crutch in order to meet the meal truck that delivers their lunch at ten each morning, and there is one chap who can be found on his own in a room, separated from the others, and simply stays in bed. I've never seen him out of it. Most of the men form their own circles, sitting beneath the trees or in the sun, talking. Some are usually found alone, seldom seen being engaged with and seldom seen outside their rooms or beds. Alternatively Indian culture is also a tender and loving one. I see this in the way one old man massages his friend's back in the sun every morning. The man giving the massage is blind, and his friend, with his shirt lifted over his head, has no fingers on his hands or toes on his feet. He is also one of the oldest men in the home; his smile, however, remains young as his back is rubbed, as his blind friend begins to feel his way up the bowed spine, feeling for ears before working his fingers though the man's short white hair.

Then my afternoons are spent sat with Jyotie. We talk about snacks mostly, she tells me her favourite ones and her least favourite ones; cake being her favourite, along with ice cream, while *Hing Goli* is by far her least, little hard balls that are salty on the tongue, reminiscent of Marmite but without the yeasty taste. The little packs of *Hing Goli* are fronted by a cartoon man with his hands drawn in the air, a speech bubble rising from his mouth, "*Aha…*" This ayurvedic medicine describes itself as being *Tasty & Digestive* and to REMOVE GAS IMMEDIATELY. American Dave always has a pack in his pocket; he and the old women in the room love them. Jyotie scrunches her sweet face up when he offers her one. We might then watch a Bollywood film or documentary, or paint pictures

191

together on a laptop, read, or take it in turns to play highly addictive games on Dave's mobile phone. So this is my day in the community; structured yes, but no two days the same, for we are working with people and life can always be relied on to chop and change.

Christmas day passed much as any other; massaging in the morning and then I hung out with Jyotie in the afternoon. Christmas being a Christian concept means it's not marked or celebrated in most of India, except in the Christian communities scattered around the country. December 26th did, however, mean something, in Anandwan at least, as it was the 100th anniversary since the birth of Baba Amte. Our routine changed because of it.

The group all came together and organised a mass movement of old folk from the home to Baba's Samadhi (in India, one definition of Samadhi can refer to a tomb for a soul who has ascertained Samadhi, a non-duellist state, before or after death. Baba Amte didn't consider himself a saint, yet the work he did over the course of his long life meant he was still honoured in death in a way reminiscent of one). A morning of celebration had been scheduled to take place around the raised flowerbed grave where Baba and his wife Sadhana were laid to rest. We unlocked the storeroom where twenty wheelchairs were kept; unfolded them and began going around the rooms offering rides to any person wanting to pay their respect to Baba. The chairs were easily and quickly filled. I happened to enter a room in the men's section; it was darker than most, and smelt as though shit or food was rotting somewhere inside it. A man was led on a wooden bed frame in one corner of the room. My first thought was why hasn't he got a mattress? He had a heavy woollen rug over him, and he sat up when I approached with the wheelchair.

"Baba's Samadhi?" I asked him.

He didn't speak but his face worked between nervousness to excitement before smiling as he looked at the chair. I'd say he was around forty; a short man, dumpy but not fat.

"Baba's Samadhi?" I asked again.

I pushed the chair close to his bed. He shakily stood, turned and dropped down into the chair.

"Alright," I said. "Let's get out the hell out of here!"

I spun him around and pushed him out of the room, out of the courtyard, and down the ramp that led out of this section of the home. The sun soon beamed down on his black short hair and occasionally he reached up with his arms, I thought he was clasping at it. Baba's Samadhi was only a five minute walk down a dusty tarmac road which is often lined by community members, digging up the weeds from beside it, or others going to and from the fields. They stopped working to see the stream of wheelchairs pass them by.

"Namaste," many of them said to my passenger.

He brought his hands to his eyes and my stomach and chest tightened as he looked like he was about to cry. It's such a simple thing, going for a walk, or going outside, that the impact it can have on someone who is not used to such things can never really be known. Small grunts and wheezes erupted from his throat as we walked; I think they were born from excitement.

We approached the tended ground on the edge of the community grown forest, a pocket of natural beauty, surrounded by miles of rural scrubland that marked the boundaries of Anandwan. Baba and Sadhana's grave is a large square raised bed of colourful flowers, his wish being to nourish life even after death. The green grass around the grave was covered by hundreds of school children and community members who had taken time off work to join the celebration. There was a speaker system set up and traditional music was sung by a group of musicians from beside the grave.

The army of wheelchairs entered the main gate. We

began to help the riders out of them, sitting them down on chairs or, for those physically able, on the carpeted ground. The wheelchairs were to return to the home to pick up more residents who wished to honour Baba on his birthday. My man stood from the chair, following the lead of others who were lowering to sit on the ground. Nathan was stood beside him in case he needed assistance; another group member stood behind a wheelchair quickly directed both mine and Nathan's attention to the ground beside the man's leg. There was a small pile of shit on the carpet, no more than 5 metres from Baba's grave. *Shit!* I said internally. The man continued to sit placing his rug over his lap, which he had brought along for the ride. I guessed there would also be shit in his shorts and down his leg. The celebration was in full swing; he sat smiling and watching the musicians play their instruments. He didn't seem in anyway disturbed or put out by what had just happened. It would have been too much to lift him back into the chair and whisk him away; too obvious and have brought too much attention upon him. The pile of shit, so far, had gone unnoticed. Another member of the group, fortunately having a tea towel, quickly hid it. The celebrations continued.

It was a lovely marking and remembrance of Baba Amte's life; little leaves were blown free from the trees and wistfully fell over the grave as the songs continued to flow out of the singer's mouth and through the speakers. Almost an hour of speakers and songs passed before we began to position wheelchairs. I had one wish; get my man out as quick as possible. Whatever happens I cannot leave him sat alone on the ground. I couldn't let him be seen beside the small raised tea towel. I wanted to get him back in the chair while there was much commotion around as the other old people were moved. I found a free chair and Nathan helped me to lift him, the rug slipped from his lap and my fears were worthy, his leg was covered in shit. I positioned the rug over him and began pushing, trying to swerve around the chairs ahead, the old people in them, teary, tired and some appearing bored, watched us rocket past them. I walked beside Nathan, himself pushing a chair and old person.

"Do you have a plan?" he said.

"No, just to get him back to start with."

I had no idea about what to do when I got my man back to the home; he was coherent in some things but the fact he barely seemed phased by what had happened showed to me that he may not be able to tend to his own needs.

"I'll help," said Nathan, stopping at Rest House on the way to pick us up some rubber gloves.

Arriving back at the home, we positioned the wheelchair outside the shower block before helping him to a cubicle. He didn't resist us manoeuvring him, he just stood like a small child waiting to be tended to by a loving parent. Nathan began taking off the man's brown stained shorts and shirt; he was covered and the smell soon dominated the wet tiled cubicle. Nathan, experienced in care work, thoroughly cleaned him and commanded me to pass the tissue, then the soap and finally some water. I felt like an assistant to a surgeon preforming a complex operation, I was pleased for his strategic approach, as I have never been in a position of cleaning the shit from another man's arse before and was relieved to simply be assisting for my first experience. The man seemed to enjoy being washed and cleaned, the soap studs soon covered his naked body, before we dowsed him in a bucket of water (we all take bucket showers in Anandwan), which made him giggle and grit his teeth as he grinned. The resident in charge of the block then arrived and wanted to take over; he led the wet, naked man out of the cubicle and back to his room. Nathan and I removed our rubber gloves from our hands. This experience was over but my engagements with this man, not one of them being verbal, were not.

The next day I found myself outside the home, working with Mark and David, two fellow Englishmen. We were massaging chaps who spent their mornings talking at the base of a big tree and in the sun. We had come to know this group as the massage club. We would normally return to this spot each morning as the men had come to expect us and we'd often arrive to see the legs of trousers already rolled up. We would soon examine the varying shapes and density of legs which were becoming increasingly drier and warm due to the hot sun. I saw the man I had taken to Baba Amte's Samadhi, the poor chap who had soiled himself. He was sat on the edge of the group of men, appearing relaxed in the sun. We had been joined by some local school boys who wanted to ask us questions about our own cultures and our reason for being in India and Anandwan. They wanted to know if I would have a love marriage or arranged.

"Love," I replied.

Their English was very good. I decided to utilise one of the boy's translation skills and asked him to come and speak to Samadhi (the name I have given him) as he remained sat in the sun. I wanted to know if he needed a mattress or if he in fact preferred not to have one. The young lad had no problem with this and promptly engaged him. Samadhi looked up at him and squinted against the sun before looking back down to his lap. The boy engaged him again with the question. Nothing. One of the old men sat beside us, turned and said something in Mahrati to the boy. A look of sudden understanding washed over his face as he straightened himself and away from Samadhi, who was now fiddling with a crease in his sleeve. The boy raised his hand to my shoulder and pushed me lightly away.

"He's mentally ill, just leave him."

"Leave him, why would I leave him because he's mentally ill?"

The late teens quickly returned to their excited conversation about American wrestling and I looked from them to Samadhi, still sat quiet and at peace in the sun.

I was disturbed by the young translator's reaction. Each of these sixteen to seventeen-year-olds already had their ambitions and careers in mind for when they finished their education; engineers, marines, and one wishing to work in government. They were intelligent and highly educated, yet their image of someone with a mental illness was to leave them be. Nothing good can come from engaging with them. Why bother? I decided to do something and went into the women's section of the home to find Zohar, mentioning to her about the missing mattress. She said she'd look into it. Shortly after this experience I returned to Rest House. I sat alone and replayed the young translator's response over again and again in my mind.

After having mentioned to Zohar about the mattress, she quickly located one and delivered it to Samadhi's room with an incontinence sheet rolled up inside it; she told me that he almost snatched it from her as she offered it to him. She told me he hugged it tight. A few hours later, and after having spent some time with Jyotie, I walked from the women's section of the home to the men's, wanting to check he had been able to make his bed. The doors to his room were closed, so I pushed them open and entered. The smell I had held my breath against in the morning had not gone away; the six beds that filled the room were all home to men of varying ages and hampered bodies. One young man's left leg was shrunken and twisted. I don't know if it was from leprosy, polio or something else. He walked on his hands and one leg, the left held fixed in the air. Another, lying in bed and excited to see me, was a regular for the daily wheelchair walks we provided; he enjoyed the chai and samosa we bought for him at the chai stand more than the walk itself. The other beds were taken up by real old boys, difficult to tell what part of them was lost from leprosy and what part had been instead shrivelled by old age. I looked to the corner of the room where I watched the man who had left Baba more than just a blessing at the anniversary ceremony; Samadhi was carefully unfolding his new mattress over the wooden bedframe, before positioning the incontinence sheet to cover it. If you treat someone with dignity they in turn have a greater chance to be dignified. He might not be very responsive to verbal engagement, but he knew the reason for the rubber top sheet, and he wanted to protect his new mattress, not only from being ruined but perhaps more importantly from being taken away.

I said *Namaste* to the men in the room, turned and walked out into dusk and another mosquito filled and starry night.

The following morning I again found myself outside the home, working my way along a line of legs belonging to men who had embraced the temporary massage club. I said *Namaste* to the men patiently sat down and expecting a massage. I was alone as the other morning massagers had instead decided to do a wheelchair run. I oiled my hands and crouched down before the nearest leg. It was hard work being crouched for so long while continually working the muscles of these old timers. Not having a language we could share, I could only imagine and invent the many stories they had lived and the different narratives that had brought them to Anandwan. Not all of the gents had leprosy, some were visually impaired and others mentally. By the time I got to my third pair of legs, the backs of my own calves were getting tight and beginning to shake as I had been crouched for almost thirty minutes. I stood and stretched out. Rotating my head I noticed Samadhi, sat in his spot in the sun, and at the end of the row of men. He was looking around him; shyly watching the men beside him, to the cars and motorbikes occasionally passing by on the nearby road, and to the fields in the distance, being ploughed by a tractor and oxen. I lowered back down to the legs I still had to massage, gradually working my way towards him. The engine of a scooter pulled up behind, I turned while holding a bony leg to see three of the young lads from the previous day, including the translator, behind me. I nodded and smiled but didn't stand to talk to them. I wanted to finish the massages. The boys watched me work. Ten minutes later and I got to the end of the run of legs, a glistening display of hairy and skinny legs shone in the sunshine behind me. Samadhi now sat before me. I sat on my heels for a moment looking at him, the small bottle of massage oil in my hand.

"Would you like?"

I gestured to the bottle, again he didn't respond verbally but the expression on his face moved in a way that might have meant yes or no. I couldn't read him. I decided the only way to know for sure was to try. I took the lid from the bottle and poured a small puddle of golden oil in the palm of my hand. I settled the bottle on the ground beside me and gently rubbed my hands together, oiling them before reaching out and taking his right wrist. He didn't flinch or pull away. He simply looked down to where my fingers now softly pressed, beginning to rotate their way up his arm. He didn't look away from my fingers and I didn't look away from his eyes, they were wide and watchful but intermittently lost as he blinked and blinked. It was the curtains that closed to keep tears away. I lowered back down his arm to hold his hand in mine as I worked my thumbs into the heel of his palm; this raised a smile on his lips. I didn't turn but could feel the eyes of the young lads watching me as they sat, all three of them, on the scooter. I massaged Samadhi for fifteen minutes, moving to his other arm and repeating the same massage I had given his right arm, finishing on the hand and fingers.

'Thika?' I asked, the Hindi for Okay?

He looked towards my mouth from where this word had parted but again said nothing. He let me place his hand back on his knee as I stood and smiled.

"Namaste," I said.

I really could see the divine in him.

XV

"Please tell me again, Manon."

I was sitting on the flat roof of Rest House, the sun low on the horizon and the blue sky slowly changing into the pale of dusk. Manon was sat on a plastic chair beside me; our chairs faced each other and I had my phone and notebook on my lap, ready to record our meeting. Manon was from Québec; she was an affectionate and open-hearted woman, and had embraced her adventure and the people of Anandwan with love and kindness. After selling her house in Canada, saying farewell to her now grown up children, Manon had felt it time to pursue her long held dream of spending a year in India. Over dinner on our last night in Somnath she had recounted her experience of arriving in Delhi, and I decided it was worth me asking her to tell it to me again. I wanted to capture it. Manon held the plastic arms of her chair and looked at me, her mind working through memories to find the one detailing her arrival in the East.

"It is my first time to India," she said. "I arrived in Delhi in the middle of the night. When you arrive in the middle of the night you don't really see the poverty or the cultural difference. It's too late at night-time. The only thing I worried about was to get to my hotel safe. I didn't look at the environment at all. The next morning I heard children laughing and playing outside. It reminded me of my grandchildren. I woke up, got out of bed, went to my balcony, and when I opened the door and saw the poverty before me... it was just beyond anything you could imagine. Because you see it on TV, you read about it, but when you're in it it's totally different, and I just couldn't believe what I was seeing. There was a field used for planting, agriculture, then the homes that were behind me were like shacks. What you would call shacks, but they were homes to these people. They were made out of whatever garbage material was lying around: tarps, ropes, everything to try to create a home. I sat there pretty well the whole day the first day, just looking and observing the scenery and the environment. You know when they say about the culture shock, that to me was my culture shock.

"So I went to bed that night and then the next morning, early in the morning, I heard the dogs barking like crazy. Now the night before it was silent, there were no dogs barking. But by early morning, the dogs were barking like there was somebody in the neighbourhood. The barking was like a warning. I decided to get up and go look outside. When I looked outside I could see that there was a young guy, and I could see that he was under the influence by the way he was walking. It made sense to me why the dogs were barking. But then what I noticed when I looked to my left, out of one of the shack homes, is this woman that came out. She was also wondering what the noise was about. I noticed that she and I were both just observing, although she couldn't see me because I was on a balcony that was much higher than her. She was just looking to see who it was and I continued to look until he made his way on and the dogs got quiet. I didn't go in right away. I was just watching her. She looked on both sides of the street. I wondered what she was looking at and I also looked to see if something was coming. She crossed the street and then looked back; she then knelt and went to the washroom. It was that moment when my whole idea of Western thinking, you know like you come here and out of ignorance you're thinking that they're just squatting anywhere and you wonder why they do that. You figure they're dirty or something and why can't they go to the washroom? It was that moment that changed everything for me, because when I saw her my heart just went out to her. I realised what else could she be doing? What else can she do? She's living in a shack, no washroom, no water. The cleanest place for her to go was across the street. Where she was living was surrounded by garbage but where she went was clean."

Manon's story had dislodged an article I had read towards the end of the summer. It detailed a warning made by the UN deputy secretary general that 2.5 billion worldwide were 'blighted' by the lack of toilets. Gender equality was weakened by this as women would often have to spend much longer searching for a secluded place to relieve themselves; men, and from what I had seen during my walks around Mumbai and later Kolkata, could frequently be seen urinating into open gutters or up against walls. Lack of sanitation is also more of a problem for women with reduced personal hygiene and health as a result. There is also risk that comes with being forced to search out secluded areas. The article stated that the warning by the UN was made shortly after two young Indian girls, having gone into a field to relieve themselves, were attacked, raped and murdered.[13] The sun was now out of sight after dipping below the horizon. We remained sat on the roof at Rest House. Manon continued her story capturing the view from her hotel balcony in Delhi.

"For the next couple of days while I was there I just watched them and what they have to do just to survive. They walk so far just to get water. During the day I wondered where they go to the washroom because it's a street where a lot of activity happens, a lot of people and where a lot of kids are playing. So I'm not too sure where they go during the day. It's just a thing you don't even think about because we have everything that's accessible. I just know that after I saw that I got to go back into my room... " Manon's eyes reddened with tears and she struggled with her words. "In the room I had two beds with a Western washroom and a duvet cover, and I couldn't even sleep because just the thought that I was in bed and yet she is so close to me. I was just one floor, two floors up from her. There she was, below, with the reality of the difference of how we are and how we live. This experience will ever change me."

XVI

Despite dusk having taken hold of the sky over Rest House, now no longer blue but a pinkish grey with darkness determinedly creeping after the sunset, I wasn't ready to let Manon go. I decided to question her about her experiences[14] at Anandwan, for she had spent the mornings in the wound clinics, cleaning and bandaging wounds of all shapes and severity for the community members who would then head off to work. I would then see her in the afternoons as I sat beside Jyotie; she offered massages to the old women in the home. Manon often moved me during these times. I would watch her hold the hands of the women she had just massaged, or lower to sit beside them on their beds, rubbing their backs. Some women were brought to tears by her touch and embrace. With night now upon us, I asked her about some of the moments that she will hold onto. She instantly reflected on an encounter from the same day, in which she had spent time with one elderly woman who is close to dying, presently in a bedbound state, frail and uncommunicative. Her existence is fragile.

"I'd been seeing her for the last three days, but today she wouldn't even drink. I'd been going there every day to do therapeutic touch on her. I took my gloves off, I can't put a glove on between somebody that's passing, it just doesn't seem right. So I'm just with her and I sing to her. Yesterday she drank water and today she can't even swallow, so what I did was take a sponge, like a cotton ball and you dip it in water, and not too much because she can

205

choke on the water. You wet her lips, so they don't get dry. That's what I did, and then just gave her a little water from that."

"And when you leave Anandwan," I asked, "what will stay with you the most? Is there something you can put into words? When you go away from here and when you look back, how will you see this place?"

Manon weighed up my question.

"Well for me," she said after a moment's pause, "it's forever changed me. The people here have so very little and where they have wounds they have different things, different challenges, and yet they just continue their day like there's nothing. There's so many things; just as you think that you saw something that is the last thing you think could move you, something else comes along and you go, 'Oh my God.' Every day I just feel that my heart space expands so much more, and the place of empathy and compassion deepens. And not just on myself, as we're tough on ourselves as well. Since I've been here I've had a problem with my knee and problems with my feet. I've been very aware every day of my own challenge of my leg, which is nothing compared to the people here, but it's a very small thing that brings me an awareness every day of what they must go through. I think that if I had not had this difficulty then I'd probably not be at that level of understanding."

"And then today," I said, "there was this lady sat on her bed in Jyotie's room and she was visibly very sad about something. We can't communicate with her through language so we might be inclined to pass her by, but I watched you rest on the bed beside her and you began to stroke her back. What was the force that compelled you to comfort her in this way and what did you feel you could bring to her?"

"I noticed that every day when I entered the room she was always very happy, always smiling to me, yet she's never let me massage her or do her hair. She seems to be a woman that needs very little, yet very content. But when I saw her today, it was instantly very different because her head was down and she stayed on her bed, there was no smile, no greeting when I greeted her. My sense was something on the emotional level, not the physical. I wanted to take the time to stay connected to her, and just by touching her and her allowing me to do that, I knew that there must be something. Otherwise she wouldn't have let me touch her and normally she barely lets me hug her, but today she was totally open. I asked if she was okay, and physically she said yes. Then I went like this… " Manon brought her hands together before her heart to show me the movement she had made. "I knew it was emotional because I could feel it from her. I felt at that time to stay with her and comfort her in the way of letting her know that I am here, just touching her back. I think that did it because she allowed me to do that for a long time."

A silence fell between us as we reflected. I wanted in some way to crystallise my being in Anandwan with regards to my notes from the gutter. It appeared to break the rules of being poor, for I found it hard to look upon the community members, their basic needs covered yet receiving a tiny stipend which would likely deem them as being in poverty, and still I wasn't sure if I could call them poor people. It didn't fit with the bountiful environment in which they lived, the crops flourishing in the fields they tended, their forest home to green winged bee catchers and butterflies, and their days spent nurturing and providing for themselves and the community. I turned in my chair to face Manon, the brightest and closest stars now faintly blinking overhead.

"When you think about poverty, and when you see the people here, do you see them as poor people?"

"I think when I first came here I saw them as poor

people. I saw that they don't have this or they don't have that. But eventually through being here, I don't see them as poor people. One of the things that Baba Amte said was that, *The poor have big hearts and the rich people have no hearts.*"

Not wanting to be side-tracked, I nevertheless feel it's only fair to say this statement could be challenged both by definition of rich and poor, and also by the examples where a rich person uses their wealth to better enable the poor, through funding of schools in deprived areas, or donations made to projects such as Anandwan. Much of its existence is dependent on the donations it receives from those financially able to give, and at the same time equally moved by the work of the community, and wishing to support it.

"I totally understand what he was saying now," continued Manon. "Even though the people here don't seem to have a lot, but what they have is joy. I see their joy. I see their pride when they're doing things. When I'm at the wound clinic, and I do a lot of women there, and then when I walk to the other end of the lake after work, I see a lot of them there cutting grass. Before I get so close to them I watch them; they're talking, and humming, and singing, and seem to have that camaraderie. To me that's rich: rich in joy, rich in happiness. I think that when you have a lot you are always looking for something else. When you don't have so much, what you really hold onto is the joy and the happiness and the community. Here you have to remember that these are people who got rejected, no one cared for them. They came here and now they're accepted. They're cared for and loved by the community."

Manon paused and bit her lower lip in thought.

"I spent some time yesterday with the ladies that are deaf and they sew the uniforms, and there is a woman there, her hearing fine but who has no legs. She is absolutely amazing. I asked her story of coming to be here.

She was born walking. She was walking until she was two and then she got immunisation and got polio from it and stopped walking. She's thirty-one. All this time until she was twenty-nine she lived at home. No one cared for her. All she did was look after the family, sweeping and all that kind of stuff. So basically she was a nuisance, and felt so depressed, no joy, no love in her life. And she heard about this place and came. Her parents gave her a really hard time about coming here, but they said okay and let her come for a year. She's been here three years. She loves it here. She's so free. She has a bike, the three-wheeled trike and she's going all over the place. Not only that, she has so much love, so much love, and she gives that to all the children she teaches to sew. And you can see that; I was there for over an hour with her and the children, they hug each other and they talk. Everything that she didn't have at home, she found here. She has so much joy because of it. She's learning English, she knows sign language and she has a life. She loves it here and would never go back."

XVII

In the final days we would spend in Anandwan, Jyotie was taken to the nearest hospital, around two hours away, for a check-up and to receive treatment for sties which had made her eyelids swell. It was meant to be a day visit, and as such I never got to say goodbye as the treatment meant she had to stay in hospital for a few days. This also resulted in me having nothing scheduled for my last afternoons. I decided to follow up my conversation with Manon and look for the woman she had mentioned, the one who had contracted polio when she was two and who had apparently found her life changed by coming to Anandwan.

Early afternoon on New Year's Eve, I walked to the textile workshop and school. I entered into a room full of desks topped by sewing machines with girls sat before them concentrating as they worked on the fabric being pulled through their machine, the needle seaming it together. Shama was sitting on one of the desks in the room; she was overseeing the students as they sewed their uniforms. The girls all stopped work to turn and wave at me as I walked past their desks. I came to stand in front of Shama. She smiled as I introduced myself and said that Manon had mentioned her story to me. The sewing machines began to fire up again as the girls were told to focus. Shama was wearing a beautiful dress that draped down from the table. If not for my conversation with Manon, I wouldn't have known that she was missing the lower part of her legs from the knee down. I wanted to hear about her coming to Anandwan in her own words and asked her about the circumstances that led her here.

"I stayed in my home," she said. "My confidence was very low. I was alone."

A machine rattled away on the table next to us, filling the room with a noise resembling the distant sound of machine gun fire.

"I was really alone. My friend told to me, 'You are alone. Your confidence is low. You go to Anandwan.' I had never been away and stayed in another place. My family said, 'No, you can't go to Anandwan.'"

"Was that because of this being a community for leprosy patients, did they fear you catching the disease?"

"No. No. No. I just one daughter, my mum and dad wanted me to stay. I came just one time to see the place, with my friend. I saw the canteen. I liked that very much, that the handicapped person has tricycle, and happiness. I decided to come for one year and I came."

After arriving, Shama completed classes in tailoring and within a short time gained the experience and knowledge to begin teaching. Her days are now surrounded by friends and students and the wide smile which often graces her face reflected this. I asked her about the polio she contracted when she was little and how this happened.

"I am two years old and I have fever in the night. My family took me to the hospital and the doctor is injection me. The following morning, both legs in polio and hands also. Another doctor told my mum and dad that my upper body is okay, but my lower body was not."

"Were you able to go to school when you were a child?"

"My dad teach me."

"Did you have any friends?"

"No, I shy. No friends, friends would talk to me but not enjoy with me. They not talk to me about boys and girls. I alone sit on my bench and read my books. But now I not shy. I got friends. I have my most friends."

"In Anandwan," I said.

"In Anandwan," she replied.

"And so what does Anandwan mean to you?"

"Anandwan is a very sweet place. Anandwan makes a confidence in the handicapped person. And Anandwan makes a happiness in your face. I was not happy in my home, but now I am very happy in Anandwan. Baba Amte saved me."

That night the meditation room was transformed into a cheap yet wonderful disco. The group all chose some of their favourite songs to dance to and we enjoyed celebrating the passing of 2014 and eventually came together to cheer the New Year in. We were soon to leave this community made up of those who had once found themselves as outcasts and of little value. My bias as a writer, a fault I am aware of, was in perhaps searching out the negative to convey the suffering I saw. However, I will always look back and see Anandwan as that special place where almost everyone walks with a smile and an eager greeting of *Namaste* when you pass them. It is a place that should not need to exist for the fact that it does show a failing in society, and this failing goes beyond the borders of India. Something Nathan said when we were first being introduced to Anandwan reinforced this:

"It's important to remember that this is not an intentional community; people don't choose to live here. They're forced to live here because their society doesn't accept them. Dr Vikas, Baba's son, who in a way is co-running the project although it's in the charge of his son, he says that he's the chief jailor of the biggest prison on earth, which is a stark way of expressing the situation here. Although I'm guessing that a lot of the people who are now living here aren't looking to escape prison, aren't looking to get back out to society. Because this is now not just a place to come because there's nowhere better to be, but a place that's better to be than anywhere else you could wish to be."

A failing, if recognised and challenged, can lead to a positive outcome. Anandwan is a living example of this. I can appreciate why it is proudly seen by those who live in and maintain it as a forest of joy.

On New Year's Day I repacked my backpack and sat on the steps leading up to Rest House, contemplating my three-day train journey to Kolkata. I was going from a place that demanded a chance not charity, to a city renowned by the life and legacy of an Albanian nun who offered charity to the desperately poor.

XVIII

Letter for V written on the Howrah Mall travelling from Chennai to Kolkata.

4th January 2015
Hello you,

Not having anything to write on, I'm afraid you get my used ticket. It's nearing midday and I have less than twenty hours of my train trip from Chennai to Kolkata to go. It's hard to write as the train is rocking and rolling. I'm in a cabin of four beds. I have one of the top bunks, the opposing one is taken by a young Indian chap, presently dozing. The bottom two beds are occupied by an Indian couple, around seventy years old. The man has a fabulous white beard, and is wearing formal white dress with a button-like hat on his head; his wife is dressed in a turquoise sari and giving out snacks to three family members who have just come in and sat beside us. Now the familiar call of 'Chai. Coffee. Chai. Coffee' is sounding from the corridor. It feels busy in here with the seven bodies making the temperature rise against the cool breeze entering through the vents in the roof. The family is now sharing ghee sweets and conversation.

The trains in India are a world unto themselves; first I've to try and learn all the names of the different things that the sellers call out as they walk up and down the carriages; to take care to always keep an eye on the train when stopped at a platform after taking the opportunity to stretch my legs, it's pulled away twice already without warning and I had to run to jump back into the moving carriage; then a chap appears holding a scrap of cardboard and pencil to ask the passengers if they would like lunch and dinner. The meal is then brought to you and always very good; normally rice, dhal and roti. It costs around 100 rupees (a little over £1).

Yesterday I passed almost the entire day hanging around Chennai Central Station. I arrived following another overnight journey from Anandwan with some of the group members. I said goodbye to them and began the work of keeping myself amused during the long wait until my train departed that same evening. The first thing I did was to go to the station's bookshop. I purchased part one of a mythological trilogy about Shiva, a fictional interpretation of him being Shiva the mortal man and becoming Shiva the Great God, or the Destroyer. It's four hundred pages long and I'm already three hundred pages through. I expect to finish it by sundown. It's quite simply written, and I wouldn't say it's the greatest writing I've come across, but the escapism is perfect. It's sold over two million copies, yet while reading it I want to colour it in more, give the characters more physical and emotional definition, and strip the contemporary slang from the dialogue as it spoils all illusion of its apparent setting of 1900BC. Not wanting to carry a trilogy around with me perhaps I'll send the book to you with this letter.

Can you read this, V? I forget myself sometimes and my words get so slim that they appear like broken lines in themselves.

Lunch, siesta, reading, and then this…

> Wow, I've got to tell you about my last thirty minutes.
> I was stood at an open door in a train carriage, holding
> onto the sides and leaning as much as I dared forwards
> and into the powerful wind of movement. The train
> rattled forwards at speed and I just stood starry eyed,
> watching the beautiful world of greens and browns
> streaming by. We travelled through a basin of paddy
> fields, rice I believe, with the occasional palm tree, oxen
> drawn plough or distant mountain catching the eye.
> It's one of those experiences that can rid all thoughts
> and distractions from the mind, a euphoria brought
> about by the dress of Nature and the awareness of
> death being just a silly slip away; falling from a moving
> train at high speed would certainly do it. I made sure I
> held on tight.
>
> I've returned to my cabin and am now sat with
> another chai; I think I've had three in the last two
> hours, but they are small and sweet so it's hard to say
> no when the 'Chai. Coffee. Chai. Coffee' appears at
> the door.
>
> The couple just pointed out that a cockroach was
> on my bag. I tossed it out into the corridor but it
> has already found its way back through a vent in the
> door. So these are a few words from a train running
> along a track somewhere in India. It will soon be
> dusk and I'm going to finish reading the last few
> pages of my book. It's not very good and I don't
> know why I can't put it down.
>
> I miss you deeply, M. x

XIX

Kolkata. Oh my, Kolkata. How to make your vividness, your yellow taxi filled streets, your constant demand to be noticed, the rubbish, the market sellers, the food stands and the people who walk up and down your dirty and yet strangely beautiful body stand out in words as you stretched out before my eyes, your limbs throbbing with life? Kolkata. Oh my, Kolkata.

It was still dark when I disembarked from the Howrah Mall. She had carried me the 1,662 kilometres from Chennai, the journey lasting almost thirty hours. A thousand or more strangers poured out onto the platform around me.

Of course they'll know, I reassured myself, spotting the yellow Prepaid Taxi Stand sign above the bobbing heads as I followed the masses out of the station.

I then waited in a long line of people for an hour; the parallel line of yellow taxis moved slowly forward in unison with the people, one step forward meant another taxi had been filled and was hurtling off into a city I knew very little about, the brake lights blinking with their horns fading into the distance. Another step forward, my backpack rubbed on tarmac as I pushed it forward with my foot.

"Hotel Galaxy, *Sudder* Street," I said quietly to myself, not knowing if I was to pronounce it *Sud-der Street* or *Sudder Street*.

I had made the classic mistake upon arriving in a new city; I didn't have the full address or a contact number of the hotel where I was staying in case difficulties arose. I could only hope my taxi driver was as hot as a London cabbie when it came to knowing the many streets of the largest city in East India, with a population swelling to almost 4.5 million. I had been complacent in not taking note of my hotel's particulars for reason that Sudder Street was renowned, or so I thought, as the tourist capital, and where many of the foreigners stay who come to the city to volunteer with the Missionaries of Charity, founded by Mother Teresa, or another of the projects that work with the poor.

"Where you go?" the man inside the booth asked as I finally got my chance to stand before it.

"Hotel Galaxy, *Sudder* Street."

"130 rupees," the man in the booth replied.

"Great," I said. *That was easy*, I added silently.

I paid the man and in exchange he gave me a printed slip of paper.

"Second lane," he said. "Taxi number, 605."

"Thank you."

I took the docket and lifted my backpack, beginning to work my way along the line of taxis, inspecting their front wings and the numbers painted on them. *605…605…605… Here.* I waved at the driver through the windscreen and he gestured for me to get in the back.

The yellow Ambassador taxis are a moving icon of the city. They are spacious, their suspension is soft and bouncy after hitting potholes or bumps, and their drivers, I was to learn, are not at all like a London cabbie. I got in the back and passed him the docket with my destination printed on it. He looked at it and then he looked at it some more before the taxis behind us began to honk their horns. He started the engine and we drove away from the station; he continued to look at the docket still held in his left hand with his right hand steering the moving vehicle.

"You go to hotel?"

"Yes, Hotel Galaxy, near to Sudd-er Street."

"Hotel Galaxy," he repeated.

"Yes, near to Sud-der street."

"Hotel Galaxy. Hotel Galaxy," he said again.

I knew there and then, he had no clue where my hotel or Sudder Street was. *Bugger it*, echoed through my mind.

"It's not too far from Mother Teresa's House," I said.

"You go to Mother Teresa?"

"No, not far from Mother Teresa's house."

"Not stay Mother Teresa?"

"No, Hotel Galaxy, near to Sudder Street."

He turned the wheel and steered the car almost subconsciously around the slower vehicles in the road ahead, with his attention remaining divided between the printed ticket and the act of driving.

"Hotel Galaxy," he said to himself again. "Hotel Galaxy." *He's no idea where to go, no clue whatsoever.*

Thirty minutes later and we pulled up alongside yet another Ambassador. My driver had already stopped next to five en route to ask for directions. He called out his window to the fellow taxi driver who was parked in a quiet street and dozing in his seat. It was still dark and around five in the morning.

"Hotel Galaxy?" my driver shouted at him.

Through a series of hand movements, the other driver indicated that it was just around the corner. He then leaned his head back on the headrest and closed his eyes. We drove on, negotiating a tight corner between concrete buildings to drive up Stuart Lane, walled by the buildings on both sides with litter having been swept and piled into the curbs.

"Here," I said, seeing the name of the hotel on the front of a building. "It's here, on the left."

We pulled up outside the building and the driver leaned forward to look up at the sign above the entrance.

"Ah, Hotel Galaxy," he said.

Three hours later I was awake and feeling very much alive

after a stroll around the neighbouring streets. Red fire engines were stationary and being cleaned outside the fire brigade headquarters at the end of Sudder Street; the firemen stood in the morning sun talking and sipping small clay cups of chai. It was still to make sense to me. The chai sellers, either the hole-in-the-wall type or wheeled carts with gas bottles beneath and hot stoves on top, heating the sweet and milky beverages in milk crusted pans, would serve their chai in these handmade and kiln baked terracotta containers, known as *kulhars*. I presumed they were handmade for the wobbles in their lips and the small differences and imperfections in their shapes and sizes. A chai would cost 4 rupees from these stands, served in a handle-less *kulhar*, its sweet and gingery tones meeting the lips with earth as I tasted the clay rim of the cup before the liquid inside it. The *kulhar*, soon empty, is simply thrown onto the ground, often cracking as it hits the tarmac. Around the chai sellers it was not uncommon to find piles of them clogging the gutters. I tried to work out the economics of it but failed; the cost of the ingredients: tea, sugar, ginger, and milk along with the cost of the gas and the disposable clay cups, and yet a cup of chai was still only 4 rupees to buy, no more than four English pence. Failing to comprehend the profit in it for the chai seller, I simply savoured the taste. It tasted how I'd come to see Hinduism: mysterious, mythical, shining bright and adorned with overtones of the divine.

I walked and I passed a run of small street stalls on Dr MD Ishaque Road, running parallel to Sudder Street. The sun warmed away the last of the early morning chill from the air and the stalls emitted scents of spices and burning oil as they made *puri*, small discs of deep fried unleavened Indian bread, a typical breakfast served with a potato based curry. A man was sat on the ground between the food stands, odd pairs of shoes scattered around him as he was in the process of repairing the sole of one, open tins of polish beside him. There was a barber too, applying foam with a brush to the chin of his day's first client; a small mirror was hung from a nail hammered into the redbrick wall the traders worked in front of. The man in the barber's chair had a linen cloth placed beneath his chin. The barber tapped his shoulder and he tilted his head back for the razor blade to gently scratch away the stubble on his neck.

I walked and I turned down Chowringhee Lane, leading back towards Sudder Street; it was still only eight o'clock so the road was quiet of taxis and people. I passed a barber's shop near the end and peered through the window, an old man was polishing the large wall mirrors above the wash basins, the rag in his hand making quick circles over the glass. I still hadn't been able to check into my room as it was too early and I hadn't showered since braving the bathing cubicles in Chennai Station, which had been a tantalising dousing in cold buckets of water. My hair was greasy and knotted. The man with the rag saw me at the door and stopped polishing.

"Are you open?" I asked.

"Thirty minutes," he replied.

"No problem, I'll come back."

He nodded and returned to his work. I walked away and joined Sudder Street, passing the many cafés and cupboard shops, as I call them; a man sits behind a counter with the three walls crowding around him and laden with snacks, toiletries and cigarettes – the staples of the Westerners that frequent Sudder Street. Taxis were parked along the road and the drivers called out at me as I walked past.

"Taxi, sir?"

I declined their offers. I approached a blue cart on my left; a man was busy behind it displaying bottles of water before pumping gas into his stove and putting his free hand over the flame to test its temperature. He saw me and waved.

"Coffee for you, I make best coffee in Kolkata. Not Nescafé, Italian coffee, fresh coffee."

I was lured. I walked over and sat on a long wooden chest placed beside the cart on the pavement, inside the chest is where he kept his stock.

"Sounds great, can you make it black?"

"Of course," he replied. "You want sugar?"

"No, thank you."

He began busying himself with grinding beans in an electric grinder while filling the bottom chamber of a stove top coffee maker with water, before inserting the basket and spooning the ground coffee into it, finally screwing on the upper chamber and resting it on the stove, the flames climbing around it. I asked him his name.

"Manik," he said. "You?"

"Matthew."

"You be happy you found me. I make good coffee, real coffee."

"Looking forward to it."

I left Manik to continue displaying the water bottles as the water boiled in the lower chamber of the stove top, before the high heat would create a pressure as it expanded, forcing it up and through the ground coffee, extracting flavour and wonderful caffeine, which would then empty into the top chamber in a treacle-like black liquid. Black gold as it is sometimes known. I wrote in my notebook as I waited for the stove top to whistle and the lid to jump as the pressure and steam escaped in angry raids. A shadow came over me and I looked up from my words to see a woman stood before me. She was an old woman, a dull sari around her small body with a veil covering the most part of her long grey hair. Her cheeks were full of dark wrinkles and the skin on the edges of her heels was cracked and dry, her leather sandals old and scratched. I looked at her for a moment, not sure why she had come to stand so close to me, but then she outstretched one of her hands with her palm facing up.

"I'm sorry," I said.

It's a foreign and meaningless word to her but I had nothing else. I decided that I could not give money to the beggars on the streets, especially in areas like Sudder Street where so many poor people cumulated to beg for money from the tourists. Giving money to her was prolonging her plight as it reinforced the expectation of receiving hand-outs, it reinforced her dependence. Yet what else could she do? I suddenly felt like a selfish prick, sat with rupees in my pocket and about to enjoy a freshly ground 'Italian style' coffee in her country where she was desperately poor. She raised her hand to her mouth and then gestured to the large kettle that was rested on the blue cart.

"You would like a chai?"

"Chai," she whispered.

I smiled and asked Manik if he could pour a chai for her and he did so, and I asked for a biscuit from one of the many jars on the stand. I stood and lifted the warm glass of chai and biscuit from the cart and offered them to her.

"Thank you," she said, which I found strange as saying thank you is not custom in Indian culture.

The woman carefully held her drink and biscuit and moved to sit down with me on the chest. Manik shouted at her and thrust his hand to signal for her to move away. She did and I felt bad for not saying to Manik that I didn't mind her sitting beside me, but I think it was not that he was thinking about me but instead potential customers passing on the street who might not want to sit near to the old woman. After all, she might have lice, she might smell of nights spent on the dirty roadside, or worst of all she might try and beg something out of them too. She scuttled a couple of steps away from the stand and crouched down in the sunshine, facing the road with the chai glass now placed on the pavement before her. She dunked the biscuit into the liquid and ate it quickly. She then reached into a fold of her sari and pulled out a parcel of tin foil. Pulling back the foil I saw a slice of white bread inside, cut into fingers like my mum would cut my toast into soldiers when I was little so I could dunk them into my boiled eggs. The old woman looked at me and lifted the bread, gesturing for me to have a piece.

"Oh, no thank you."

She continued to gesture and I could not refuse her. I stood. I felt the pavement move like a current of water beneath my feet as I walked over to take a piece of the bread between my fingers, I was swept away with her wanting to share her food with me. She had most likely begged for it and it was likely to be all she had until successfully begging something else.

I returned to the chest with the morsel of bread and thanked her. She smiled and sunk a piece into the tea and I too took a bite. It had been simply buttered and sprinkled with salt. The lid of the stove top began to jump and the steam whistled as it was forced through an escape valve in the lower chamber. Manik lifted it from the gas and poured my coffee into a glass. He placed it beside me on the chest. I sat chewing my bread and sipping my coffee and the woman, crouched two steps away from me, sipped her chai and chewed her bread.

I suddenly recalled a scene from part one of the Shiva trilogy that I had finished on the train the previous evening. Shiva had embarked on a righteous war with the Meluhans, an almost utopian society who had welcomed him as their leader, battling against the neighbouring land home to the Chandravanshis, who lived, Shiva had first thought, in a base and broken society, where poverty was ravenous and lurid acts of debauchery were on public display. After winning the war, Shiva arrived with the Meluhans to the enemy's capital city where he began to search out the evil he had wrongly envisaged the Chandravanshis to live under. Lost in his thoughts about perhaps not having been right in his decision to conquer these people and to then civilise them, he walked to the temple where he saw a man, appearing as though starved, on the ground. He was nursing a small portion of food which he invited Shiva to join him in eating. Shiva refused, not wanting to take anything from the man for he surely had so little. Yet the man insisted and Shiva realised that by not accepting the man's gracious offer he was insulting him, seeing him as something other than himself, and denying him the presence of his company. This hungry man humbled Shiva to such an extent that Shiva became angry with himself for being so ignorant as to think he could ever redeem such a man, for the man had instead redeemed him. The Great God Shiva prostrated before him, touching his feet, forever changed.

My first day in Kolkata passed with many wanderings. First I explored the neighbouring Muslim quarter, with the market stands along the roadside busy with trade. Streams of small flags were hung up across the roads between the buildings displaying a star and crescent, a symbol associated with Islam. I believed they were to mark *Milad un-Nabi*, a holiday to commemorate the Prophet Muhammad's birthday which had passed the previous day. I then lost myself to the smaller alleyways where tiny shops were hidden away, similar size to the cupboard shops along Sudder Street. In one, two men were pressing t-shirts using a square sandwich iron; it reminded me of a giant toasty maker. Chai dens were spotted along the alleyways with men and their shadows drinking their glasses of chai and watching me walk by. I loved ambling through the veins of the Muslim quarter. When I arrived back to a main road, I would quickly scan the pavements for another break in the buildings and another alleyway, leading me deeper into the heart of the city.

Later I stopped for a bite to eat outside a restaurant on Alimudden Street. I had vegetable noodles and two veg rolls (not like Chinese rolls, bigger and with delicious chunks of stir-fried vegetables inside cooked in a sauce I can't name but a fine and fitting taste all the same). It cost me 54 rupees altogether, around 50 pence. I got to talking to a chap sat on a bench in the street beside mine, long beard growing from his chin and his belly a little paunchy. He questioned me about why we don't live with our parents in the West, or our parents live with us throughout our/their entire life. I explained a little about the difference in our culture, about the rarity for a child to grow up and stay in the same place as they are likely to go off to do degrees and seek employment. He chewed his food slowly; I think he was a little disgusted. Still, I liked the Muslim quarter, although the roadside butchers were quite the startling sight. After leaving the restaurant and heading back to Hotel Galaxy, a man cycled past me with over thirty live chickens tied upside down by their feet from the frame and handlebars of his bike. The noise they made was truly terrible.

Evening fell. I decided to head to a chai den I had passed earlier, one which I would soon come to see as my local. First entering Dr. Kamales K. R. Kapat's Sweet Shop the same feeling arose in me as the times when I had slowly entered into a cave, not knowing what I would find in the dark. It was a cavern of a place where the walls had been blackened by two centuries worth of wood smoke; the scratched and knotted wooden tables and benches were frequented by men of varying ages, eating samosas, sweets or sipping at their glasses of chai. It was a hangout for locals and I fell in love with it instantly. A middle-aged man greeted me on entry; he was sat next to a clay fire pit with a big metal drum placed above, water boiling inside. He made the chai and collected the clients' money. His friend and colleague, having worked at Dr. Kamales K. R. Kapat's Sweet Shop for over forty-five years, was stood behind the glass cabinets displaying trays of sweets, plating them for the customers. A boy, around nine or ten, would tarry between the tables, serving the plates of sweets and collecting empty chai glasses and finished plates. He would wash them at a sink beside the entrance. My chai was poured and the boy brought it over and I sat with my notebook and etched out a fabulous long history which I adorned to the blackened walls with my mind, dreaming up smuggling stories or it being a hideaway for the wanted or a chamber of secrets for the lost. I dreamed up so many things in that sweet and smoky cavern along Hartford Lane.

Saying goodnight to the men and boy I left the worlds I had been imagining behind me and stepped out onto the road. It was now busy as people walked from Sudder Street towards New Market, a massive bazar that had every material possession, and no doubt more, that a person could ever want or need in a lifetime. I followed the flow of human traffic. I arrived at a large road, the pavement clogged around the food stands and the many lights above the shops distracting. A dishevelled man was stood in a doorway, a crutch beneath one arm. He stumbled towards me.

"Please," he said, reaching out the hand not holding the crutch, "I am poor and handicapped. Please give me some change."

He limped to my side and I said I'm sorry, still unable to right or wrong my decision to not give money to beggars, no longer sure in myself or my convictions. I walked and he was no longer beside me. I turned and saw him now holding out his hand to the world, leaning on his crutch, as the waters of people broke and flowed around him. I thought back to those with physical impairments in Anandwan, how they lived and worked and supported themselves. The man being buried alive by society in Kolkata had two crutches, really; the one beneath his arm and the other being his dependence on another's goodwill and charity.

XX

Morning mass was held in a large room. The dawn sky was grey outside the windows, it was a grey I would ascribe to pollution but it wasn't entirely pollution, the sun had simply not fully arisen. A sister set about closing some of the windows, seeking a silence fitting for contemplation and yet the drone of the cars on A J.C. Bose Road below fought through the thin panes of glass, the horns pulled the mind from its prayers. The sisters took up the most part of the room, sat in still and silent lines on the floor with their study books in little stacks beside them and their bibles open on their laps as they worked through their morning prayers before the start of mass at 6am. A corner of the room, free of nuns, slowly began to fill up with internationals: Europeans, Latin Americans, Asians and Americans. They too entered the chapel and sat on the floor, most on their knees with their backs straight and palms pressed together before their chests as they faced the altar and closed their eyes.

A young woman from Argentina, also staying at Hotel Galaxy, had offered to show me the ropes of attending mass; she led me in and we sat also. She then passed me a laminated piece of paper listing the prayers which were to be said. I sat looking over them, and then I looked around and observed the gentle effort on the faces of the sisters, bringing forth a communion with God. They all faced the altar, their attention either with the written word of the Bible opened before them or the unwritten devotion to a god who they had committed their lives to. They wore the familiar white saris with blue bands. Seeing so many together I immaturely remembered seeing a video clip online; everyone in it was doing the same dance routine to Michael Jackson's 'Thriller', and they had all dressed like a zombified version of him, torn red leather jackets and their faces painted to be wretched and hungry for life after having come back from the dead. They held their crotches and thrust their hips in the trademark Jackson way. I looked at the sisters and saw one hundred or so women in Mother Teresa costumes. It was silly to think in this way, but then I looked at the framed pictures of Mother, as she was fondly called, on the wall, with her old and kindly face framed and protected from dust by the glass, her head covered in a white veil with three blue bands just above the forehead. The sisters in the chapel mirrored her image as they sat before her, as they mirrored her intentions to give their lives to doing 'God's work', after they had first renounced a worldly and material life in order to better understand His will, and to be closer to Him and their prayers.

The room was becoming smaller and smaller as more internationals arrived, searching out a space to sit. A sister at the back of the room began to speak, reciting a prayer and the sisters sat before her followed her lead. Some of the prayers I found beautiful, others wishy-washy, while one or two of them were simply divine, such as the Peace Prayer of Saint Francis of Assisi:

Lord, make me an instrument of Your peace;
Where there is hatred, let me sow love;
Where there is injury, pardon;
Where there is discord, harmony;
Where there is error, truth;
Where there is doubt, faith;
Where there is despair, hope;
Where there is darkness, light;

And where there is sadness, joy.
O Divine Master, grant that I may not so much seek
To be consoled as to console;
To be understood as to understand;
To be loved as to love.
For it is in giving that we receive;
It is in pardoning that we are pardoned;
And it is in dying that we are born to eternal life.

The mass began and I stood and I sat, then I stood and I sat again, as each new prayer was said and finished. I hadn't slept so well the previous night and all the standing and sitting was making me dizzy. Then some priests came in who were also volunteers for the Missionaries of Charity, they performed the Eucharist and those who wanted to share in the body of Christ lined up and stuck out their tongue for the priest to place an unleavened wafer onto it.

I sat and watched and didn't get it but felt something in the way the room was moved by a higher presence. I think I was looking for Jesus and couldn't see him. I wanted the rebellious and charismatic leader, downing the wine and tossing the shards of bread and his broken body into the air, yelling at us to be cautious of institution and religious rule and to be playful with the god in our hearts. I imagined Jesus dancing around the room, to 'Thriller', and yawning as the more mundane passages of the life he'd been ascribed were read aloud in order to remind us that we were all sinners, and Christ was our saviour and redeemer. My Jesus then jumped onto the altar and moonwalked backwards along it, his long hair flying and the candles falling onto the floor and the carpets bursting into flames; they climbed and he screamed above them as he spun like a skater on ice before grabbing his crotch and thrusting his hips forwards for his finale, *Don't follow me like little lost lambs, I'm long dead.* I shook my head and the altar, Bible again peacefully placed upon it, was no longer on fire and Jesus had returned to the cross on the wall, nails through his palms and feet, his head limp and fallen to one side, suffering. I was wrong to think mass was going to be dull.

J-e-e-e-zus, I said silently as though waking to find myself in a strange world after a trippy dream.

The mass came to an end and the sisters, following the priests, left in a slow line, their Bibles and study books held in their hands. The internationals made their way downstairs and past the chamber where Mother Teresa's white tomb rests; an Asian tour group was stood around it taking pictures. The volunteers amassed in a room where they were given breakfast: two slices of white bread, a banana and cup of chai. More internationals made their way in, those not moved to go to mass or perhaps not Catholic, but still wanting to join the Missionaries of Charity and go to one of Mother's houses where they could serve the poor. This was my reason for coming, and I had gone to mass to get the full Mother Teresa experience. More and more bodies crammed into the breakfast room. I was amazed how many volunteers there were, enough to form a small army. I nibbled on my slice of unbuttered bread, washing it down with chai and again retreating into my thoughts as my friend from Argentina was in a conversation with a Mexican, their Spanish beautiful but too quick for me to keep up with. I instead recalled what had moved me to come here, to this house now overseeing Mother Teresa's legacy.

Two months before leaving for India, I was sat in a friend's garden in Bath when she asked me about my travel plans. I told her about joining a community where people with leprosy could find inclusion and purpose, and then how I might travel east to learn more about extreme poverty by volunteering with Mother Teresa's charity. My friend's response was immediate and stayed with me as my notes from the gutter finally led me to Mother House on

A J.C. Bose Road in the Indian city of Kolkata.

"Mother Teresa?" said my friend. "She wanted to keep them poor."

This conversation in an English garden turning red and brown with autumn was enough for me to want to know more about Mother Teresa, and to try to see beyond the saint she had been likened to. I also wanted to recognise the controversial aspects of her life and work. So I read a book written about her by the late Christopher Hitchens; the book itself was received controversially, as he presented a sound and rather unglamorous portrayal of the Albanian nun who gave her life to serving the poor. Hitchens was attacked by many for his work and others said that his dislike of institutionalised religion meant his argument was biased against Mother Teresa. I disagree. *The Missionary Position*, as the book was boldly titled, is a piece of clear and concise journalism, written by an excellent writer and professional. His presentation of some of the more ugly truths is backed up by records and testimonies and he doesn't write with anger or bitterness, but with clarity and judgement. The book questions Mother Teresa's engagement with some not very savoury world leaders and powerful figures; it reflects her strict view on abortion, including her counsel given to rape victims to maintain the life savagely implanted inside them; he raised questions about where the vast donations of money the Missionaries of Charity received were channelled, and the thing that struck me the most was Mother Teresa's view that poverty, for those afflicted by it, was a gift and a means to strengthen their commitment to God. I finished the book the day before I left England, and I didn't read any others about her life or work, and I know there to be many more publications that pay homage to her rather than attack. Still, it was enough for me to want to see the work the charity does, and how the poor are treated.

As breakfast ended a sister stood on a bench to rise

above the volunteers and make a speech, pleading with us not to make relationships with the paid workers in the houses where we were to volunteer, that our intention was to serve the poor people and not to make social engagements with the staff. "They are paid to work," she said.

A shutter at one end of the breakfast room was then opened; the pavement and the road were on the other side of it, now coloured by daylight, traffic and people. The volunteers began to go out in their groups, to scatter across the city and to the different poor houses established for the old, the sick, the young, the mentally ill and the dying. I waited in a small group of new arrivals for the sister to instruct us as to where we would be going. When it was my turn to stand before her, she asked my age.

"Twenty-nine," I said.

She stood and thought for a moment as her pen waited over a small slip of paper which was to inform the sister in the house where I was going to volunteer that I would be joining them. The sister before me began to write.

"I'm going to send you to Nirmal Hriday."

Outside Mother House I joined with two Latin Americans who were also heading to Nirmal Hriday, which means the home of the pure heart. It was located in Kalighat, a busy and colourful area in Kolkata and also home to the Kalighat temple, one of the main tourist attractions in the city. The temple was built in honour of Kali, the fierce Hindu goddess of empowerment, or *shakti*. After a bumpy city bus ride from Mother House we walked along Kalighat road past the *holi* sellers, their tabletops displaying bags of the deep coloured powder which is used to colour the world during the *holi* festival in spring, a celebration of colour and love. Ahead a white building rose up before us. I saw Jesus first, on a cross near the roof; *I Thirst* was written on the wall beneath his crucified body. Steps led up to the door; there was a ghost of a man lying on the stone beside it and pressed up against the building, a poor man at the door to a poor house. We climbed the steps and I read the words written above the entrance, *Mother Teresa's Home for the Dying Destitute*. I braced myself for what I was about to see.

We entered into a large building separated into two quarters, one for men and the other for women. I was taken to the men's section; two groups of volunteers were already washing clothes in large baths, wringing out the water-heavy blankets in pairs. The men were sat on benches and they fronted varying degree of ages, disfigurements or mental disorders, and some didn't display much in the way of suffering or illness at all. I was expecting a squalid den of meek lives having prayers said over them as they lay dying. I instead found large organised rooms of stone floors which could be easily cleaned, wounds which had been neatly wrapped and then covered by a plastic bag to stop flies getting to them. I instantly recalled massaging legs in Anandwan with the flies terrorising some of the wounds and wounded. The men were all wearing green and tidy clothes, and the band of volunteers busied around them comforting, massaging, later feeding and then washing the many plates. Out of the forty or so residents, there was one man in the home who was not sat in the dining area but instead under a blanket on his bed in the dorm; half of his face was lost to a gross cancer and he really was there to pass into the beyond. Yet fluid was given to him, and he was cleaned and made as comfortable as possible.

I pitched in. First hand washing clothes with a group of Germans, and later giving massages with coconut oil. I was moved as a man took my hands after I had finished massaging his arms, bringing them to his mouth and kissing them. I watched a charismatic Frenchman from Dijon go around with a razor blade, shaving foam and small cup of water, a towel over his shoulder. He placed a stool before the men and shaved their cheeks, chins and necks. I tried to talk to the one resident who spoke English well enough to converse. I asked him how long he will stay in the house and what had led him to be here. He was spritely and cheery and liked to tell jokes, and replied to my questions with a jovial smile and kept leading me back to Genesis, explaining it was all because Adam and Eve had eaten the apple, which angered God as he had forbidden them to. I thanked him for talking to me. We washed the many steel plates in a system of four sinks and then helped the paid workers to fold some of the now dry clothes. A bell then rang loudly and the morning was done. The residents were to go to their beds until 3pm and rest; the volunteers' service was complete.

I went upstairs to grab my woolly hat I'd left in a locker, a morning chill now breezes through the city as winter fluffs the folds of her dress. I chatted to the other volunteers for a bit and then we left, passing the men now under blankets or sat on their beds. We walked out the door and I looked down at the hungry man still pressed up against the base of the wall, with a framed picture on Mother Teresa beside the entrance and above him. *He's poor*, I thought, turning as Nirmal Hriday's door was pushed closed to visitors between the hours of noon and three.

I have nothing bad to write about my morning with Mother Teresa's charity, and perhaps my imagination will have some riled and angered by my lightness of experience during morning mass. At Nirmal Hriday I was pleasantly surprised to see how clean the house was, and it was fun to work with the other internationals and learn their stories. In truth I don't really know where my thoughts rest about the charity, it is clearly feeding and helping those who need food and assistance, yet what that means in the long run is hard to say. When does the poverty end, or doesn't it – is this what I must accept? I thought about the temple to the Goddess Kali just a stone's throw away, and the meaning of *shakti*. Had I been sent to another house, the children's perhaps, would empowerment have been more central to the charity's aims? I don't know. Leaving Kalighat and passing the low tables of *holi* powder, the road around them coloured red from where the powder had been spilt, I made the decision not to return to the Missionaries of Charity. I was in Kolkata for a relatively short time, and the ghost of the man at the door to Mother Teresa's first home established for the poor in 1952 was telling me I needed to take my notes back to the streets and write from the gutter.

XXI

Message sent to group members from Anandwan, Monday 12th January 2015.

Dear all,

I have been in Kolkata for almost a week. I had planned to join the Missionaries of Charity and went along one morning to one of the poor houses where I worked. For various reasons I have decided not to volunteer with the sisters, primarily because there is already an army of volunteers and I also wish to use my time to better understand poverty in the city, whereas in the homes it is dressed-up and tended to, still real but with the roots now hard to see.

On my second evening in Kolkata I was walking down a dark and busy road towards some food stands. In the doorway ahead a man was propped up on a crutch. He saw me approaching and he stepped out and towards me, limping to my side and raising his hand. 'Please,' he said. 'I am poor and handicapped, please give me some change.' I instantly thought back to the forest of bliss where hands were raised to tend to something or work something into being, not to beg. The following night I saw a man pull a wooden plank on wheels by a rope along Sudder Street, the main tourist street. On the cart a deformed and immobile man was on his back, there was a speaker playing music and a dish containing coins placed on his chest. He was pulled close to a group of tourists, and they were asked to be compassionate and help this sick and handicapped man. I can now quite clearly see the joy that Anandwan can bring to a life which is impaired by sickness or ill health, whereas the city can be unaccepting and as a result a showpiece is made of suffering and begging is all that is left.

It was lovely to have shared a moment in time with you all and I wish you well for your onward journeys.

My warm wishes, Matthew.

XXII

I'm in my room in Hotel Galaxy. It's now early evening and quite dark already. I can hear a wooden cart being pulled along Stuart Lane below my window, and the all too familiar sound of hooting car horns echoing over and around the city. My German roommate, tall, blonde, always to the point, who speaks English with a Canadian accent, has gone out, leaving me to potter around the room with my thoughts. I spent the day catching up on my notes, rereading some of my reflections and questioning my sanity for having shared my vision of Jesus moonwalking across the altar in Mother House. I then had a vision of my editor pulling out her lovely hair. Still, I feel no more sane or insane than days past so I have decided not to omit it.

After sitting with my own words for much of the morning, I then opted to take John Green's *The Fault in Our Stars* for a walk to find a quiet spot where I could read. After the film adaption had left me shattered on the flight from Heathrow to Mumbai I wanted to see how the book compared. I think about V a lot as I read it, not that either of us has cancer or is terminally ill, but still she comes to me. I guess the narrative brings about uncomfortable images of something happening to her/ me while I'm away, and that we only shared a fleeting few weeks together. My mind runs away and I think up all the things I should have said before saying goodbye to her in Bath Spa Station on an otherwise non-descript late November day. I should have let her know how much she means to me or how it feels to hold her in the early hours of the morning, our breathing filling the night-time silence. Distance and separation is a constant reminder to the things we hold dear in life.

It's hard to find a quiet spot to sit and be still in Kolkata; the city whirls on like a spinning top that never slows. A wheel of fortune that people can't step off of as being out of the game is not an option; it's not a question of being in it to win it, but being in it to survive. Society is demanding and life has its costs. We all have to pay for it somehow.

I ended up resting against a tree trunk in Maiden. The expanse of open grass was being enjoyed by many of the city's inhabitants, playing games of cricket, football, or simply sat in pairs or groups as the sun began to lower into the rose sky with its flaming body smeared by haze. I read three chapters, enjoying the feel of bark on my back with the mad rush of the city momentarily put to the back of my mind as the car horns honked and billboards lit up behind me.

Walking to Maiden I was approached by five separate people on the pavement; they begged for money. I also passed three people under filthy blankets, the Living Dead I have come to think of them, their hearts beating but not much life to be seen. What can be done to alleviate the streets of such a terrible thing? Yet there are so many people in the world, is it just a case of simple mathematics and logic to suggest that there will always be some who don't make it? They instead fall out of employment, out of an income, a home and society altogether. Poverty is messy and ugly and circumstantial. So far all I could conclude with conviction was that poverty was not going to go away anytime soon, if ever.

The sun sank some more and I closed my book. I stood and walked away with my back to the sunset as I headed towards a busy carriageway with concrete buildings rising up alongside it. I ran across the road holding *The Fault in Our Stars* and my notebook tightly in my hand, stopping and starting in order to negotiate the lanes of traffic bearing down on me. Across the street I saw a big billboard beaming Mother Teresa's face over the heads of those clogging the pavement below; it was a photo taken of her when she had been very old, her palms are pressed together and raised before her mouth, her eyes are closed and she appears to be in prayer. The billboard was advertising a philanthropist exhibition and in the top right corner was a quote attributed to Mother Teresa: *If you can't feed one hundred people, then feed just one.* I looked up at this little old lady turned black and white and then saw images of the men in the Home of the Dying Destitute where I had spent a morning, being fed their meals and then moving to their beds to follow the schedule outlined for them by the sisters. How long will they be fed for? What happens if they don't die and they live long lives, will the feeding keep on going?

The pavement was no place to stand still and gawk up at Mother Teresa as I was being bumped and pushed by the bodies passing me. I turned and walked. Not fifty yards from the billboard, the pavement now wider, I saw a young girl sitting crossed-legged on the ground; there was an even smaller boy outstretched on his back across her lap, his head flopped back for his crown of glossy black hair to rest on the pavement. He was asleep. On the pavement in front of the girl was a small silver dish with a couple of rupees in it. My sight lingered on her as I neared; my stomach began to fill with this horrible emptiness that I ascribed to helplessness. There was something different about her, about the way she begged. She wasn't engaged with her begging like those I had passed earlier. Normally a beggar's eyes would be fixed on trying to meet with those that are walking past them; their hands would follow the passer-by and guide them to the silver dish and they would say something, they would plead with them to part with some rupees. Yet this girl's eyes were fixed on the window of the Domino's pizza restaurant which she was sat outside of. I thought it must have been the sight of people eating their pizza out of the boxes inside, the slices dripping with melted cheese and tasty toppings. I slowed as I passed her and turned my head to look through the window. Above the hatch where the pizza boxes were distributed a flat screen television was fixed on the wall, playing a music video. I looked back and down at the girl on the pavement; she was so glued to the television that she hadn't seen me pass her. *She's just a normal child*, I thought. *She likes television and music and escapism.* But then she wasn't a normal child, really, for no child should be sat on the pavement holding another child and stricken. Her little brown eyes remained on the window and the television behind it. I lowered my head and continued walking. I wish I didn't count and paint a memory for all the beggars and Living Dead I passed, as they all stay with me, they all haunt me. I feel weaker too for all I can do when I pass them is say a pathetic and disempowering, *I'm sorry.*

XXIII

I like to walk. It's a way to better taste and feel the environment around me, often becoming a blurry or fleeting snapshot of life when travelling in a vehicle. In a new city and wanting to go somewhere, I look on a map and find my direction and any landmarks en route to maintain my bearing and then I set off, walking and soaking in all I can as I go.

This morning I decided to walk to the Botanical Garden that is located on the other side of the Hooghly River. The river slices between Kolkata and Howrah, a separate city that nevertheless falls into the Kolkata metropolis with Howrah Station being one of the main transport hubs. I was drawn to the garden because, quite simply, I had heard it was lovely, but I'd also read a research paper about the city's slums and learned there to be a small slum lining the canal which flowed next to the garden. I thought I could see how this slum compared to the tent homes I had seen pitched with sticks and fabric outside Bandra station in Mumbai. I carried my notebook in my bag and had taken the effort to properly tighten my shoelaces as I believed the walk was going to be an hour or more. I stopped only at my favourite chai stand at the end of Stuart Lane.

Sweetened and warmed with chai, I set out across the Maiden; the wide open field was covered by a hazy white sky and the many cricket and football games were interspersed with herds of goats, a strange sight with the tower blocks and Victoria Memorial, the city's white marble wonder, rising behind them. The goats chewed on the greenish-brown and rather lifeless grass, and the games played out with cheering, shouting and the sound of cricket bats hitting tennis balls. The landmark to keep my direction by was easy enough to follow; it was also my means of crossing the Hooghly. I could see the steel cables of the Vidyasagar Setu Bridge rise in a fan over the treetops surrounding the Maiden. I amended my course slightly, realising I was overshooting the bridge, and continued to walk. A herd of goats was rounded towards the edge of the grass where water trickled along a concrete gully, flowing slowly around the rubbish in its path. The goats drank and the city shepherds leaned on their sticks and waited.

At the far side of Maiden, I lost sight of the bridge; I thought this impressive considering there was very little else of much height that its 127-metre high steel pylons could be hidden behind. The Vidyasagar Setu, at just over 820 metres long, is the longest cable-stayed bridge in India. The road widened into carriageways and the traffic moved fast and chaotically along it. I ran across the lanes, calculating the speed and distance of the motorbikes and cars coming towards me. I sprinted towards the sign and road I needed:

Bridge

I stopped at the beginning of the slip road, hugging the curb, and looked along it as the traffic raced by with the road beginning to rise and curve. There were no pavements. I sighed and knew then that the Vidyasagar Setu was not for pedestrians, unlike the Howrah Bridge, over 3 kilometres upriver and around a five-hour detour in order to get to my destination by foot.

"Bollocks!"

I turned away from the deadly carriageway and bridge road and took a slightly less deadly carriageway which led me towards a sort of mini spaghetti junction (M.S.J., my own abbreviation) as highways circled round to join the bridge road which rose above all others and finally over the river. I could see its massive steel cables again, rising high into a blank canvas of sky. I walked and passed beneath a concrete overpass, the moving vehicles creating claps of thunder as their wheels beat against the seams in the road. Fabric walls, similar to what I'd seen at Bandra, were raised in the shelter and shadow. The bamboo supported structures were pulled tight with string at their corners, clothes were hung up to dry from makeshift washing lines and children ran in and out of the little houses, disappearing behind the fabric walls. I walked past them and found a large open and dusty area in the middle of the looping highways, for some reason I drew up the image of a Roman amphitheatre. This arena, however, was not meant for spectator sports.

In the dusty heart of the M.S.J. the community of people who lived under the roads were gathered in a circle of sorts, the highways busy with traffic all around. Men and women were stood or sat on pieces of tarpaulin, talking to each other. Some ate and others were drinking out of plastic containers. Horses were tied by ropes to spikes in the ground, the earth around their hooves nothing but dust and dirt. The horses didn't even attempt to eat from it. Beyond these, surprisingly strong and nourished animals, I saw the carriages they were used to pull. The wooden wagons were spectacularly adorned with shiny silver panels, red *romantic* seats, and all manner of details to make them appear luxurious, but never quite succeeding and often appearing over-the-top and garish. One particularly silver carriage reminded me of the sledge ridden by the Snow Queen in The Chronicles of Narnia. I'd seen many Cinderella carriages, as I called them, pulled by horses up and down the seafront in Fort in Mumbai, offering rides to the many tourists milling around The Gateway of India. I figured providing horse-drawn carriage rides around Kolkata to be the main source of income for the people who lived in the dark under the highways.

I observed the community relaxing together in the sun, their homes without electricity or water behind them, their horses flicking at flies with their tails and ears twitching, and their children smiling as they ran round and round under the highways with the traffic looping round above. Standing still, a memory of being a boy overcame me, strong and fast, and I let myself be taken by it; Kolkata, busy, foreign and new, was replaced by oak trees and the familiar stillness of being in the New Forest in southern England, and my childhood home. The engines and horns faded and the forest grew around me.

I was sat in the rear of my grandparents' car driving out of Poulner, a small suburb of the old market town of Ringwood, and the place in which I grew up. My sister was sat beside me in her horse riding clothes and the car drove over a flyover; the lanes of the A31 below were thick with traffic stuck in a jam, most of the drivers and passengers wanting to reach the seaside town of Bournemouth. My Granddad was smoking his pipe as he drove, which, when in the moving car and tasting like over-seasoned wood smoke in the back of my throat, made my stomach feel light and my head feel funny. My grandmother sat in the passenger seat. I could see her reflection in the wing mirror as I was sitting behind her chair; she was looking out the window and over the fields ahead, the cows in them munching grass. We turned down Eastfield Lane and headed towards Hightown before turning right at The Elm Tree and beginning to enter the forest. The Elm Tree was a thatched and traditional inn and a place where, reaching drinking age, I had stumbled home from on many a Friday night bleary-eyed and no doubt singing to the stars. Living in a small town meant the pub became the focal point of engagement, culture and existence.

It was a hot day, perhaps even the summer holiday, which would explain why my grandparents were taking us out as my parents would have been at work. I wasn't wearing any horse riding gear, because I didn't ride horses. I'd probably have been wearing my Adidas popper tracksuit trousers because I tried to wear them every day. I had been bought them on a family holiday to France and they made me feel cool because they were still to be discovered in Ringwood. These synthetic trousers were the type with poppers running high up the legs which served no practical purpose other than, once they became fashionable and everyone wore them to school on non-uniform days, to chase the girls around the playground and un-popper them in order to get a glimpse of their legs. The girls in turn chased the boys and our trousers then flayed at the bottoms like sportswear flares as we eagerly renewed chasing them.

I was never very good in the classroom, my mind always fighting to free me from the regiment of sitting still and trying to remember all this stuff which ignored the principles of dynamic learning and gave no space to creativity. So once outside on the playground I would run and play and try to forget that it would soon end and the bell would ring and the prison of the classroom would rise round me again. One day education must be redressed to complement the world we live in and the mind and soul of the child, but that's perhaps not for these pages. Although I could argue that the standardised and out-dated module of mainstream education is a real source of impoverishment, even detrimental to the health of both individual and collective wellbeing, as more and more children are medicated in order for them to fit into the classroom, a fabricated and restrictive environment which their beautiful minds are too great for. They are introduced and moulded into the framework of factory line production. *Come along now, children – produce, produce, produce.* There is great poverty to come from this, yet the ministers and policy makers are blind to it, or worse they are not but press on regardless; the tests increase, as do the years in the classroom and the piles of data and detail to remember from six years old, five years old, no why not make it four until, *What was the time of birth, please, the schooling starts this instant?* It's no surprise little minds are cracking more and more, and teachers are unable to free themselves and their pupils to a world of spontaneous and wonderfully exciting life learning.

As a boy I was afraid of riding horses because they were big and I was small and they didn't speak my language and I didn't speak their language and so I could never know what they were thinking, and if they didn't want to carry me, not being able to tell me, they'd likely buck me off. This is what my young mind told me. Even today I am indifferent to being on a horse, I'm just as happy to watch them in a field or observe the ponies in the New Forest just doing their thing, eating the grass and avoiding the bracken. My sister had loved riding horses, and was very good at it, until she was thrown off one day, a year after this memory. I then got to write silly stuff on the cast over her broken arm.

Sat in the back of the car and peering out my open window I noticed the distance between the houses on the roadside increase and the trees thicken with their branches reaching over the road for sunshine to shoot between the leaves in golden streams. We drove deeper into the forest. I loved it, every time: the old wrinkled and knotted tree trunks, the occasional thatch cottage which I told myself was where I would live when I won the lottery or became a famous footballer and married one of the beauties from *Baywatch*.

I was in love with all of the red swimsuit adorned *Baywatch* Babes; my young eyes would remain fixed to the screen and I'd be jealous of the guy plucked from the watery depths, unconscious and dragged onto the sand for a wet and heavily breathing Pamela Anderson (C. J. Parker in the show) to give him the kiss of life. Then David Hasselhoff would ride up on his quad bike and steal the limelight and I'd be impatient to see C. J. Parker again. It's hard being a boy entering those troublesome and unknowing teenage years with *Baywatch* on television. I'd come to see Los Angeles as the true home of angels in red tightfitting swimsuits. I wanted to drown and to be brought back to life by C. J. Parker, and then we'd marry and forgo L. A. because I felt insecure about my puny and pale English body next to the crafted muscles of the L. A. hunks. We would instead buy a little thatched cottage in the New Forest and it was hard for me to keep finding a good reason why C. J. Parker should want to continue to wear her red swimsuit, the nearby brooks and streams being only ankle deep.

My sister rode at the Bagnum Riding Stables; the road there narrowed and passed beneath an old and dilapidated redbrick railway bridge with ivy growing over it. The track would have once connected Ringwood to the national railway network until much of the railways were removed, leaving the small towns dependent on tarmac and cars to travel to and from. Before reaching the bridge I remember there being a fork in the road, with a little pond and green in the middle. There would often be ducks on the surface of the water and the nearest house to the green, my memory paints, used to have a dove house on one side. White doves would sit high up in their little white home and watch the world around them.

'Look!' I shouted, pointing to the green.

My grandfather slowed the car. There was an old hand-painted horse-drawn caravan beside the pond. A man with a thick grey beard, braces over his shoulders and a heavy cotton shirt, was sat on a stool sharpening a knife. His horse was chewing the lush green grass around the edge of the pond. The man was a roaming traveller, living on what he could find in nature and the little money he made from sharpening garden tools and kitchen knives. My childhood mind could not comprehend that the caravan was his home; yes, it was beautiful, the wooden sides baring intricately painted patterns, mostly red and greens with a dome canvas roof, but what about heating, electricity, water and *Baywatch*?

The traveller smiled to himself as he worked, the horse chewed the grass and the sun hit against the water. We drove slowly past.

'Nanny?' I'd said. 'Is that man a poor person?'

I don't remember her reply but I don't think she would have said a conclusive yes or decisive no, for the traveller, looking back, was then the perfect figure of what poverty now means to me, unclear and subjective. In terms of financial and material wealth the traveller was poor, although a caravan, horse and tools put him above many others who may only have the clothes on their back. He appeared healthy, content and nourished. How poor was he, really?

I turned on my seat, pulling the seatbelt from my neck, to look back at the grey bearded traveller, and wondered where he would go next. Would he eat the raspberries from the bushes on the roadside for breakfast, or drink from the streams when he was thirsty? I wondered if he went to bed at night and also thought about C. J. Parker running, in slow motion, along the sand to dive, in even slower motion, into the ocean. What did he think about life? We passed under the old redbrick railway bridge and the traveller was left behind me.

At the riding stables I stood on the wooden fence surrounding the paddock, my grandmother to one side of me and my grandfather the other, tapping out his spent tobacco against the fence. We watched my sister going round and round the paddock on a black horse, her riding hat bobbing up and down on her head.

Growing fidgety and impatient I began to think about the hole I had made in the knee of my favourite pair of Adidas popper trousers, I thought about C. J. Parker saving me from a shark attack and our subsequent wedding, and then I imagined Ryan Giggs scoring a hat-trick for Manchester United with his infamous left foot. Finally, with my grandfather lighting his pipe once more, the smoke trailing and fading away into the forest scented air, I thought about the traveller and his horse, and how poor he must be. I already knew what poverty was, and this man was in it, or so my childhood self believed.

A horse neighed and rubbed one of its front hooves back along the dust; I was back in the M.S.J., freed from memory and again looking upon the poor people before their Cinderella carriages that glittered and beamed in the sunlight. They were poor; I know this for reason that they lived under highways with their fabric and tarpaulin walls having been scavenged and erected using rope and bamboo. Houses made in the dark and in a place where nothing can grow. It was a place in which there was nothing to compel one to be there, what with the noise, the dust and the dirt. Yet the community smiled as they talked in their large group; they shared bottles of water and pieces of food and the children continued to run and play, trails of dust rising behind their scampering feet. The picture I had always painted of poverty was one of bleak and despairing isolation, where nothing good can come from the day as living to survive is not an enjoyable pursuit, but a necessity filled by anxiety, uncertainty, and a long, hard cycle of deprivation. I had blamed society for this, believing it had failed the individual and closed the door, locking the poor person out. Now I don't know.

The community of the M.S.J. were living to survive but they also showed signs of vital life, unlike the Living Dead who spotted the pavements and bridges, lying still as corpses under blankets and the weight of being poor. This community had family, friends and meagre possessions. Yet it didn't feel right. It wasn't right, to live in such basic and unsanitary conditions and a life in the shadow of an overpass. But it was life, to these people, and their children, and they lived it, and I'm left not knowing what's right or wrong. They have to live somewhere and with so many more people, with the Kolkata Metropolitan Area projected to rise from 14.1 million in 2011 to a population of '21.1 million by 2025',[15] perhaps it's inevitable that not all will be able to afford or hope for conventional bricks and mortar. Affordable housing, in the UK, India and the world over, is essential if such a worthy dream as the eradication of global poverty is ever to be entertained.

I turned and walked away from the horses, Cinderella carriages and the poor – yet not completely deprived – people living beneath the M.S.J. I passed back under one of the highways and followed it as the raised road became lower and lower to ground-level and the fabric walls became lower and lower until there were homes erected under sections so low that one could not stand up straight. I spotted a yellow Ambassador parked at the side of the road; I walked towards it and spoke to the driver through the passenger window.

"The Botanical Garden, please."

The garden did not disappoint. I walked in the shade of the coconut trees and my steps slowed as the stillness deepened. Quiet. Thick and beautiful quiet. I knew the city was noisy but hadn't noticed just how brutal. With just the occasional caw of a crow in the treetops, I fell into a silence so new and noticeable that my footsteps were loud against it. The path traced the edge of green lakes, the water lilies big with pink lotus flowers teasingly closed just above the surface. The garden grew beside the Hooghly River and I came to stand beside the tall fence and held onto the iron bars as I looked out over the wide expanse of water. A cargo ship, a giant made of steel and yet so buoyant, was slowly turning after having completed an unknown voyage; it dwarfed the tiny motor boats further upstream and the black plume of smoke rising from its funnel stained the white sky like a pot of spilt ink stains paper. I watched as its bow turned to point downstream and towards the ocean it had crossed, I thought about the distance it had covered and the journey. I then reflected on my journey and the worth of my notes and reason for me capturing them. I had doubts. To understand poverty I first had to see it, I once wrote, or close to, when my journey commenced. Now that I have seen some of the different dresses of poverty I'm still none the wiser as to a way to alleviate it; if anything it had made me want to run away from it, because I felt powerless to help all of the beggars on the streets in Kolkata and Mumbai. Mother Teresa had said to just feed one person, if not a hundred, but how to pick that one person out of a line of many all sat on the pavement with their hands, palms open, before them? The ship's anchor clattered and then boomed like a firing canon as it was dropped; the vessel was now still on the moving water.

"Poverty," I whispered. "Poverty?"

I knew it was complicated and I didn't think I would find an answer to it. I was even surprised to learn that, in the global fight against it, poverty was decreasing. 'Every region of the world has seen a decline in poverty over the past fifteen years,'[16] an expert working on the new Sustainable Development Goals had said. The SDGs are to replace the now expired Millennium Development Goals which, he also said on the online broadcast, had reached its target of reducing the number of people living under extreme poverty by half by 2015. The SDGs are to keep the fight going; one of the aims is to eradicate extreme poverty, as defined as someone living on less than

$1.25 a day, by the year 2030. The expert was reservedly optimistic that this could be achieved. This will of course not be the end of poverty, those living on $1.26 a day will also feel their poverty to be extreme and no doubt grinding.

Listening to the expert speak, I got the uncomfortable feeling that I had neglected the bigger picture of poverty, that there are trends reinforcing it and work being done to tackle it. I watched the fast flowing Hooghly kissing the side of the ship it carried.

"Poverty?" I said again.

I let go of the iron railing and walked away. Outside the gardens I moved between the buses to find the slum which was built beside a canal. It was a narrow run of small brick buildings and I passed between a gap in them and into the internal passageway. Women were washing clothes on the concrete steps, using buckets of water to get them wet before rubbing the fabric back and forth over the step. They looked at me and I said, "Namaste." They did not say anything back but maintained a look of distrust and suspicion. I was then shouted at by a man stood in a group of men and resting on the front wing of a taxi on the road. It was an angry shout and basically told me to leave. I walked back past him and his wide piercing eyes followed me; I guess he saw me as a foreigner finding the slum of cultural amusement, when really I just wanted to better understand the lives of the people that lived there. Unlike the fabric and bamboo houses under the M.S.J., the brick buildings were well established and, like many of the slums in the city, now formed a permanent shelter to the people that lived there. With the saris hanging up to dry between the buildings and the children stood on steps at the doors, and the little passageway swept and free of rubbish, I knew then that the slum wasn't just a slum or needed shelter, it was home.

XXIV

I am in the city of Janakpur, central Nepal. The city is not on the foreign tourist trail, I'm still to see another Westerner. It is however popular with Indian and Nepalese tourists who want to pay homage to the lavish temple built out of devotion to the Hindu goddess, Sita. Legend goes that Sita was born in Janakpur and the temple that has been built because of it is truly fit for a courageous goddess looked to and worshipped as an inspirational figure by Hindus. Richly adorned, the temple is a jewel in the centre of an otherwise small yet burgeoning city. A luxury hotel, Hotel Sitasharan, has been built next to the bus station on the outskirts of Janakpur and caters to the Indian businessmen and wealthier tourists. I am staying in the Sita Palace Hotel, primarily because I arrived in the dark and had nowhere to stay and a kindly passenger on the bus told me to stay here. The room is mid-range at 800 Nepalese rupees per night, approximately £5.40. In Nepal there is around a ten-hour power outage each day. The power is out now as I write this, so I am restricted to the battery life of my laptop. There is only one water tap in the shower cubicle, *cold*, and I had to do battle with a small army of mosquitoes when I arrived in my room. My net kept me unbitten during the night.

I wish to include a pencil sketch outline of my journey from Kolkata, not to make it too thick with content or capture every detail or toilet stop along the way, just to mention a couple of encounters which stood out and also left me thinking about being poor.

At the end of Stuart Lane the cars and auto-rickshaws drove past in a messy blur of noise and chaos. My backpack was on my back and I stood on the edge of the road trying to wave down a yellow Ambassador. I had checked out of Hotel Galaxy and was about to check out of Kolkata, my destination Nepal. It was early evening and already dark; the Darjeeling Mall was scheduled to leave Sealdah Station at 10pm. I had given myself plenty of time to get to the station, and didn't get too anxious when taxi after taxi passed me by, already taken with passengers.

"Rickshaw, sir? You want rickshaw?"

I turned towards the voice to find it belonged to a man; around fifty-five to sixty years old, lean verging on skinny with his gums housing a run of yellow and black teeth. He smiled.

"I take you, where you go?"

He pointed to the wooden hand-drawn rickshaw beside him, two big wooden wheels with a seat above them, and two wooden poles protruding out the front which he would stand between and lift in order to pull the cart. The hand-drawn rickshaws, an old and now iconic means of travel, can be seen all over the city, carrying people above the heads of those on foot with the drivers hitting the bells held in their palm against the handles in order to run through the parting crowds.

"I go to Sealdah Station." I said. "Too far, no?"

"Sealdah Station. I go. I take you now. Not far. Twenty-five minutes, sir. Come, I take you now."

He was so desperate to take me that he was already helping me lower the backpack from my back.

"How much?" I asked.

"Not much, only 120 rupees. Much cheaper than taxi, sir."

"If you're sure it's not too far," I said, letting him take my backpack and place it onto the cart.

I stepped on and sat rigid as he arranged the bell in

his palm and began to position his fingers in a way that didn't put too much pressure on the blisters I then saw on his hands. I instantly regretted my decision to be carried and pulled by him. He bent his knees and shook his small shoulders before hoisting the handles; I was tilted back as he began to walk, pulling the cart forward. Stuart Lane was quickly lost in the depths of the city behind me.

The rickshaw driver wore a pale blue turban-like cloth around his head. I don't think he was a Sikh or that it was a sign of religious obligation, but more in the function of a large sweatband. Ten minutes later I began to notice the first beads of sweat trickle from beneath it. He was running, and running hard. The bell in his hand chimed against the wooden handle and the wheels bashed against the potholes which I felt in my coccyx; there was nothing but wood for the vibrations to travel and dissipate through. I began to notice the want for the driver to get me to the station as quick as he could. He was relieved to have found a passenger – what with so many auto-rickshaws, pedal-rickshaws, taxis, and trams – and he wanted to satisfy me. I couldn't believe his stamina; twenty minutes in and his pace hadn't dropped, running along the side of a busy carriageway, holding the weight of the rickshaw and pulling it forward. The man was double my age and I would have been on my knees after only five minutes, gasping for fresh air amongst the pollution.

Eventually he was forced to slow as we entered a wall of bodies, all moving forward in a hurry to get to the station. I saw it approaching over their bobbing heads. We bumped and rocked over the potholes in the entrance and he moved to the side of the road and set the handles down, tilting me forward. He didn't even stop to catch his breath as he was helping me to get my backpack onto my back. He had just run over two kilometres; the sweat poured off his face and I was torn between feeling grateful that I had given him some custom and an arsehole for having exhausted him. A hand-drawn rickshaw driver will earn very little for their sweat. They charge less in order to tempt riders away from the taxis and auto-rickshaws. I looked in my wallet and gave him 300 rupees, more than what I would have been charged by a taxi. He quickly stowed the money into the front pocket of his shirt and pointed to the big clock shining bright over the entrance of the station.

"I made good time. Yes?"

"Really good time, thank you."

I walked toward the station but turned after a few steps. I looked back to see him rubbing at the bleeding blisters on the inside of his fingers. I shook my head and felt guilty again. The thing I find when I travel is – and not just to distant lands but even across the UK, past large industrial estates or the graft of labourers, to the hours behind a desk in office blocks – that for the majority of people, it really is a hard life. I moved into the swell of bodies once again and entered into Sealdah Station, my exit from Kolkata.

The Darjeeling Mall choked and grumbled throughout the night. When I woke and first looked out the carriage window, I found a world cloaked in clouds and mist. There was nothing but white; occasionally I could see a figure walking beside the track or the silhouette of a building but the morning fog was thick and impenetrable. The rising sun slowly burned it away and the sky began to turn blue and the earth different shades of green; the train rattled through the tea plantations, the low growing plants stretching for mile after mile in plotted lines. We were nearing Darjeeling and tea growing was also the mainstay of the surrounding region. I shook out my neck and shoulders after a fine sleep and continued to stare out the window wanting to watch the morning colours being painted ever-deepening shades; the train howled past small wooden shacks with people showering outside them with buckets. I noted the never ending stream of litter beside the tracks, all having been tossed out of the moving trains, and tainting an otherwise beautiful scene.

A chai *wallah* moved through the carriage. "Chai, Coffee… Chai, Coffee…" I looked to see what cups he was serving his sweet milky drinks in – paper. "I'll take a chai, please."

The paper cup would at least break down and degrade once it also found itself beside the track. I handed him ten rupees and he passed the small cup with a teabag in and warm sweetened milk, the white liquid turning brown as the tea infused. I sipped it and returned to the moving view outside the window. Another voice called out and moved closer to me, "Story book. Story book to read." I leaned forward to look along the carriage. A young man was approaching with a stack of paperbacks in his hands so tall he had to tilt his head back to be able to see over them. Most of them were English titles and second-hand, *The Da Vinci Code* and *The Fault in Our Stars* were amongst the creased spines. He stopped at each chair and displayed them to the sitting passengers, "Story book," he said again. "Story book to read." He worked his way along the length of the carriage, not selling a single book. I watched him struggle out of the door and into the next carriage, the stack of books wobbling as he went. I returned to the window, sipping my paper cup of chai and trying not to let the sight of thousands of discarded cups on the ground outside make it taste any less sweet. The sun shone on the tea plantations and workers moved amongst them. Such beauty, such ugliness, and both tended to by human hand.

I was sat in the passenger seat of a moving car. The driver was a young and fashionable man, his hair styled and spiked at the front and his shirt tucked into his fitted jeans. At first he was only going to be driving me from

New Jalpaiguri train station, the end of the line for the Darjeeling Mall, to the Siliguri bus station. I was then going to catch a local bus to the border town of Panitanki, walk across a bridge over the Mechi River and into Nepal on the other side. For an extra few hundred rupees, he offered to take me directly to the border. Knowing the bus would have added extra hours and the train already having being delayed, I took him up on his offer.

One hour later and we drove straight through Panitanki and onto the bridge, the Mechi rippling beneath, skirted by riverbed on either side as it flowed low in the dry season. There were small groups of people working beside the water, digging up stones and loading them into baskets. We raced past the pedestrians and pedal-rickshaws moving across the bridge, either heading away from or towards Nepal. The driver pulled up outside the barrier and border post. I got out of the car, paid and thanked him and he again told me with pride how he had said he would drive me all the way.

"Great job," I said.

The car sped away and back across the bridge to India. I turned to Nepal. I took my passport from my bag and walked past the barrier and into the small white immigration office to request a thirty-day visa. Inside, something instantly didn't feel right. I waited behind a young couple of backpackers, their passports being inspected by a suited man over the counter. I swore silently. *I didn't go through immigration in India. He's driven me straight into bloody Nepal.* I was told on a later bus journey that India and Nepal have a relationship where their citizens can move between the two countries without a passport, which would explain my driver's neglect. I did need to show my passport on leaving and entering. I turned and, without showing any alarm, walked out of the office. My pace heightened as I walked away from the border post; the bridge over the Mechi lay ahead. I had heard a rumour that there was going to be a general strike in Nepal the following day (like many countries, its political establishment is a bloody mess and around the time of me walking across the bridge the rival political parties, unable to agree on the new constitution, broke out into a brawl in parliament, throwing chairs and slanderous words at each other) which meant the border would be closed, so I needed to get in before the immigration office shut that evening. It was hot and I began to sweat on the kilometre or so walk back into India. Indian soldiers waited at the entrance to the bridge, spot-checking peoples' possessions. Slowing my pace, I then causally made my way into the immigration building. A guard with a rifle over his shoulder welcomed me, "Coming in or exiting, sir?" I smiled, "Exiting." He pointed to a table. "Sit down and I'll get you a departure form to fill out." Twenty minutes later I was again walking over the bridge, this time with the needed exit stamp in my passport. The river flowed far away into the distance, trees lining the stone banks and the sky mottled blue overhead. Holding the straps of my backpack I walked back into Nepal.

That night I stayed in Kakarvitta, the Nepalese border town. It appeared to have been built around the bus station, with the surrounding streets filled with guesthouses, hotels and shops. I walked along two of them, unable to choose between the many hotels. In the end I decided simply to go by the name, and that's how I came to check into *Hotel Orchid*. My room overlooked the street and my first impression of Nepal was one of family; children played below and their parents stood at the entrances of their shops and hotels and watched, joining in with their games on occasion. The sound of play was so welcome after a fortnight in Kolkata, with its brutal and unceasing noise. This isn't to say I didn't like the city. I loved it, truly.

In Kakarvitta I spent some time walking around the

town, surprised to see how much fashion played a part in the younger generation's appearance and lives. I saw leather jackets, women with finely applied make-up and wearing skinny jeans, as were some of the guys. I was a creased linen mess in comparison. I don't know what my expectation was of the Nepalese people, I guess mainly poor rural folk who tilled the land and didn't have time to think about hairstyles or eyeliner. I was of course ignorant and wrong.

I had dinner at a small fast food restaurant with only one table outside; two men worked it and shook their woks over a gas stove. My vegetable stir-fried rice was being cooked in one of the woks. After the long journey I also indulged in a beer and it tasted malty and familiar and took me back to The Griffin and fond memories of pulling pints and catching up with the locals. The man stirring my rice confirmed that there was a strike planned for the following day and I would be lucky to get a bus. I asked him what it was over and he said the government were trying to bring in a new constitution and the 165 or so different political parties, unsurprisingly, had failed to agree on its draft. He turned back and flicked the wok with his wrist, tossing the rice and vegetables into one another. I drank my drink and looked along the quiet road; dusk had settled and was inviting the night. The chef lifted a bottle of soy sauce from a wooden shelf and added some to the wok, it hissed and spat and scented the air.

"Janakpur? I'm looking for a bus to Janakpur?"

I worked my way along the ticket offices at the bus station in Kakarvitta. The morning sun was spellbinding and showered the town in radiant sunbeams which eased away the chill I had awoken to.

"Janakpur?" I said to another man behind a counter.

He shook his head, "No morning, night bus only."

After an hour of asking departing bus after departing

bus if it was heading to Janakpur, I cut my losses and decided to search out a coffee and internet connection so I could write to V. If I was destined to be catching the night bus then I had a whole day to spend in the border town.

Fusion Coffee Lounge was less than a minute's walk from the station; it served espresso coffee with the choice of ordering a cappuccino or Americano from the menu. This was reflected in the price, a chai from the roadside stands cost 15 Nepali rupees (around 10p) and an Americano in Fusion cost 80 Nepali rupees (around 65p). I was the only customer and I think this contributed to the changing of the music from a loud and repetitive sacred chant to 'I want to know what love is' by Foreigner. An inside joke amongst the staff, I thought. I wrote to V to tell her I had made it to Nepal and that I missed her.

An hour later, fuelled by caffeine and determination not to die on a bus in the dark, having read how treacherous the roads and driving were in Nepal, I was back at the station.

"Janakpur?" I said to every person who looked to have some role in the directing of buses to the stands.

"You want to go Janakpur?" said a guy in a hooded tracksuit top.

"Yes."

"There's a bus leaving in an hour, that one."

He pointed to a white and blue bus that was parked at the edge of the stand.

"It's going to Janakpur?"

"In one hour," he said again.

Thirty minutes later the bus drove away from the Kakarvitta bus station. Fortunately, I had run straight to Hotel Orchid, picked up my backpack and was back sitting on the bus and relieved to be so when it pulled away from the stand early. I subsequently couldn't think about anything else but the six hours on the road to Janakpur and that we were never going to make it. The driver was a bloody madman and possessed by some demonic urge to overtake absolutely everything in his way. Nepal did her best to distract me from the heightened risk of death by putting on a fine green streaked dress to soothe the eye. My image of Nepal had been of snow peaked mountains, pure white against steep rock faces, but the land we drove through was flat and expanded as far as the eye could see: rice fields and tea plantations. The majority of the bridges we crossed carried us over dry riverbeds of white stone. I wondered how different the landscape must be by the end of the monsoon with swollen rivers flooding the surrounding flat lands.

The journey was painful and long and the bus bounced and rattled when the roads turned from tarmac to dirt tracks, before returning to tarmac for the driver to be able to press down hard on the accelerator once again. Four hours in and I was now sat next to a woman holding a sleeping baby in her arms, the child's tiny head was rested on my forearm and she slept deeply. I envied her, not being aware of the journey she was partaking in. We passed two completely totalled and wrecked buses on the roadside. I thought it morbidly ironic that our own bus sped past the wrecks and the sight of them did nothing to lessen the driver's speed or lust for overtaking on corners. I should write that I was probably the only passenger on the bus who was envisaging death at every bend, for the Nepalese passengers thought nothing of it; it was just a typical bus journey. *Still, had this been at night,* I thought, *it would be far worse.* Not long later the sun dipped and night fell over the dastardly bus.

We tore through the dark and it was not as bad as I thought it would be. The darkness hid any danger so I simply looked out at a moving black curtain and wondered what was behind it. We then stopped in a small town, I have no idea where, and the driver got out. Ten minutes passed.

Twenty minutes passed. And after another five minutes a young Nepalese guy came up to me, clearly reading the confusion on my face, with the other passengers visibly frustrated.

"Are you afraid of the situation here?" he said.

"I don't exactly know what the situation is to be afraid of it," I replied.

He told me that the driver was refusing to drive the rest of the way to Janakpur and he wanted us all to get off the bus.

"You've got to be kidding me?"

The Nepali didn't know the exact phrasing but he got the gist of it.

"Some things are not as good as they could be," he said.

I thanked him for informing me. The driver could not be persuaded to fulfil his duty and our options seemed limited. Fortunately, Nepal is like India in that something always comes along, even during a strike, and twenty minutes later another bus was waved down. The mass transferral of passengers began. We set off; sixty-odd souls in a tin can rocketing down the dark roads. An hour later we pulled up again and another passenger waved at me.

"Janakpur. Janakpur."

I looked out the window at the dusty pavements and dimly lit shops with a couple of big buildings behind them.

"Here, Janakpur?" I said.

"Yes, hotel." He pointed to one of the large buildings.

I checked with another passenger and he confirmed that it was Janakpur. I got off the bus and crossed the road covered in a static mist of dust and darkness. I dropped my backpack from my shoulders and sighed as I checked into the Sita Palace Hotel.

XXV

The bus was scheduled to depart from Janakpur at 6am. The roads were laced with darkness as people stood around the gas stoves boiling milky coffee on the stands, warming their hands. A group of lads had set fire to a pile of newspapers and stood over the flames, turning to warm the backs of their legs. The nights and mornings in Nepal were cold, the days so far sunny and pleasant. The bus pulled away to begin its long journey to Kathmandu. I wasn't travelling to the capital, not yet, for I planned to disembark at a town called Sauraha, located on the edge of the Chitwan National Park.

I knew little about Sauraha or Chitwan before arriving, my main reason for stopping here was that it broke up the journey to Kathmandu and meant I could avoid taking a night bus on the mountain roads. I rented a small place on the edge of the community forest, with a river and the boundary of the reserve beyond. I placed my backpack on my bed, boiled some water in a pan over the stove to make coffee and then stood on the balcony, looking out towards the treeline. I was told the reserve was home to wild rhinos, elephants and tigers, with a panoply of birds, insects and no doubt serpents. I only had three nights scheduled here and I was already convinced it would be too short.

My little home was owned and rented by Sushilla and Hira. They used the money, around £7 per night, to help fund the orphanage they ran less than a minute's walk away. It was what had drawn me to stay in the first place, happy to know my custom would benefit a greater project. After settling in, Hira came round and invited me for a walk followed by *dal bhat* (a staple Nepali dinner consisting of cooked lentil soup and rice) with the children at the orphanage.

We set out through the community forest and it opened to a wide flood plain, the Rapti River, flowing low and slow, tracing the edge of the reserve. We followed the dirt paths through the wild grass and pursued the river's course. We passed an elephant breeding centre; the animals would grow to provide rides to the many tourists or labour for the villagers. They seemed healthy and well looked after but it still stirred uncomfortable feelings to see the thick chains around their legs, tethering them to posts in the ground. We walked through another pocket of trees, past a small woman herding goats with a stick, and I saw around one hundred people stood by the river in the distance. They all held cameras at their necks and were pointing them down to the water, concealed by the bank.

"There are a lot of tourists here," I said to Hira.

"Chitwan is the third most popular tourist destination in Nepal," he replied. "Many people come to see wildlife. The park is 932 square kilometres, very precious."

A man standing amongst his grazing water buffalo shouted at Hira, pointing to where the tourists were stood.

"Rhino!" said Hira. "Come quickly."

We hurriedly walked to the riverside and joined the many Chinese and Western tourists already marvelling at the great beast stood in the shallows, drinking. It was a formidable sight and yet so big and heavy that it was easy to forget the explosive power underneath that hard grey skin. The rhino had small tusks and three black winged and white-breasted birds perched on its back. It moved slowly and occasional stopped drinking to look at the line of people all stood staring at it. The camera shutters snapped and the sun lowered over the park. The sky paled and it was then that I faintly made out the rise of the Himalayas in the far distance, their white tops kissed by the setting sun. *I can see why this place is so popular.* I looked back at the river to watch the rhino drink some more.

"Come," said Hira. "Around the corner I'll show you crocodile."

We left the tourists and walked on a path above the river; it joined the East Rapti River to flow much wider and faster, the bottom no longer visible as the water turned brown.

"See, down there."

On a bank where the two channels of water merged, a plump old crocodile was outstretched, still as a stone. We were stood on a high manmade flood defence protecting the many restaurants and hotels from the rapid rise of water during the monsoon. Many tourists were again stood taking pictures of the crocodile, Nepalese tour guides moved amongst them selling tours or canoe trips as well as a small boy selling packets of popcorn for 40 rupees.

I noticed during the short walk how little rubbish there was to be seen on the ground, not to say it was litter free but overall far better than anywhere else I'd visited in either Nepal or India. Beside where we were stood, a soldier was sat in a wooden hut with a tin roof, using the vantage provided by the defence to look out over the flood plain and towards the national park. On the sides of the hut were two banners, like the pictures of blackened human lungs on the side of cigarette packets; these banners were meant to make an impact. One displayed a collection of photos taken of people who had the most horrible deformities or massive boils on their bodies; a baby lay with what looked like another baby being born from the side of its cheek. The banner said this was a result of burning plastic. I thought back to Hotel Galaxy, waking in the morning to the nauseating smell of burning plastic seeping through the cracks in the window frames, as a small pile of rubbish was set alight in Stuart Lane. It was common to find fires burning away in the gutters, yet Kolkata was one of the most efficient places I'd visited for its management of waste disposal. Many sweepers could be seen piling the rubbish into their carts and taking it to modern compactors from where it would be taken, unless incinerated for energy, in trucks to the dumps, which of course hasn't really solved the problem of waste management. I recalled a video blog I had been asked to write an introduction to, the speaker was Jamie Cloud from the Cloud Institute for Sustainability Education:

'We are inextricably linked to the living systems upon which our lives depend,' Jamie said. 'The health of cultures and languages is linked to the health of ecosystems. In order to be *sustainable* […] we want to contribute to the health of the systems upon which we depend. In order to be *sustainable* certain things need to be preserved and certain things need to change over time. We're pretty good at changing what should be preserved and preserving what should be changed, but if we could get that right that would be extremely powerful. We also want to make sure that young people understand what the operating instructions are for the planet; things like the first law of thermodynamics, which in English means: There's no such place as away and yet we keep throwing things there. And it doesn't' exist. So we want to make sure that they understand how the planet works so we can thrive over time and contribute to the health of those living systems.'[17]

To reinforce this point, the second banner displayed on the soldier's hut was of a dead bird; the side of its body had been cut open. The animal looked like it had been made up of litter; a blue disposable cigarette lighter and plastic foil filled the bird's stomach. Despite Sauraha being much better than other places I had stayed, I still found it remarkable to have walked past stricken plastic bottles on the riverbank, not far from the thirsty wild rhino, or to have picked up two empty foil packets that had contained instant noodles, being tossed along the path by the breeze. *Who would throw their rubbish on the ground in a place such as this?* It was a poverty of appreciation for the Earth and her continual blessings, a poverty of care and responsibility. If Nature is not protected from the impacts of humanity then all life will be poorer in the end. The late E. F. Schumacher wrote a much needed book in 1973 and *Small Is Beautiful* still holds as much truth, relevance and importance today:

'If we squander our fossil fuels, we threaten civilisation,' wrote Schumacher, 'but if we squander the capital represented by living nature around us, we threaten life itself.'[18]

There is perhaps no greater poverty to become us all, and a result of the reckless exploitation of nature for profit. Yet Sauraha showed a different way, for the town's wealth now relied on the wealth of the environment around it, the people profited from nature but in ways that compelled them to protect it. (Again, this is to a degree, for the rubbish was mostly in the community areas, the places where the tourists were less likely to visit. I am still to learn whether this was cultural or a lack of viable waste management alternatives, or both.) Without the eco-tourism enterprises that flourished as a result of the Chitwan National Park, the majority of the villagers of Sauraha would be mustard plant farmers, or goat or buffalo herders, and many, unable to make a living, would leave their community to make a go of it in the city. With the National Park the town has a bright future, the many mustard farmers and herders included, which is only sustainable for as long as the park, and the wildlife it is home to, remains protected. Of course not all rural communities have a nature reserve to boast, and this is why the regard for rural living and farming must be valued more highly in society, and much work done to innovate means of production that protects the capital found in nature, not as something to squander and take from but something to invest in. All lives, more importantly all spirits, will be the richer for it, no matter the figure in the bank. A fitting passage echoed through my mind which I had recently copied into the front of my notebook, taken from a lecture John Ruskin had delivered in Tunbridge Wells in 1858. It was titled, *The Work of Iron, In Nature, Art, and Policy*:

'But this is not all, nor the best part of the work of iron. Its service in producing these beautiful stones is only rendered to rich people, who can afford to quarry and polish them. But Nature paints for all the world, poor and rich together: and while, therefore, she thus adorns the innermost rocks of her hills, to tempt your investigation, or indulge your luxury, she paints, far more carefully, the outsides of the hills, which are for the eyes of the shepherd and the ploughman.'

"Come," said Hira, "I take you to orphanage now."

I was staring at the banner of the dead bird, lost in thought. I turned and smiled at Hira, the sun no longer visible after it had dipped behind the trees, leaving the sky a silk sheet of pink, the river musical as it flowed over the stone banks.

"It is pretty here, Hira," I said as we began descending the flood defence to walk towards the dusk waiting beneath the trees ahead.

"Yes," he said, "our home is very precious place."

to be continued…

XXVI

I'm in a guesthouse in Kathmandu, my belly burping as I write. I've been sick, a stomach bug and the type which has left me with no control over my bodily functions. I'm staying in Thamel, the famed backpacker area in the heart of the city, with the streets lined by travel agencies, clone cashmere clothes shops, Tibetan thangka shops, t-shirt shops with most of the t-shirts displaying Mount Everest. There are many cafés, restaurants, bars and *gack* shops – as I've come to call the stores or holes-in-the-wall that just sell biscuits, chocolates, soft-drinks and cigarettes. It's busy in the centre of Kathmandu; some of the roads are dirt with the same volume of traffic bumping down them to be expected of a capital city; this means there is no end of dust in the air and no surprise to see many walking the streets with masks over their mouths and noses. It's pretty in places, mostly the views of the surrounding mountains which contain Kathmandu valley in majestic greens and offer a taste of the high Himalayas beyond.

After a few days staying with a Nepalese family in a quieter part of the valley, most of it spent on the toilet or in bed, I had planned to leave Kathmandu today but my body and bowels were not stable enough for any kind of journey so I found this cheap guesthouse hidden along one of Thamel's colourful and *have me want me taste me* streets. Except for the odd Fixed Price shop, all is available and all is negotiable. My room, the man who had welcomed me into the guesthouse first told me, was 700 rupees. He then showed me the room and I looked at him and he said,

"Okay, 600." As we walked down the stairs he asked me where I was from. I told him. "You're from England and you look for cheaper room?" I simply wanted to check into the room and be near to the toilet so I just filled out the arrival form and thanked him.

The room is how I see the inside of a depressed person's mind to be; things are out of place and some things are broken and can be fixed but for some reason there is something stopping them from being fixed, something invisible and untouchable. There is a bed in the room, a single bed which has a pillow at one end and a sheet, blanket, towel and roll of toilet paper at the other. The bed is pressed against one wall, there is a wooden stand beside it and two sofas which could seat six people – god knows why there are two sofas which could seat six people in a single room, the smoking chair next to one of the sofas would have been sufficient alone. There is a sink in one corner of the room; it drips one drip every two minutes, not the worst leak I've come across during my travels. There are light fittings without light bulbs, a wooden framed mirror on the wall above one of the sofas, it is crooked and one corner of the glass has broken away and is now held in place with black tape. Beside the mirror is a window with a curtain, I keep the curtain closed as the window looks out onto a tiled stairwell that is sterile and has nothing going for it except to make passage up or down. The floor of the room is covered by scraps of laminate which have been poorly cut in waves with the swirly patterns not even close to lining up where the scraps join. The room's depressed.

I spent the morning on one of the sofas, weak from three days of diarrhoea and vomiting, and wondering whether sunlight would help, but the sofa was comfortable and next to the toilet so I stayed under the blanket and continued to devour *My Friend Leonard* by James Frey. It's a good book, well written. Made me want to sit up and write, which I'm doing although my belly wants to buckle in the middle and for me to curl up under the heavy blanket and keep reading *My Friend Leonard*. I like it because it's in tune with life, shows how fucked up it can be and yet how people can still find a way through, to revel in it, to feel love, to taste sweet things, to see beauty even if it's temporary and we fall back into ourselves, into horrors, or into a life we didn't want or choose but hey, here it is, let's see what comes of it, work at it.

Being alone and looking back over my winter I become agitated as I think about all the people that work damn hard, the blood and sweat of society, who put in their hours, give their souls to their jobs and their careers and still find themselves short at the end of the month, struggling to get food on the table or heat in the house. I think about the upcoming general election in the UK and try not to shun it, try not to look at parliament as a playground of puppets who don't really have the power to implement real change for society and the poorest members of it as they are merely the awful actors, the needed distraction, on stage while the vested interests behind the curtains maintain a steady hold over policy and protect the evil rich. I think it's important to define the rich in terms of good and bad, as there are many rich folk who use their wealth to do the most amazing things for others, who invest in culture and community. They are beautiful people.

A March for Homes protest took place in London over the weekend, thousands gathered to protest against the lack of affordable housing and the way the government has welcomed wealthy investors to buy up chunks of the capital, pushing up housing prices and forcing born and bred Londoners out of their homes. I try not to become disillusioned, to tell myself that voting matters, but often I think it doesn't and it won't until the House has been truly shaken and the profiteers are exposed and curtailed.

Democracy. Bullshit.

I then put down *My Friend Leonard* and lie under my heavy blanket and think about what can be done, what needs to be done to better the lives of the majority – to stop forcing people down, to stop pushing people out. I think about mass peaceful defiance where millions decide enough is enough: *Fuck it*, they cheer, as they head out of their front doors and join with their neighbours and take time to engage with those around them, make new friends, have street parties, and not feed into the system for a day, for two days, a week, and more importantly not allow the system to feed off them. I then think about my friends' coffee shop in Bath and if they had to close for a week and how this would hit them hard and tell myself this won't work. But then maybe there will have to be pain in order to make something better. If it was a pain shared by the majority, it would be easier to bear.

I think about education. I don't know why but I do. I think about how the children I've met so far in Nepal are so hungry to learn, so happy to go to school, and so bright. They smile and play, their faces brim with excitement as they carry their books under their arms. *Why did I not smile when walking the twenty-six minutes to school? Was I not appreciating? Was I a no good brat? What do these children find in it that I did not?* Simply, I believe not all minds are suited to the classroom environment, and those that aren't are unfortunately made out to be strugglers or labelled as not applying themselves, or in special need. I lie and I think and then I want Sir Ken Robinson, my favourite expert on education who advocates creativity to be a core principle of learning, to be invited by the UK government and given charge of overhauling the education system. *Why the hell hasn't the government pleaded with him to help?* I lie under my blanket and I think about all these things. A voice then sounds in the back of my mind. I know the voice, and it's hard to say whether we're friends or enemies as our relationship is complex. Still, the voice is rarely comforting: *Fucking joke you are, lying under a blanket in a shithole of a room in a city where no one knows you and you know no one, and fantasising about bettering things you know fuck all about. Loser.*

I hear the voice and then carry on; it's best not to give the voice too much mind space. A few years back it tried to kill me. I defeated it then and now hold control, and purposely hold the reins tight as I don't want to go back there again. The abyss of the self is dark and terrorising.

A drip just sounded in the sink basin, another two minutes has passed. The power is out across Nepal as the load shedding is in operation; the guesthouse has a backup supply, perhaps a generator out the back. Being that my window looks out onto the stairwell I can't tell if it's dark outside yet or not. No. It's 5.30pm so the sun would have just set behind the mountains and the sky would be slipping into her grey dusk dress. Bowels and belly permitting I plan to leave Kathmandu tomorrow; despite the dust and trippy streets of Thamel, it is a magical city of old bazaars with whispers of the ancient sown so haphazardly within the rapid modernisation that's taking place. In years to come the roads will no longer be dirt and the electricity will run all day. I've heard there are plans to build the world's largest hydro dam up in the mountains; many rural villages will be flooded in order to provide the power the country needs. Tomorrow I plan to go to a small town 32 kilometres away. I will then return to the orphanage in Sauraha and continue my notes from there. *Drip.* Another two minutes has passed.

XXVII

A letter for V – 5th February 2015

Dear V,

I'm going to write to you about my days even though I can't send this to you for a while, but I miss not writing to you and this is as close as it gets to feeling near you.

I'm in a town called Panauti. It's around a two hour bus journey from Kathmandu, and I've just had an exceptional day.

I arrived yesterday and found a little guesthouse which is basic to say the least; the internal walls are bare boards of plywood; the water doesn't flow out of the taps but instead drips pitifully, as though each drip might be the last, but it's quirky and old and the food is made with vegetables from the garden. I can lie on my bed – as I am writing this – and listen to the conversation of two guys drinking coffee in the garden beneath my window, the swallows chattering on the terracotta rooftops and the bells of the temple next door. It's an old town, very auspicious.

Arriving in Panauti my heart pained instantly to see the amount of rubbish everywhere, and everywhere I've been, town or city, is the same; it's horrible to project what the toxicity of the soil and water will be like in these rural places in years to come, once some of the plastic, foil and other unnatural materials break down and spread into the surrounding farmland. It's the thing I will take away most from this winter, the problem of waste. Something has to be done: global initiatives, scientists set to work, national commitments, focused funding, education in order to clean and implement some sort of waste disposal in these places. The people are poisoning the very thing they're dependent on. I stand on the bridge over the river in the centre of the town, I look down at the water and see more rubbish than stones on the banks, see a family of ducks bobbing next to plastic bottles and I watch the drowned plastic bags on the riverbed. I look up and see the beautiful green mountains, the wooden carved temples and old wobbly buildings and it's so special, but I can't appreciate it because my attention falls back to the rubbish at my feet, the rubbish under the little ducklings' webbed feet and the locals tossing more of it on the ground, so carefree and apparently so unconcerned by what they are doing. Do they have an alternative? That's what needs to be asked. I don't want to come back to India or Nepal again as it makes me too sad. I know the UK is not a success and we probably ship our shit out to these poorer regions, and we pollute and poison like the rest of the world, but to be in such naturally rich environments and to see them being spoiled and foreseeing that it will only get worse is too much to bear. I can't watch it happen.

This comes after the most magnificent walk to a Buddhist monastery on a mountaintop, Namo Buddha. It was 9 kilometres from the town and I set off around nine o'clock. There was a funeral taking place beside the river and I watched for a while and was going to wait for the cremation out of morbid fascination to see a body burn but it took ages so I carried on walking. I have never before seen valleys so extensively cultivated; it was almost like a lunar landscape, so changed that it didn't appear to be Planet Earth any longer – miles of brown terraces that have been dug into an intricate network of gullies for the water to channel through and feed the crops. In winter the farmers grow potatoes and then they reseed and grow rice in the summer. The roads cut through the terraces, sometimes dirt, sometimes tarmac, sometimes rising, sometimes falling, and the morning mist was pooled at the foot of the mountains. I breathed deep and smiled. So pretty. Around an hour in I saw Klaus on the road ahead; a Danish sixty-four-year-old birdwatcher who walks around 10 kilometres every day. He's staying in the same guesthouse and we had coffee together in the morning; he's a nice man, a happy man and loves birds, adores birds. I caught him up and we walked together. His binoculars were held round his neck and his eyes lingered on the sky and the trees. I like Klaus; he's easy to be around. He spots a bird, tells me what it is. I see something pretty, mustard plants dancing in the breeze in yellow waves, and we stop and enjoy the view together and then we walk some more. At Klaus' insistence, we stopped in almost every tea den we passed. 'I just love these little places,' he said every time the tea arrived. We reached the foot of the mountain with the monastery dazzling in the sunshine at its top. I walked ahead as Klaus wanted to break up the climb and sit alone and look through his binoculars and be with his birds. When walking with another he also ends up climbing too quickly and needs to keep a slow and steady pace. So I climbed into the trees and out of the trees, and to the mountaintop. It was jaw dropping: the high Himalayas in the distance with their white snow peaks and wide expansive views over the tended valleys, the surrounding green mountains visibly breathing. There were many monks; many of them were young boys (which I don't like in any religion because I end up questioning if it's a thing of faith or conditioning). They entered the red monastery which is clearly getting large amounts of money from somewhere with its golden roof and more dormitories being constructed. Klaus plodded up the last incline and we had lunch on a terrace with a panoramic view a dream would have found hard to paint. It was so wide and magnificent that it made me dizzy. We talked about some of our previous travels. I asked him about his life and he told me he lives on a small Danish island close to Sweden. His first wife died of cancer and he raised his two children alone. He's not married now. "I have a good girlfriend," he laughed. "We kiss once in a while." He worked as a craftsman for thirty years and gets his pension in five months which he's looking forward to. He said it's not much but will keep him. He lives a simple life in a converted chicken shed: no television, no computer, the water source is 70 metres from his home which he fetches as he needs it, and he likes his radio and of course his birds. Apparently, so Klaus tells me, the swallows presently in South Africa will arrive in Denmark on the 20th April. I laughed that the swallows have taken the trouble to set an exact date of arrival.

After walking around the monastery we then headed back down the mountain and waited for the bus back to Panauti. The village at the bottom of Namo Buddha is made up of orange growers, the surrounding hills filled by trees all dotted by little balls of tangy sunshine on their branches. The houses were clay or brick with chickens and goats running in and out of them. Apart from the rubbish on the ground and the occasional power cable, I doubt much has changed in the village for hundreds of years. While waiting for the bus we had our fifth tea of the day, no wonder I need to pee again. Sipping my drink I watched a cockerel chase after a hen before standing on her back and pinning the crying thing to the ground; she did not consent. The bus left and it was noisy, the roads rutted and dusty, and after half a kilometre I patted Klaus on the shoulder and said I'm going to walk back. "Good idea," he said, "I'll join you." So we stepped over the wicker baskets of potatoes in the way and got off the bus and began the 8.5 kilometres back to Panauti. We stopped for tea again and the sun slowly lowered behind the mountains and I could have just kept walking, walking, walking. I forgot how much I love to walk in the countryside, even the rubbish on the side of the road couldn't diminish my happiness to be outside and observing the darkening greens and browns of the earth. Then we walk back into Panauti and cross the bridge and I look down at the River of Litter (Punyamati) and something inside me gets angry, and I want to blame someone for being so irresponsible but I don't know who that somebody is, the person who litters or the society and systems in place that have created a culture like this. If it's because of lack of money, because they're 'poor people,' then stop all the silly war shows and power displays which I saw in the big park in Kathmandu before leaving, with thousands of men and women in camo walking in step and saluting in unison. There's a lot of money being spent on shiny metal killing machines, I fear more than is invested in keeping towns and villages clean.

So I'm back within my plywood walls and it is dark outside and the one lightbulb is struggling to rid the dark from the corners of the room. I'm going to go and pee now as my bladder is telling me it's overdue. I miss you, V. x

XXVIII

After leaving Panauti I returned to Kathmandu for two days before catching an early bus heading back to Sauraha. The Kathmandu Road, when hurtling down it in a bus with squealing brakes, is at once thrilling, terrifying and, if free from contemplating the fleetingness of existence and about it ending in a fiery blaze, truly spectacular. The many vehicles appear to be in a race to get up and down the steep winding road and the slow moving transport lorries, with loads sometimes so heavy they appear on the verge of rolling backwards, are simply obstacles to beep at as the bus veered out into the oncoming traffic to overtake, now beeping at the bus flashing its lights and honking its own horn as the fatal crash was narrowly avoided. We passed six wrecks; one lorry had suffered a blowout and the weight of its load had caused the vehicle to topple onto its side. It was left in a perilous position as it balanced on a concrete barrier, the other side of which was sky and a long way down. The bus sped past the crumpled metal and shards of glass. *Still*, I kept reminding myself, *at least it's not as bad as the journey in Bolivia.*

I once took a bus travelling north to the Amazon basin from La Paz, the world's highest capital city; if the lorry had had the same blowout on that road then the driver would not have had long to say his goodbyes as the vehicle was lost into the clouds below; there were often only millimetres of dirt between the wheels and the near vertical drops.

Nevertheless, I was relieved when the mountains

flattened and the roads became horizontal and the bus turned east to trace the edge of the Chitwan National Park. Two hours later I was standing on the veranda of my little home, happy to be drinking a bittersweet cup of coffee, and looking out towards the community forest. I was back in Sauraha and, calmed by the birdsong and revived by caffeine, thought it would be fun to hang out with the children at the orphanage.

When I first visited the orphanage with Hira on my previous stay the dusk was becoming thick and the light thin as darkness fell. There were two buildings either side of a square courtyard of dirt with a swing in the middle; a vegetable patch grew alongside it and the surrounding fields were sown with mustard plants with the small yellow flowers becoming harder to see as the night took hold. We walked across the dirt to the building which housed the children's bedrooms, reading area and kitchen. Small figures began rushing towards us, their faces awash with smiles as they crowded before me.

"Hello. What's your name? Where are you from? Do you play chess? Are you married?"

Their questions came thick and fast and I answered them and asked them their names and ages. There were twelve children, all coming to the orphanage after finding themselves alone or unable to be looked after by their parents. Hira left me to go and help make *dal bhat* with Sushilla. She was a middle-aged woman with long and wavy black hair, a rounded body wrapped by a sari and happy face. Sushilla and Hira were assisted by one other woman who was tending to the rice over the fire. She was the mother of a little boy who was stamping his feet beside the swing and laughing as he did so. He clapped his hands and appeared unaware of anything else except the sound of his clapping hands and stamping feet. I learned his name to be Babo (*little brother*) who Hira later told me has no memory. My hand was then taken in the hand of another boy, older, perhaps ten years old, with short black hair and dark eyes. His name was Rahal.

"Come see," he said.

He led me to the building and a board on the outside wall which had many pieces of paper stuck onto it displaying pictures and words: *Pilot, Teacher, Engineer, Doctor, Rocket, Policeman* and *Climb Mt. Everest.*

"Dreams," Rahal said. "These are our dreams." He pointed to one of the pieces of paper. "I am Pilot."

I read the words above the colourful pictures and ambitions, *Express your dreams.* All the other children came over to point out which dreams belonged to them before they returned to their learning with two Danish women who were volunteering at the orphanage. The children were working through mathematical problems and I soon felt redundant when a seven-year-old had to explain how she went about solving an, from my side, incredibly challenging equation. Rahal ran off to join two other boys who were playing with their *lados* on the dirt – spinning tops made of wood carved into a pine cone shape with a nail sticking out the bottom which are wrapped by string and then thrown with a good flick of the wrist to the ground. If the lay of the land and throw was good, it would spin like crazy. The boys then used the string to lift the whirling *lados* and perform tricks with them. A cry like a high-pitched caw sounded and I turned to see Babo reaching up his arms towards me. I lifted the little boy and he instantly pressed his wet lips against my cheek and continued to make his high-pitched calls, which I made back to him and he liked the feel of the vibrations this made on his lips. He then pulled away and began to drum my face. Babo, I learned, liked to drum things.

"Wash hands!" Sushilla shouted and all the children, except Babo who I had placed back down to resume calling his calls into the dark at the edge of the dirt courtyard, ran to a water pump and frantically pumped it up and down to then dash before it and put their hands beneath the flowing water. They ran to the kitchen and sat in a circle, each receiving their plate of *dal bhat*. Babo's mother came to collect him and sat him down next to the children where he was instantly silenced by the bowl of food before him, lifting the rice and vegetables with his fingers and sticking them into his mouth. I had already come to the conclusion that he had some form of memory, but something was clearly impeding his development. He was four and showed no real signs of language development, except when he drummed my face and cried "Noooo." I sat with Hira and the Danes and we ate our plates of food. The children's laughter escaped from the kitchen to continue playing outside in the shadows as they remained inside and ate.

I pulled the gate to my forest-side home shut. It was only a short walk to the orphanage, a little over a minute. I still had the taste of coffee on my lips. I walked out onto the dusty road and passed the *gack* shop on the corner, expanding its stock of biscuits, chocolates and cigarettes to also include bread and a limited display of toiletries. I turned off the road and onto a narrow dirt track; there was a buffalo tied to a wooden post outside a clay home and, as I passed, it raised its head and began grunting and chewing its thick lips. It was an old and cantankerous thing, and it made the most peculiar expressions. Its lower jaw would move to the left and lips fold back to show its crooked teeth and it left me thinking of Steptoe, the old miser from *Steptoe and Son*, a sitcom my father watched and enjoyed when I was a boy. Not far past the buffalo was the rear of a hotel, there were two large baths filled with wet white sheets covered in white foam. Two women walked back and forth and round and round over the sheets, treading the soap into the fabric with their bare feet and then adding more water to begin the rinsing process. The hotel kept its own elephants for providing rides to its guests and they were chained beneath a concrete shelter, rocking back and forth on their big old legs. Poor things looked bored of rocking but there was little else they could do, the chains didn't allow steps. Their ears flapped, and tails and trunks swayed. I felt tension growing inside me so I hurried on. The orphanage was a stone's throw from the hotel. I arrived to find Hira working on a gate and fence.

"Is this to stop the rhinos at night?" I asked.

"No," he replied, wetting the fresh concrete posts to make them expand, "it's for Babo."

Babo showed no sense of fear or danger and had a tendency to walk out of the orphanage, day or night. The little boy was alone in the courtyard, holding a yellow plastic container, which once contained five litres of cooking oil, and, now empty, was a perfect drum. He held it with his right hand before him and hit it with the palm of his left, calling his Babo calls in-between. I left Hira to move along the fence line and walked over to Babo. I crouched down and drummed with him. This ended, as it normally did, with him wanting to drum my forehead and cheeks. He then made his calls and pressed his lips on my cheek to feel the vibration of the calls I returned to him. This seemed to content him and he returned to his oil drum and, beating it hard, showed no more recognition of my being there. I stood and made my way across the dirt courtyard to rest on a bank beside a large dusty field. The remainder of the children were playing cricket with a Brit volunteer, a Londoner by birth who wanted to return to the city but couldn't afford to from the income he made from the Eastern jewellery and scarves he imported and sold at local markets. He was a tall man, a tower when stood beside the children, and had come to Nepal to volunteer for four weeks, happy to gain new experiences, especially with the markets being quiet this time of year. A girl bowled the ball at the stick stumps and all of the fielders, no matter the distance, ran for it when it was walloped by the 4-foot batsman. The sun was beginning to set and the game would soon be suspended due to poor light. Babo's calls echoed across the land and I came to think about the dream board and there not being one for him. He was in a good place, he was loved and allowed to drum and sing. I couldn't help but think that in another setting, more advanced, he would have child development specialists working to better understand his condition, and neurologists trying to locate what's firing and what's not in his brain. A part of me longed for Babo to remain a lost boy, never growing up and always thrilled by the simple act of stomping his feet and beating his oil drum. It's hard to know what life will be like for him as a man, I fear troubled and confusing. I watched the other children chasing the ball, eager each day to learn and chase after their dreams. I remembered there being three more pieces of paper on the dream board, the words on them written by a child's hand:

FAITH	**ACTION**	**PATIENCE**
"Anything is possible."	"Willing is not enough, you must do."	"Let it go, it will come back."

The cricket game continued as the sun went down, the sky awash with pinks on one horizon and deepening greys on the other. I sat on the dry earth, smiling, as I looked out upon a field of dreams before me.

XXIX

Om Home Guest House is tucked away down one of the narrow passageways in Shivala, the old town in Varanasi. Looking through the parts of my window which aren't boarded up by newspaper I can see a slim stretch of the Holy Ganges. On the far bank there is a large white riverbed which offers an insight to how the waters swell during the rains.

I left Om Home around seven o'clock this morning for a chai and ended up first finding a good *puri* stand, three *puri* and a dish of vegetable curry cost 20 rupees. I was one of the day's first customers and before being served, the boy in charge of taking orders made four offerings in four points around the stand, placing little dishes of tiny *puri* and deep fried sweets down for the gods. He touched his forehead, mouth and chest each time he set down the dishes. Once the gods were catered for he began to serve the waiting customers. His father, I presumed, sat before a wok of oil, rolling out the sticky dough balls into discs before sinking them into the oil which bubbled and hissed and made them swell and turn golden. I sat on a wooden bench and looked at the little paper plate of food on the ground beside me, untouched. I tore the unleavened bread with my right hand and used it to eat the curry. I then found a chai den and sat inside drinking a glass of chai and watched the men outside talking and drinking their drinks. Cows moped up and down the street, the rickshaws swerving round them. The shop shutters began to be lifted and the city stirred to life.

The first thing to stand out is how filthy the city is. The sacred cows leave runny patties behind them, their diet of picking through the rubbish heaps means they lack the needed fibre to shit solidly. People, many barefoot, step around the shit, including dog and human waste, and the rubbish, as well as the red trails of spit which is coloured by the tobacco many people chew. I passed women with brooms sweeping the rubbish out of the gutters and into small piles which are then collected and brought to a square compound, it spills out of the open gates and back onto the roadside; cows and dogs and an old boy are free to sift through it. You'd have to be hungry or desperately poor to want to. I guess this will be later collected by trucks and burned or dumped.

I finished my chai and returned to Om Home to finish writing my notes from Suaraha. I wrote little during the two days of travel it took to reach Varanasi from Nepal. I wanted to get my experience and memories on the page while they were fresh and before new experiences demanded to be written. I sat cross legged on my bed with my laptop and wrote for two hours, it felt like minutes. I had almost written my way back to the present and was thirsty for chai and to stretch my legs. I rose from my bed and looked out my glass and newspaper paned window. The River Ganges called to me.

At the end of the narrow passageway I saw a large building used by the Missionaries of Charity. It was at the entry to Shivala Ghat, one of many ghats where stone steps lead down to the river. I began to descend and stopped to soak in the scene. Boats were slowly moving along the river, carrying tourists and providing them with the iconic view back towards the famed ghats of Varanasi, where so much is to see and so much to learn. The water flowed brown and the only clear thing about it is that it's terribly polluted; it's revered and abused with equal fever. I walked and sat on one of the steps to observe a holy man overseeing a group in their religion as they had likely journeyed to Varanasi to pay their blessing to the Holy Ganges. He spoke fast words and with magnanimity, his large round belly wobbling as he reached out his arms and gestured to the flowing water. I looked too.

A herd of buffalo were bathing in its shallows; no more than a stone's throw away a group of men were dunking their heads into the water and washing under their armpits. Beyond them I could see the mounds of ash where some of the cremations took place; rubbish spoiled the banks and much of the stone sloops around the steps were used to dry saris and sheets as men and women washed their clothes on large flat stones purposefully positioned in the river. There were many beggars, so many I had to, like in Kolkata, walk past them all and feel helpless and worthless as I could offer only an apologetic smile as they reached up their wanting hands. Despite my previous spiel about compassion, I don't know how to be with suffering here; there's a point when it becomes too much for one heart and mind to comprehend and respond to.

Climbing a ghat further downstream I entered a covered passageway that ended in a narrow street lined by fruit and vegetable sellers. I bought a kilo of oranges and then returned to the river. Drumming ahead quickly stole my attention. Men descended the steps, a body held on a bamboo stretcher above their heads, covered in orange blankets and flowers. They walked to the river's edge where they rested the stretcher in the shallows and began to scoop up handfuls of water and pour it into the mouth of the deceased old lady. The water is said to purify the body. I stood and watched this ceremony take place below when I felt a tug on the bag of oranges in my hand. I turned to see a young boy. He pointed to the oranges. I took one and gave it to him and he scampered away. In an instant his cheers and cries had lured six more children to me and they instantly snatched at the bag, despite me telling them to wait. The bag tore as they yanked harder and the oranges dropped to the ground for the children, smiling and now wrestling on hands and knees, to retrieve them all and run away happy as could be. No begging. No please. No. See. Want. Take. I would have given them all the oranges anyway. It was their way that upset me, as though it was perfectly fine to take, to snatch something that doesn't belong to you and see no wrong in doing so. I guess I was shocked more than anything. I don't know their poverty or the hardships of their little lives, despite their cheery smiles and the games they played with each other.

I turned back to the river; a pyre of wood had been made. The body was lifted from the stretcher and placed upon it. She had a large protruding chin and deep concave eye sockets, she had died very old. Her small body was wrapped in a white sheet which was sprinkled with sandalwood to scent it. She was also covered with oil to help with the burning. I overheard an Indian man explain the ceremony to a couple of tourists sat on a nearby bench. It takes three hours for the body to burn and even then parts remain, normally the chest of a man and the hips of a woman. These, he said, are placed into the river and fed on by the fish. I again looked to see the bathers, soaping their bodies before sinking beneath the surface. The man explained to the tourists why only men attended the funeral. "Women do not have a strong heart," he said, suggesting that women were likely to break down and cause troubles for the departing spirit. He said women might also jump onto the fires of their burning husbands, a practice known as *Sati*. Two sons of the dead woman were crouched down near her feet, weeping as they said their final goodbyes. A priest then came with a hot coal burning in some long grass. He circled the smoke around the body four times, once for each of the four elements: earth, water, fire and air. The grass was then shaken from side to side and the oxygen brought the heat into flame. He placed the now burning grass beneath the woman and the wood soon began to catch. The sons would remain beside the burning pyre until the bones had turned to ash, and that which hadn't was offered to the current of the Holy Ganges. The flames quickly embraced the body. I walked back up the steps of the Shivala ghat and into the warren of passageways, wondering what I might stumble upon next.

XXX

I pulled open my glass and newspaper paned window to look upon a golden haze. The morning light poured past me and into my room. I put on my trousers, a t-shirt and my denim jacket and left the room, slipping my feet into my trainers outside the door before bolting it shut with a small padlock. There is a communal sink on the landing which has a plastic framed mirror above it and an energy saving light bulb; hundreds of small flies clung to the wall, fascinated by the light. Many had drowned in the sink basin, their tiny wings stuck to the porcelain. I turned the tap to stop it dripping and descended the stairwell, to then walk through the internal courtyard with the guests' clothes hung up on the washing lines, mostly baggy linen trousers and shirts, good to stay cool in the heat and light when folded into a backpack. I left Om Home Guest House and turned left down the narrow passageway, it was only a minute walk to my favourite chai den. I passed a hole-in-the-wall *gack* shop where a teenage girl, early teens, was reading a study book with the walls of biscuits rising around her and a cigarette stand beside her crossed legs, the small boxes all displaying blackened lungs. She did not register my walking by her, so lost was she in her learning.

I turned the corner onto an even narrower passageway, just wide enough for a cycle rickshaw to pass a pensive cow. Stone slabs formed a bumpy surface underfoot and the low sun was still to show her gracious face over the rooftops. I heard the sound of metal scraping against stone ahead. Beside an old rubbish cart, metal framed with wooden panelled sides, a young girl, no older than eight or nine, was crouched down gathering a pile of rubbish between two metal scoops. She pressed them together and strained as she lifted the slushy waste to drop it into the cart. She had black hair and bubbly cheeks and she was attentive to her work. I walked past as she crouched back down using one of her scoops to pull at the wet dirt, a composite of shit and rubbish, dampened by gutter water and piss. Her hands were covered in filth as was the front of her brown full-length dress. She wore a long green scarf around her neck and her appearance was that of a little lady, no matter the dirt. She worked alone and appeared not to be disheartened by the filthy work she was doing. She was focused and after I had passed by her rubbish filled cart I instantly noticed the tidy little passageway she had left behind her, the stone slabs free of biscuit wrappers and discarded chai cups, the gutters free of the wet filth which normally scented the air with urine.

I arrived at the main street, rickshaws honking horns and swerving around two bulls mooing and clearly disorientated. I sat on a wooden bench outside the chai den, unable to see anything else but the little girl with dimples that deepened with her smile as she tidied up other people's waste. She had a radiant spirit burning inside her and it reflected in the tidy passageway she herself had cleaned. I wondered what she was paid and how poor her family must be for her to be sweeping some of the dirtiest streets I've walked instead of being at school. Finishing my chai I headed back down the same passageway; the girl had just emptied her cart at the rubbish heap and was pushing the rickety thing before her, eager to finish collecting the last of the waste. She retrieved her metal scoops and set to work; scraping, piling, gathering, lifting and placing the rubbish and dirt into the cart. She was an adult in a child's body, or a child forced all too quickly into an adult's world. She worked.

I walked away and passed the slightly older girl who was still reading her study book amongst the biscuits and cigarettes. Two doors down and I walk by another, younger girl, maybe five years old, who was sat on the stone step leading into her home. She wore a burgundy red jumper and grey school dress. Her pupil-lit eyes were fixed on something I couldn't see in the blue sky above. She was passing time with the worlds inside her before being collected for school, her young mind a fountain of possibility.

I don't believe in fate. I try to believe, which is still not easy, in making the best of the here and now. Thinking about the young road sweeper, I don't know if I could have found her smile or eagerness to collect every last bit of dirt and litter. I don't know if I could have pushed the rickety cart with wobbly metal wheels with her straight back and purposeful steps forward. She walked her full load to the concrete compound, for it to be chewed over by the cows and dogs before being taken to the dumps, and then she returned to her passageway to finish her work and, for the first time since arriving here, showing me the sacred heart of the city – its people and their spirit. In my eyes, this little road sweeper, this little lady, with dirt down her dress and other people's shit under her nails, is a living goddess. It's not right, her lot in life. But her energy, her enthusiasm, and that smile she smiled to herself, she brought me inspiration in equal measure to heartache. This is Varanasi, such beauty born from the cradle of human waste.*

* In my haste to capture my experience fresh on the page, I overlooked the caste system that is ingrained in Indian society and explains why this girl was not in school but instead cleaning up other people's filth. I was recently told that sweeper children are increasingly being permitted an education. For now, however, this girl was born into the sweeper caste; she was born a sweeper and, unless a shift occurs that can tackle this rigid and soul defining system, she will always be a sweeper.

XXXI

Sitting on the stone steps of Kedar Ghat, their vertical sides alternating between red and white. It's calm on the ghats today. I'm sat high up, close to the buildings to be able to rest in the shade for it's too hot in the direct sun. There are a few rowboats out on the water, carrying tourists and a couple of motorboats. Two cremations are taking place to my right, at the Harishchandra Ghat and the smaller of the two cremation grounds. One of the bodies is close to ash while the other is still whole but blackened and alive with flames. Kites are swishing high up in the sky, lower down the steps boys control their dives and tug on the string in their hands to lift the kites and send them shooting back upwards on the breeze. Unfortunately the breeze is also carrying the scent of urine...

... My passage was broken by a young Chinese woman who lowered to sit on the step beside me.

"Are you a writer?" she asked gesturing to my notebook open on my lap and my scribbled words inside it.

"I'm just capturing a little of today," I replied.

"You're the first person I've seen keeping a journal since being away."

"Really?"

She nodded and smiled.

"Can I read it?"

I closed the cover.

"Ah, no, it's just random thoughts really."

She nodded and smiled again.

"What's your name?" I asked.

"Chris, c-h-r-i-s. And what's your name?"

"Matthew."

"Matthau, a nice name."

Chris was wearing a black baseball cap and held a small backpack over one shoulder. She wore green baggy trousers, a plain t-shirt and black plimsolls. She turned to face the river and then looked to the burning pyres; a *dom*, an outcast who oversees the cremations, was pushing the burning wood and stoking the fire with a bamboo stick. His clothes blackened with smoke and ash.

"I have a question to ask, can I ask you?"

"Sure," I said.

"If one day we die, just die, then what's the meaning of being here?"

The sincerity in her tone stemmed my laughter, which I had felt rise from the pit of my belly at being asked such a thing. I wondered if she had mistaken me for a Sadhu who had forgotten to undress and cover my naked body in ash.

"Ah… well… I guess… that's… I guess that's something people have been trying to make sense of since the beginning of humanity, and no doubt will continue to question until humanity's end."

"I just think about it a lot when I travel," she said. "When I'm in Beijing I work all the time and become lost to it – the city, the busyness, the earning money. Then I come away and I have a chance to think about life, but I only have two weeks before I go back to Beijing. I work ten hours a day. Everyone's working for the future."

"It's tough," I said, "a lot of pressure and expectation."

"I have met some Europeans during my time here and they told me they just work for some months, save some money, and then they go away travelling again. I could never do that. I have to think about the future. It's always there, isn't it?"

"Yes, I suppose it is."

Our conversation eased into a silence; a minute passed,

two minutes, and we simply continued to look out over the river. Finally, Chris smiled.

"I won't disturb you any longer; I'll let you return to your writing."

"Ah, really it's nothing important, more just sitting here and thinking."

She stood.

"It was nice to meet you, Matthau."

"Nice to meet you too."

"Bye."

"Goodbye."

Chris turned and slowly descended the steps. I watched as she came to stand beside the river, staring down into the murky water. I opened my notebook and lifted my pen:

The Ganges is a core part of Hinduism and a Hindu's life; it is said to be pure, purifying and transformative, able to wash away the dirt or sins of those who bathe in its holy waters. And I see life in it; its sacred spirit, its magnificence, how it has become polluted beyond belief, and its continual flow. I still don't know the meaning of life or why, as the burning bodies to my right confirm, one day it just ends, leaving so many to question, what's the point of it all? I just know that I respect it, appreciate it, that I'm in love with it and pained by it. I know only that I am in the midst of it, with all its murk and seeking the rare hidden pool of clear water. I am at the mercy of its flow.

I look up from these pages and my scribbled notes and see an Indian man wearing what from a distance look like orange Speedos. He dives off the front of a wooden boat and belly flops into the river. He's now paddling about in a current of sacredness, swimming in the depths of human pollution, dunking his head, before turning on his back and lying still. He floats on the river's surface. He is at peace.

XXXII

It was just another day on the banks of the Ganges: cremations, devotions, bathers, shady men who try to sell drugs through whispers, and kite flyers. I walked along the ghats in the morning sun and sat on the stone steps to watch the abundance of life and the wonderful array of colours, the air tinted by the sandalwood. The smell is much more pleasant than the occasional waft of urine. I was enjoying my last day in the city, setting the wonder of the ghats to memory and the feel of the warm sun on my neck. My time in India was near its end.

Embracing this time alone I thought about what I had first set out to capture and better understand, and a part of me felt I had failed to see the heart of what poverty is and means. I am not afraid of failing; it is an integral part of learning and moving forwards. India is a land offering an experience like no other. I find it hard to believe that anywhere else in the world could accumulate the same daily filth in the streets and still leave the traveller feeling as though they are in a sacred place. It is a true wonder, India. These notes have meant my eyes have been drawn to the filth and deprivation, and as such the reader may feel my view of India is one of degradation and squalor. This is not to do the country, as with Nepal, justice. Had I set out to make notes on Indian architecture, culture, religion, food, language or the spirit of the people then of course my notes would have painted a very different picture. My concern, however, is that which has been shared by many and a word that has been increasingly used over the previous decade, *sustainability*, or, as E.F. Schumacher gave upmost importance to achieving, 'permanence'. I am not an economist, or a specialist in any field for that matter, but through the winter months of observing different aspects of poverty, both home and abroad, I am left in no doubt that a shift in the present make-up of humanity, from one of the great consumer to that of loving producer and carer, is paramount. This will not be an easy transition. Humanity, on the whole, is shackled to a system that is fed on greed; the powers who determine policy, who have the abhorrent status of being able to put people in poverty, to force people out of their homes, are themselves overseen by an established few, the evil rich I like to call them. If a world without poverty is wanted, then the beautiful power of community must make its power known, the people must make their power known. If the world is being poisoned and natural laws violated, as I believe to be the case, by the spread of unchecked, sexualised and violent consumerism, then the power really is in us, the consumer, to change it. I firmly believe we are at war and it is a war many do not even realise they are engaged in. It is the War of the Spirit, and its outcome will determine humanity's continual existence. It is of vital importance for the higher spirit that dwells in each soul to be reconnected to all aspects of life: education, livelihoods, and the way we engage with each other and nature. The eco-systems which sustain life are being butchered by the heavy trudge of the human race, and it will take orientating and then acting upon the human spirit to turn instead to slow wisdom, not quick knowledge, to save what's left and to nurture life to flourish again in those places already left barren or polluted.

Alone on the steps beside the River Ganges, I watched the brown water flow by. I am small and insignificant in comparison. This one body of water gives life and supports many millions of human beings and wildlife, feeds without judgement. And it is being killed. I find it sickening that people then lovingly bathe in it and dare to call it sacred. All life is sacred, and as such all life should be treated so. I stood and turned, climbing the steps before heading into a covered passageway that leads to a small market street. In the dark, four men in orange robes were sat with their backs against the stone wall. I passed and one began to chant, pointing to his begging bowl before him. The other three simply stared up at me with sad eyes of need, their bowls empty. I couldn't help but think that, what with their bony legs, the dirty sheets beneath them and rats running past them, their spirit had also become empty, drained by their prolonged poverty.

Ten minutes later, I turned off the main road running through Shivala, onto the stone slab passageway that would take me back to Om Home. There was a girl sitting on a step outside a building ahead. I didn't recognise her at first, without her rickety cart beside her and muck down her dress. The young sweeper, who I will name Little Lady, for she appeared nothing less, had finished her morning's work, and now she sat down the same narrow street she had just cleaned. She watched it. As I neared a long line of children in blue school uniforms walked towards her, they were around her age and were a chorus of laughter, a parade of holding hands, happy smiles on their faces. I slowed and watched Little Lady; her eyes were not focused as they had been when I had passed her working, her shoulders were not straight but slumped as she rested her arms on her knees, her head raised slightly to observe the school children. She did not smile that dimple sweet smile to herself. She looked sad, lonely and lost. The school children kept on coming, I presumed they must have finished their morning classes and were returning home. Little Lady's eyes followed them all, the children made no visible indication of having seen her. I stopped and turned, watching as the school children hurried excitedly home while Little Lady remained alone on the step. A man walked past and threw a plastic chai cup on the ground before her.

The following morning and just after eight o'clock, I left Om Home Guest House with my backpack on my back. My train to Mumbai was scheduled to depart in two hours. I made my way down the stone slab street, towards the main road. Little Lady was standing in the middle of a heap of rubbish, her rickety cart beside her and overflowing. She looked strained and tired. The shit covered metal plates she used to scoop up the waste came to her side after she saw me approach. Our eyes met.

"Namaste," I said.

She didn't reply. She looked as though she wanted to hide from me. A puppy was pawing at the rubbish which would have been swept into the heap by another sweeper. Little Lady's job was to come with her cart and gather it up, before walking it to the compound on the main road. There was so much of it, two carts' worth in this one pile alone, and the piles were found all along the passageway. Little Lady turned away from me and hit out at the puppy now under her feet. She had aged fifty years since the first time I saw her, had become hardened and unhappy. Her small body and mind battled against the filth, with crisp packets and god knows what escaping the metal scoops as she tried to lift it to the cart. I walked and I turned, before walking and turning again, and what I saw was a young girl, a little lady, being buried alive by the muck and waste society had created. She had been born into the sweeper caste; this was her life, daily.

BATH
March 2015

The wind planted cold and chilling kisses on my cheeks. A clear water sky rested over the limestone city, the sunshine painting the buildings golden. I crossed the road to move from shade into a little winter warmth on the other side. I walked toward St Michael's Church; scaffolding climbed the side of the spire and held workmen in hard hats as they tended to the structure. Outside the city centre supermarket I watched a *Big Issue* seller, a woman around fifty years old with short bristle hair and tired skin, being beaten by the cold and the long hours of forcing herself to smile against it.

"*Big Issue* for you my darlings?" she said to a couple walking hand in hand, displaying the magazines that she held close to her chest. The couple shook their heads and walked by. "Oh please," the seller's voice rose, "I've only sold two all day."

The couple walked away. Beyond her I saw some down and outs sitting under the covered passage that spanned the front of the supermarket. They were holding sleeping bags to their chests and were paled by the cold – four men, homeless, spending the day reflecting on and recovering from the night. I slowed as I passed them.

"I had guys coming to my pitch," said one of the men whose small body was lost within a heavy coat; his cheeks carried thick stubble and his eyes were watery, "too cold they were."

The men remained sat outside the supermarket, the day slowly passing them by. I entered the public toilet at the end of the building. I closed the doors of two cubicles to find them broken, their locks missing. The last cubicle was occupied; I glimpsed a backpack and pair of black boots beneath the door. I knew he was also homeless, locking himself in the cubicle, toilet seat down, for him to get away from the finger-biting cold and wind. I turned and left as the automatic flush flowed down the face of the urinals.

Outside in the wind I walked back past the four men. I passed the *Big Issue* seller who was spinning in circles to tempt the shoppers leaving the supermarket and the people passing on the pavement behind her. I walked towards the big and beautiful bulk of stone and stained glass at the end of the High Street, the Abbey's tower shielding the low winter's sun. The pavements were dotted by pedestrians moving between the shops or to their offices and work. I saw Dean standing at his pitch outside T. K. Maxx. I crossed the road and he smiled as he saw me approach.

"Hey Dean."

"You're back then."

His big blue bag was on the ground beside his feet, stuffed with a greyish white duvet and scrunched up sleeping bag. His long earthen hair fell straight to his shoulders and his face also carried a layer of stubble, his skin was pale and coloured by the cold. The wind carved around us.

"How've you been?"

"Alright," he said.

I gestured to the blue bag. "You sleeping outside at the moment?"

"Yeah, it's okay, got used to the cold now."

"And how's the selling going?"

He held one magazine in his hands. "I had to borrow 25p off a friend this morning to buy a magazine. This is only my second one."

"And how's the winter been?"

"Alright I guess, I don't think about it too much now, just get on with it don't you."

Dean's eyes flickered from me to the people walking by.

"I'll leave you to it, how you doing for books?"

"I'm okay."

"Would you like some?"

"Yeah, alright, yeah, thanks."

"Cool, I'll bring some in tomorrow. Catch you later."

"See you around."

Dean returned to displaying the magazine to those who passed him. I walked away as the wind continued to plant ever colder and harder kisses on my cheeks.

The following day and the sky was like looking into a blue and unending mirror of yesterday; the wind had softened to a chilling breeze, nibbling at my nose and ears. I had left V to go and meet a friend for coffee. I walked away from St Michael's Church, the workmen lifting planks of wood up the face of the spire using ropes and pulleys, the scaffolding rising higher and higher. I held two books in my hands, paperbacks. I saw Dean from a distance, his red coat bold against the dark winter coats of the people walking past him on the pavement; his blue bag stuffed with sleeping bags and duvets was pressed up against the wall outside T. K. Maxx.

"Hi Dean," I said as I neared him.

"Hey."

"I brought you these." I offered him *My Friend Leonard* and *A Million Little Pieces* by James Frey, which he took in his bone-white hands. "I read them while I was away. I thought you might like them after we spoke in the café and you told me about non-fiction becoming fiction. The writer elaborates on the truth in these books to craft a good story. I thought they were brilliant."

"Cool, thanks a lot," said Dean.

He held onto the paperbacks and rubbed their blue

and white covers. The cold remained.

"Did you sleep outside again last night?"

"I did, yeah."

"How was it?"

"It wasn't too bad. I've lost my gloves so my hands were real cold, otherwise it was alright."

Dean leant over and placed the books down onto the grey duvet in the blue bag. He stood for his long hair to again frame his cheeks and the focus of his eyes to return to the pedestrians passing by.

"Hopefully catch up with you soon," I said. "You can tell me if you liked the books or not."

"Yeah, cool. Thanks again."

"No problem. Take care."

"See you around."

I smiled and Dean smiled back. I turned and walked away, passing the entrance of T. K. Maxx; warmth from the overhead heaters flowed out of the doors. I looked back over my shoulder to see Dean blowing on his hands, one by one, before holding the magazine in them and showing it to those walking by. Winter continued her slow dance around the city streets, taking all into her cold embrace.

One hour later I returned to the High Street with V's soft fingers between mine and a pair of gloves in my free hand. I had mentioned to V about Dean not having any. V said she had a gift card for a department store that she hadn't used so we walked down to South Gate shopping centre, and then back through the Abbey square with a street performer entertaining the day-trippers. I saw The Pigeon Man dressing those who wanted with birds beneath the colonnade at the end of the Pump Rooms. He had become a snapshot of life in Bath; that grey leather coat, the bowler hat with orange feather, the birdseed, the work. V and I arrived outside T. K. Maxx. The stone wall where

Dean was normally stood was bare.

"He must have finished for the day or gone to pick up some more magazines," I said. "I'll come back tomorrow."

I returned to Dean's pitch the next morning, then the day after that; in my mind I conjured up the image of him hiding himself out of the cold and immersed in *My Friend Leonard* as I had been immersed while sick and weak in a depressed little room in Kathmandu. But what if he wasn't hiding himself somewhere and kept warm with feeling by reading? Another twenty-four hours passed, and I walked the city with the new pair of gloves in my hand. I failed to find him. The next day V and I left Bath, the unworn gloves came with us in the car as we drove towards Folkestone.

Afterword
Paris, 18th March 2015

"It's not far now."

A metro train's steel wheels beat against the overhead tracks as I walk beside V away from Barbès station. Men in dark coats loiter beneath the overhead tracks, their eyes meeting the eyes of the passengers pouring out of the station exit. I look into the eyes of one of the men, they speak a knowing look of someone who resides in a shadowed world, a place unknown to many, yet a place of solace, hurt and risk for others, lost souls. I hold V's hand, she holds mine. We cross the Boulevard de la Chapelle, out of the shadows trapped beneath the tracks and into the light of the warm spring sun. The sky is thickly spread with blue, no clouds, just a sun slowly sinking towards the rooftops and faint jet streams in the distance. We walk, nearing the bridge just north of Gare du Nord.

"It's here."

The traffic slows and begins to build up over the bridge, we start to walk across. Much of the bridge's grey metal body has been painted in graffiti; a wire fence rises to our right, preventing someone from flinging themselves onto one of the many railway lines below. I see a Eurostar train slowly come to a stop beside a platform, its journey from London St Pancras completed. Carriage doors open. Its passengers, luggage in their hands, some suited, some not, hurry on their way along the platform. A siren rises behind us. I turn to see a police car, two wheels up on the pavement as it tries to pass the stationary line of traffic. It races past us. The siren is loud and drowns out the normal hum of the city. Across the road, between the breaks in

315

the cars, I look to spot where I had first seen a community of down and outs, sheltering beneath the overhead tracks on bare mattresses at the end of summer. Six months has passed. No time has passed. A village of pop-up tents now fills the central divide of the bridge, the little domed structures a strange sight in the city, a cluster of canvas more fitting for a field or festival.

"Do you think a charity provided them?" I ask V.

"Maybe."

A group of dark skinned men are standing beside the fence and road, one is stood before a large freestanding mirror, shaving. The car fumes sit heavy on the bridge, the traffic moving slower and slower as the city streets begin to stress on the edge of rush hour. The traffic slowly, even at a snail's pace, moves forwards, the men around the tents stand still. They are, as they were yesterday, down and out today.

Acknowledgements

It's not a nice feeling to wake up on a morning and feel inferior to the subject you are seeking to write about. I have felt this often over the past six months. Poverty is complex; the picture cannot be identified without looking at the whole. Yet in this book I have frequently engaged with only parts of the picture, often being the people at the bitter and hard end of being poor. On the other hand if someone's poverty can be easily traced back to an event or circumstance, or to a policy or system which places us on the chequerboard of life, is it then a thing of chance or control? I may have done this subject justice or, more likely, I have merely scratched at the surface; my want as a writer was to share with you my journey along the way.

I will not be shy about admitting that the idea to write this book was partly motivated by George Orwell's *Down and Out in Paris and London*. I am also not embarrassed to admit that I am no George Orwell, but I thank him for his books which continue to ignite the minds of future generations.

Thank you to V for letting me introduce her in this book, and for also reading the first draft and bringing encouragement and her endearing presence. I thank my editor, Lauren Parsons, for again helping to refine my story and make it into a book I am deeply proud to say is mine. This extends to all at Paperbooks who have done much to search out new voices in the world of non-fiction.

Finally, my sincere thanks to the people I encountered throughout the writing of this book, first in Bath, and London, then India and Nepal. I have been moved, saddened, uplifted and inspired in equal measure. I have only to write now that this concludes my notes from the gutter.

Matthew Small.
22 April 2015

References

1 – 'Food bank demand up 54 per cent in 2013' by Maev Kennedy, *The Guardian*, 9 June 2014

2 – 'Annual Fuel Poverty Statistics Report' by Department of Energy and Climate Change, 12 June 2014

3 – 'A Tale of Two Britains: Inequality in the UK' by Sarah Dransfield, Oxfam, 17 March 2014

4 – 'Millions of families living in poverty despite being in employment says new study' by Kashmira Gander, *The Independent*, 08 December 2013

5 – 'Record numbers of working families in poverty due to low-paid jobs' by Gwyn Topham, *The Guardian*, 24 November 2014

6 – '10 Countries Spending the Most on the Military' by Thomas C. Frohlich and Alexander Kent, *24/7 Wall St*, 10 July 2014

7 – 'The Mumbai Slum Sanitation Program : partnering with slum communities for sustainable sanitation in a megalopolis' by The World Bank

8 – '54 per cent of Mumbai lives in slums: World Bank' by InfoChange India

9 – 'Holding on to the Lively Traditions' by Matthew Small, *The Journal of Wild Culture*, 13 December 2012

10 – From *Letters from Westerbork* by Etty Hillesum, translated by Arnold J. Pomerans. Published by Jonathan Cape and reproduced by permission of The Random House Group Ltd.

11 – 'ADHD drugs increasingly prescribed to treat hyperactivity in pre-schoolers' by Sally Weale, *The Guardian*, 21 December 2014

12 – Starlight Appeal, Age UK Bath, more information available at: http://starlightappeal.tumblr.com/

13 – 'Lack of toilets blights the lives of 2.5bn people, UN chief warns' by Sam Jones, *The Guardian*, 28 August 2014

14 – Visit Manon's blog for a detailed and personal account of her service in the wound clinic: http://innersacredness. wordpress.com/2014/12/22/being-in-service/

15 – 'The Slums of Kolkata' by Shanto Baksi, *academia.edu*, September 2013

16 – 'Can We Really End Extreme Poverty?' by Mark Leon Goldberg, *UN Dispatch*, 14 January 2015

17 – 'Introducing Schools to the Future' by Whitney Smith, *The Journal of Wild Culture*, 28 September 2013

18 – From *Small Is Beautiful* by E. F. Schumacher, published by Hutchinson. Reproduced by permission of The Random House Group Ltd.

Come and visit us at
www.LegendTimesGroup.com

Follow us
@legend_press